SUCCESS METRICS

A MULTIDIMENSIONAL FRAMEWORK FOR MEASURING ORGANIZATIONAL SUCCESS

Martin Klubeck

Apress®

Success Metrics: A Multidimensional Framework for Measuring Organizational Success

Martin Klubeck
Niles, Michigan, USA

ISBN-13 (pbk): 978-1-4842-2585-1   ISBN-13 (electronic): 978-1-4842-2586-8
DOI 10.1007/978-1-4842-2586-8

Library of Congress Control Number: 2017932532

Managing Director: Welmoed Spahr
Editorial Director: Todd Green
Acquisitions Editor: Robert Hutchinson
Development Editor: Laura Berendson
Coordinating Editor: Rita Fernando
Copy Editor: Corbin Collins
Compositor: SPi Global
Indexer: SPi Global

Distributed to the book trade worldwide by Springer Science+Business Media New York, 233 Spring Street, 6th Floor, New York, NY 10013. Phone 1-800-SPRINGER, fax (201) 348-4505, e-mail orders-ny@springer-sbm.com, or visit www.springeronline.com. Apress Media, LLC is a California LLC and the sole member (owner) is Springer Science + Business Media Finance Inc (SSBM Finance Inc). SSBM Finance Inc is a Delaware corporation.

For information on translations, please e-mail rights@apress.com, or visit http://www.apress.com/rights-permissions.

Apress titles may be purchased in bulk for academic, corporate, or promotional use. eBook versions and licenses are also available for most titles. For more information, reference our Print and eBook Bulk Sales web page at http://www.apress.com/bulk-sales.

Any source code or other supplementary material referenced by the author in this book is available to readers on GitHub via the book's product page, located at www.apress.com/9781484225851. For more detailed information, please visit http://www.apress.com/source-code.

Printed on acid-free paper

Apress Business: The Unbiased Source of Business Information

Apress business books provide essential information and practical advice, each written for practitioners by recognized experts. Busy managers and professionals in all areas of the business world—and at all levels of technical sophistication—look to our books for the actionable ideas and tools they need to solve problems, update and enhance their professional skills, make their work lives easier, and capitalize on opportunity.

Whatever the topic on the business spectrum—entrepreneurship, finance, sales, marketing, management, regulation, information technology, among others—Apress has been praised for providing the objective information and unbiased advice you need to excel in your daily work life. Our authors have no axes to grind; they understand they have one job only—to deliver up-to-date, accurate information simply, concisely, and with deep insight that addresses the real needs of our readers.

It is increasingly hard to find information—whether in the news media, on the Internet, and now all too often in books—that is even-handed and has your best interests at heart. We therefore hope that you enjoy this book, which has been carefully crafted to meet our standards of quality and unbiased coverage.

We are always interested in your feedback or ideas for new titles. Perhaps you'd even like to write a book yourself. Whatever the case, reach out to us at editorial@apress.com and an editor will respond swiftly. Incidentally, at the back of this book, you will find a list of useful related titles. Please visit us at www.apress.com to sign up for newsletters and discounts on future purchases.

—The Apress Business Team

This book is dedicated to all those who want to find true success in their life or in their business.

The correct path to success is easier to find than we think. Staying on the path, focused on our destination, is the hard part.

Contents

About the Author

Martin Klubeck is a strategy and planning consultant at the University of Notre Dame and a recognized expert in the field of practical metrics. His passion for simplifying the complex has led to the development of a simple system for developing meaningful metrics. He is author of *Metrics: How to Improve Key Business Results, Planning and Designing Effective Metrics, The Professional Development Toolbox: Unlocking Simple Truths*, and is coauthor of *Don't Manage… Coach!* and *Why Organizations Struggle So Hard to Improve So Little: Overcoming Organizational Immaturity*. Martin is the president of MK Knowledgebuilders LLC and the founder of the Consortium for the Establishment of Information Technology Performance Standards, a nonprofit organization focused on providing much-needed standards for IT performance measures.

Martin is available for keynotes, guest speaking, teaching, workshops, and seminars. He has a weekly newsletter for visionaries, providing encouragement toward staying on the path to success.

Acknowledgments

Once again I find myself facing the most stress-filled part of writing a book. What if I forget someone who helped in the creation of this work? What if I leave out someone's name?

This work, like the knowledge I used to write it, is a result of a lifetime of experiences, input, thoughts, and ideas. It's influenced by acquaintances, coworkers, teammates, clients, and family. I don't believe we can come up with anything new in a vacuum—instead we find new ways of combining or interpreting input from others. We can break the rule of *Garbage In, Garbage Out* because our minds allow us to extrapolate and create new things from old, good from bad, treasure from trash.

So, thank you to all who have ever influenced me. Thanks to all those who have shared their lives with me, especially my friends, my family, my wife, my children, and yes, even my enemies.

I'd also like to thank all those who took the time to share their views and ideas about Success Metrics with me. Lisa Dolly, Ron Kraemer, Ron DiCiccio, Ruth Riley, Dennis Monokroussos, Nathan Havey, Colin O'Keefe, Carmen Macharaschwili, and Sarah and Jeff Saylor.

Introduction

It's time to refocus our measures. I wrote *Metrics: How to Improve Key Business Results* because too many people were collecting the wrong things, for the wrong reasons, and using the results of their metrics in the wrong way. Metrics were (and still are for many people) doing more harm than good. We needed a dose of cold water splashed in our faces—and I tried to provide that.

It's time to grow. It's time to find our way to not only using measures correctly, but using measures to be truly successful—not just momentary success, but true, long-lasting, life-changing, legacy-creating success.

Small wins are nice, but we're talking about how to achieve greatness.

It's time.

How This Book Came to Be

This book is born from my experiences in trying to help individuals and organizations create "living" strategic plans.

I thought I knew all about creating strategic plans. I learned from the best, and I'm a good learner. I was on the front lines when Total Quality Management (TQM) took off in the U.S. Air Force. I helped facilitate numerous strategic plans from departments and whole squadrons.

And the plans lived. They were carried out. They were used as a guidebook for achieving long-range goals.

After I retired and started helping non-military organizations create strategic plans, I came to learn that my previous successes weren't due to my singularly spectacular ability to facilitate planning sessions. I was successful because the Air Force is an awesome institution made up of people who embody the American spirit. They never give up, they never surrender. They get the job done. And they can follow orders—even ones captured in a long-range plan.

They made the plans work. It hadn't mattered how well I facilitated the creation of the plans, how well the plans were written, or whether the plans were documented in an easy-to-follow format.

Later, when I tried to replicate this success and help others outside of the military, I thought I was doing everything necessary to continue being successful. I came to learn after many successful (actually failed) strategic plans, that none of them was alive. They were at best stillborn attempts. They were paper. Nothing else. Well, some ink. But nothing else.

They didn't inspire action. They didn't motivate. They didn't provide any long-range guidance. They failed.

The funny thing is, these failures didn't hurt my reputation or popularity. The thing was, my customers were totally satisfied. They loved their strategic plans. They were very, very happy with the product. They were happy to go through the process of defining long-range goals, breaking those down into mid- and short-range goals. The were happy with the final product and proudly displayed it on their shelves.

I was the only one that was unhappy with it. I was the only one who saw the effort as a failure and a complete waste of time.

The question I was faced with from that point forward was why?

Why did the process fail to produce a living plan?

Why would it work in the Air Force, but not in corporate or academic institutions?

Why were my customers happy with these dead plans that represented days of effort, hours and hours of high-paid leaders valuable time, to say nothing about my fees?

And then I found the answer, thanks to Carmen.

I helped Carmen find her dream and change her life. But I'm pretty sure she helped me more than I helped her.

I facilitated Carmen's organization through a strategic planning session. Carmen wondered if I could do the same for an individual—for her. I am always game for a new twist to an old wrinkle, so I accepted the challenge.

When we started working on her strategic plan, I realized I needed to know something about Carmen that I had never bothered to ask an organization. I needed to know if she had any dreams. I needed to know why she wanted a strategic plan for her life. I needed to know whether she had a life-changing vision or if she just wanted to be more goal oriented.

Luckily for me (for her, and for you), she had a vision for her future. We focused our time on fleshing out her vision in detail. And then we built a strategic plan to make it happen. The plan had a purpose: to make the vision come true. The plan had a pulse.

The plan still lives today (over five years later).

There was a way to have the plan live without having an airman's determination to make it work.

It required a core cause. It required a bigger *why*. It required a vision. To make a plan live required a vision—a reason to make it happen.

While I was helping Carmen, I was writing *Metrics: How to Improve Key Business Results*. I was helping leaders develop meaningful metrics programs. I couldn't help but apply what I knew about metrics to my efforts with Carmen. How would I know if I had gotten it right? How would I measure whether Carmen's plan was living?

And I realized that wasn't the right thing to measure. It wasn't the root question.

Question: Why did I want Carmen to have a living plan?

Answer: Because if the plan were alive, she might actually achieve her vision.

And if she achieved her vision—if she changed the world—she'd be successful. She'd be my personal hero and a shining example of how a strategic plan should be created.

That was pretty simple.

And I liked it that way.

I'm pretty sure you will too.

Why Should You Read This Book?

So why this book? Why now?

Have I told you about Stacey?

Stacey Barr is the only contemporary I have whom I trust to consult on metrics. She gets it, from the beginning to the end. I "met" Stacey while researching for my book *Metrics: How to Improve Key Business Results*. She has a nice online presence through her website and newsletter. We hit it off right away because we have similar ways of looking measurements. She focuses on performance measures and helping organizations develop programs based on them. I focus on helping people find their root questions and finding the measures they need to improve their organizations and their lives.

Although Stacey is on the other side of the world (Australia, to be exact) and we've never met in person, I feel very close to her—because of our common views on metrics.

Even so, it was a surprise when I read her latest newsletter, which referenced a book she was writing, due out early 2017. *Prove It!: How to Create a High-Performance Culture and Measurable Success* proposes that leaders should measure how well they are fulfilling the mission. I immediately emailed her because this was bordering on spooky. I was nearing the completion of this book, and I find out that Stacey was writing a similarly focused book, independently but simultaneously.

We both had individually come to the realization that it is critical that organizations (and leaders) measure how well they are fulfilling their missions. Of course, we address it from different directions—we have very different backgrounds, experiences, and histories.

Add to that my meeting Nathan Havey. Nathan is the CEO of Thrive Consulting, a company that believes every business can thrive, in spite of the economy or other outside influences. They can thrive if they embrace the higher purpose behind their existence. They can thrive if they find their mission. And of course, the mission is not making money—that's just a means to an end. Nathan is working with businesses and chambers of commerce to help companies find their mission and work toward this higher purpose.

I met Nathan because one of his executives read my book *Metrics* and contacted me. When she did, she asked if I could meet on the phone with her and Nathan. After discussing metrics—how Thrive Consulting could measure their success—I knew I had found another kindred spirit. And fate kept playing a happy tune. I found out that I was due to be in Nathan's neighborhood the next month for a presentation. We were able to meet in person over lunch.

This confluence of events only served to strengthen my resolve that it's the right time for this book.

We need a new focus for our businesses, our organizations, our nonprofits, and ourselves.

It's time to realize our purpose and to dream big dreams.

Our country was founded with a sense of purpose. Our founding fathers believed in our nation having a greater purpose. They believed the United States was a promised land, and that its people have a mission to create a special nation. We haven't realized their dreams yet, nor have we completely fulfilled that mission.

Each of us has a calling. Each of us has a purpose.

Each and every business can also find a greater calling. It can be much more than a means of income. And to truly thrive, to become something great, organizations must find that calling.

To change the world, we have to dream. And we have to fight to make those dreams come true.

These are the measures of success.

This book will help you find your measures of success.

It's time.

This book should challenge you. It should push you past the normal wordsmithed rhetoric we use to create long, dull, uninspired mission statements. It should push you to find your organization's true calling. The *why* behind the *what*.

This book should illuminate you to the power of a vision. It should help you dream big and understand why it's not only healthy to have a vision, but why it will actually push you to grow.

But most importantly, this book will show you how to measure success.

Preface

Tl;dr

I was recently introduced to *tl;dr*. It stands for *too long; don't read* or *too long; didn't read*. The idea is when you write a long email, you can write a short synopsis and put it at the beginning of the email, with a marker of *tl;dr*. It allows the email reader to read a short version of your email and decide whether they want to get the details or not.

So I wondered. Should I write a tl;dr or should I write a summary? The major difference is where you put it. Tl;dr should be at the beginning, and a summary at the end.

Another way to think about it is I'm providing you an option. If you don't want to read this book, but you want to know how to measures success, read this synopsis.

Why Measure?

Why measure success at all? Most measurement efforts are wrapped around performance. But performance only tells you how well you're doing what you do. It doesn't tell you whether you're doing the right things or whether those things are going to make you a success. We spend way too much time measuring effectiveness and efficiency. Instead we need to focus on measuring whether we're successful or not. Our stakeholders should want to know how successful the organization is. Stakeholders don't (and shouldn't) care about performance measures.

What to Measure?

The key message is extremely simple: You measure success by how well you fulfill your mission. At a personal level, it's based on how well you fulfill your purpose in life. At an organizational level, it's how well you fulfill your mission.

The other way you measure success is related to the first. It's based on how well you're moving along the path for achieving your vision.

Can't get simpler than that.

Success is not measured by wealth, fame, or fortune. It's not measured by net profit, customer satisfaction, or your net promoter score. It's not that these measures aren't useful, but they don't measure success. And success is the first measure. Why measure anything else if you don't know whether you're successful? Why measure anything else if those measures won't let you know if you're going to succeed or fail?

It doesn't get any simpler than that.

Mission

Now, if it were easy to define your mission and create a vision, you could stop now. But of course, there's more to it.

The first requirement is to clearly identify your mission. I believe every person and every organization has a purpose—the problem is to find it. The mission is the *why* behind what you do. Too often we measure how well we do things, or what we're doing. This is a big mistake. You have to measure how well you're fulfilling the *why*, the reason the organization exists.

A mission is why you exist. It needs to be understood and embraced by everyone in the organization. It should not be a complicated "statement." It should be clear and easy to understand. Everyone should be able to understand it. Every member of the organization should be able to articulate the mission in their own words. More importantly, every member of the organization should want to share the mission. They have to believe in the reason the organization exists.

Vision

A vision is a very large, scary, hairy, audacious goal. It's the *why* that drives innovation, change, and creative thinking in your organization. It's the basis for your research and development. It gives you a foundation for long-range planning. Without vision, you will likely find it impossible to have a strategic plan. Like a mission, everyone has to know it, believe it, and articulate it in their own words. Unlike a mission, not everyone has one. It's not mandatory.

The How Matters

Your values and principles matter. They guide you in how you behave. They define how you fulfill your mission and how you go about achieving your vision. But they are not success. Granted, you may not feel like a success if you go against your values, but success is not defined by how well you adhere to those values. Although they won't define success, they will define your ability to enjoy your success.

Passion

One constant in defining success is passion. You should be passionate about your purpose—if not, chances are you're in the wrong business. And with passion comes engagement. I'm willing to bet most leaders lament a lack of engagement by their employees more than any other deficiency. If you believe the secret to success is employee engagement, than you have to share your mission and vision (if you have one) with passion. Passion begets engagement.

Nonprofits and For-Profits Alike

There are a lot of differences in how nonprofits and for-profit organizations are run, function, and deal with finances. But there is no difference in how they measure success. It's based on fulfillment of mission and achievement of vision—regardless of the organization's profit status. From experience, I can tell you it's easier for nonprofits to find their mission and to create a compelling vision, which just makes it more important for other organizations to get it right. Besides it being easier because of the nature of the organization, it's also easier for nonprofits because for-profit organizations incorrectly believe their mission is to make money, and that's just not true. There's a reason behind their existence. A for-profit's mission is no more "to make money" than a nonprofit's mission is to lose money.

Sharing Your Measures of Success

Just do it. Share your measures of success early and often. Far and wide. With everyone. Yup, everyone. If your Success Metrics are the right ones, you can share them with anyone and everyone. Competitors, peers, collaborators, stakeholders, boards of directors, investors, suppliers, vendors, and employees. You can share them on your website with the public.

Leaders notoriously hoard or hide their metrics. I'm not going to validate the excuses for this, mostly because I fully understand the reasons. And those reasons are not present with Success Metrics. Success Metrics are at the top level, telling you overall whether your organization is fulfilling its mission or achieving its vision. These measures have none of the fear, uncertainty, and doubt (FUD) that accompany performance measures. They are as close to an empirical truth as you'll find, so share them.

Stop

So, that's it. You can stop now.

Unless you need more.

If you want motivation for finding your mission, read on. If you want inspiration for creating a vision, which will focus your future direction, galvanize your stakeholders, and inspire deep and lasting change, read on. If you want to know how to create a metrics program that will pay dividends today and far into tomorrow, then read on.

It's critical for you to know the *why*. It's impossible to succeed without it. The *why* doesn't change easily.

It's required that you know the *what*. The *what* can define your level of success. The *what* changes reluctantly.

It's important to know the *how*. The *how* of your values and principles define who you are. The other *hows*, the specifics of how you fulfill your mission, can change. They will change.

If you want to know any of these things, read on.

If you want to create a metrics program of worth, one that will help you know if you are on the proper path toward success, read on. If you want to know whether you are already truly successful, read on.

And if you choose to read on, I hope you get even half of what I put into it out of it.

What Is Success?

What is success? This is a tough question—tougher than it would seem. It's also the first question among a list of questions we have to answer. When I get introduced, invariably people ask, "What do you do at Notre Dame?" Lately I enjoy answering, "I help people find the questions to their answers." I say this with sincerity and only a hint of a smile.

"Don't you mean you help people find the answers to their questions?"

"No. When it comes to metrics, most organizations have a ton of answers but have forgotten to figure out the questions." The first answer I find most people think they have is how to be successful—the problem is they haven't asked the right questions.

Where to Begin?

I have taught classes, written books, and presented seminars, and in every case I've championed starting at the beginning. It might sound funny (and obvious), but I find it's not. People tend to skip planning and want to get right into solving. They also like to jump over problem identification and get right into resolution.

My wife says it's a male condition. She says we like to skip over reading the instructions and get right into putting the bike together. It happens with new games also—"Let's play," my ten-year-old daughter will say, while I try to get us to slow down and read the rules first (so much for it being a male thing).

© Martin Klubeck 2017
M. Klubeck, *Success Metrics*, DOI 10.1007/978-1-4842-2586-8_1

So, I take the time to stress the importance of starting at the beginning when you are trying to get things done. Sure, keep the end in mind, but make sure you're not skipping over any important steps along the way. I don't see this as conflicting advice: keep the end in mind, start at the beginning.

Start at the Beginning

Usually you have to start at the beginning by measuring how well you're doing at getting to where you ultimately want to end up. And if you don't know where you're going, measurements become only "interesting" tidbits of information.

To have useful, meaningful metrics, you have to know where you're going. To have metrics that help you improve, you have to know what end game you're moving toward.

And this is true when undertaking a task.

But when measuring success, I've found that you have to do just the opposite.

In measuring success, we actually have to start at the end. We have to measure success in its full glory, not simply the steps along the way.

Start at the End

We need more time to discuss what success really is and how to measure it. But to explain starting at the end with our measures of success, we can use any goal. Let's say your goal is to lose 20 pounds. If we were to measure success for this goal incorrectly, we'd start at the beginning and measure your current weight to establish our baseline. Then we'd measure your weight periodically (even daily). If (and hopefully when) you weigh 20 pounds less than on that first day, we can claim success.

And that's the problem.

We would incorrectly claim success. The reason we'd be wrong is that we were measuring the wrong thing. Success means accomplishment—long-lasting, not momentary. You know of someone who has lost pounds and put them right back on. You know someone who quit smoking only to take it back up again years, months, or even days later. Sure, they were successful in achieving the weight, but they didn't sustain it. And in most of those cases, we don't lose the weight or quit smoking as the end goal! They are wins along the way. They don't equal success in themselves because they're not the end.

So you may be thinking, this is easy! Just change the goal to being "lose 20 pounds and keep the weight off" or "quit smoking forever." Right?

You'd still be wrong. That's still the same goal just extended over an infinite time.

The end for losing weight or quitting smoking isn't sustaining it. There's a reason behind these "goals." As I've proposed throughout my metrics consulting: you have to find the root question. What is the real underlying goal? Why were you losing 20 pounds? Why were you trying to quit smoking?

It doesn't have to be that you want to be in "good" health, although that's logical. But there's usually a why even behind that! Things like: you want to be around to play with grandchildren. It could be that you want to enjoy your life more. It could be that you believe you will be more comfortable and happier. And that's the point: whatever your reasoning for the change, that's more important than the change itself. You have to know the end you're shooting for.

And then you realize pretty quickly that you need other measures. If you lose the 20 pounds but are unhealthy in other ways, you're still in trouble. If you quit smoking but increase your drinking, are you successful?

This is why we have to dig deep and find the end. By finding the root question, the root goal, we can ensure that we are heading in the right direction.

Both of my parents smoked. I grew up in a cloud and didn't realize it. Everything smelled of smoke. Everything. Even the dog. But I never noticed because it was always there. Although I didn't smoke (what parents would let their children smoke?), my clothes smelled of it. My hair smelled of it. The cloud filled our house.

Much later in life, when I was grown and out of the house, my parents decided they wanted to quit smoking. I was so happy for them. And it wasn't just to quit. It was driven by the need to combat other health issues that were appearing on their horizon. They had actually quit multiple times in their lives—only to return to tobacco road. And the return was easy. Besides nicotine being one of the most addictive substances you can purchase legally, they didn't have an end to measure against.

In the past they quit because they thought they should. They could save money. Things would smell nicer. They'd have less trash in the house—no ash-filled dishware. But those were just benefits of quitting, and after a while the addiction would win out. The "pleasure" they got from smoking outweighed those small benefits.

It wasn't until the end was bigger—and big *enough*—that they quit and stayed that way.

This is tough for people and organizations. We love small wins. We love making headway along the way. We want to see success as we go along. And you can, of course. You should celebrate whenever you can. But you have to know the end, the root goal. And measure that. Otherwise you can continually win battles but lose the war.

So the answer to "where do you begin?" is "at the end." We'll come back to this soon (at the end of this chapter).

But first, what exactly is *success*?

Types of Success

There are many ways to interpret success. While writing this I struggled to keep from using the words *success, successful,* or *successfully* in the wrong sense. We can claim success when we achieve a task—cracking an egg into a pan without breaking the yoke. We can also claim success when we win a game, reach a goal, or get a promotion. It's important that we clarify what we mean by success, especially since this book is all about measuring success.

Success Is More than Winning

The simplest way to look at success is to see if you won. I enjoy sports, a lot. Not watching them, although I prefer watching a good college ball game (almost any sport) to much of the rest of what television offers today. I mean I enjoy playing sports. From the youngest age, I learned that competition was a normal way of life. My mother (yup, not my dad) was a fierce competitor and would even talk smack to us kids. Then I found myself playing sports almost every day, especially when school was out, on the playground, in front of our house on the street, or through the backyards of our neighbors.

As for a lot of people in the world, this kind of sport wasn't organized with referees, an audience, and doting parents watching. It was just for the love of the game. And some days were much better than others. I'd have to say we won a lot more than we lost.

But was I successful?

Each day I could judge my wins vs. losses, but my feelings of self-worth and achievement weren't ruled by my record at the end of the day.

Success wasn't based on wins and losses. It was based on "having a good day," which translated to playing well, avoiding any serious conflicts (fights), and doing well as a team. Even though my team was different from day to day. On a bad day, it would be different game to game!

As I've aged, I still play sports. And I still love the competition—the physicality of the sport, the exhilaration of making a great play. I assure you, winning always feels better than losing, but I still don't judge my success by wins and losses. Today I still judge it on how well I played, how well we played as a team, healthy and good sportsmanship (no fights), and now I've added "lack of injury." Funny how that has become more important as it takes longer for me to heal.

Getting old isn't fun.

Playing sports is.

But no one I know would consider me a success in any of the sports I play.

Even when I've won a tournament or a league championship, the joy and glow of winning is temporary. For me to be a "success" in a sport, I'd pretty much have to make it to a Division I college, or later the pros. And even then we have levels of success based on our roles on the team. Being a "role" player on a professional team is better than being a practice squad player. Being a second-string player is better than being a role player. Being a starter is a lot better than being second string, and of course the best players on the team are considered, well, *the best*.

But we judge each of these people on more stringent criteria for success as players.

No, *wins* are too fleeting and temporary a measure of success to be valuable.

In 2016 the Golden State Warriors (National Basketball Association) lost only 9 games in an 82-game season. A record! An amazing record! They also lost only nine games throughout the playoffs and championships. But they are still seen as a failure by some because that year they were also the first team to ever lose the championship series when leading three games to one in a best of seven series.

Last night my wife and I were walking (walking is her preferred means of exercise), and I told her I had a "good" day at basketball.

"I had a good day today." I said, mostly as small talk. She knew I meant basketball.

"Really, why?"

"Well, we went undefeated (winning four games), I played well, and no one got hurt."

Yes. Success in basketball is very heavily weighted based on the number of injuries to the coworkers I play with.

So, although you can measure success at the minute level of wins and losses—this is not "success."

Success is More than Being the Best at Something

One of my best mentors while in the military was a chief master sergeant who told me how to live up to the Air Force Value of "Excellence in All We Do."

It was great advice at the time because I felt trapped in a job that I didn't like. Rather than complain or try to change jobs, he said I should strive to be the best. He said, regardless of the job I'm given, I should work hard to become the best of anyone at that position.

I thought this was an interesting way to deal with a job I didn't like. Most people would just do enough until their tour was up or they could finagle their way into a different position. But rather than try to get away from the job, he suggested that I master it.

After being in the civilian workforce for 15 years, I can say that I'm not sure this would work for the corporate world. If I were to become the expert at a job, I'd likely be trapped doing that job forever.

This wasn't a risk in the military because assignments were normally not more than two or three years.

Becoming the expert, the best at a job, was a great way to focus on the role and better serve my organization. By becoming the best (or just striving to), I learned a ton about the job and the organization as a whole. It gave me a great feeling of self-worth and accomplishment. It garnered me accolades and awards. It helped put me on a faster track for advancement.

But was I successful? At that particular job? Maybe. I could be the expert and not be considered successful. Let's say I was a pilot (no, I wasn't, but it's an easier job to explain than a communications officer). Let's say I was the best A-10 Warthog pilot in my unit—or even in the Air Force. But let's also imagine that I never flew an active mission. Let's say I never destroyed an enemy's bunker, took out an anti-aircraft gun, or defended a critical position. Although I may have been the acknowledged "best," if I didn't get to put those skills to use at a critical time, I wouldn't be considered a success at that job.

Imagine a fireman—the best in the county—who never had to respond to a fire or other emergency. Imagine a lawyer who never tried a big case, or a doctor who never had to perform surgery in an emergency room.

I'm CPR certified. But am I successful at it? Am I only successful if I have to use it to save a life?

Simply being the best doesn't equate to being successful.

Feel free to argue with me.

I can hear some of you saying that Michael Jordan was successful—perhaps one of the most successful basketball players of all time. And you may even argue that he was successful because he was (and still is) considered the best to ever play the game.

But *was* he successful?

If you say, "Of course! He won the NBA championship six times!" you would, of course, be right about the number of championships. But that's only good enough to tie him for tenth place. And we've already discussed why wins aren't a good measure of success.

"How about all his records? MVP awards? All-Star team appointments?"

We can stop arguing. I think of Michael Jordan as one of the best that ever played, one of the greatest players of all time.

But that wasn't the question. The question was: does that make him successful? Of course, if you tell me he was successful at the sport, I'll agree. But to know whether he was an overall success, we'd have to look at so much more. His image. His brand. How he ended up after his career. And like a superhero endowed with special powers—did he use them for the betterment of mankind?

There are many awesome athletes endowed with incredible talents who don't wield their power in such a way that even their mother would be proud. Are they successful?

One of the best leaders of all time, who pushed a nation to singular heights of power and achievement, could be considered successful—up until the time he overreached and was defeated.

Being the best or an expert is a great achievement. But it doesn't mean you are a success.

Success is More than Being Happy

Winning is better than losing any day of the week. Even when you had a good day, a competitive day in which you played well, if you lost every game, it just wouldn't feel as good as it would if you'd won a few. And if you won every game, even if you didn't play as well, you would definitely feel better. Better about yourself, better about the day, and better about life.

Winning feels good.

For some, it even makes them happy.

Being the best at something can also make you feel very good. You feel good about yourself, about what you do every day (especially when you use your knowledge and expertise to help others), and about life in general. It feels good to have mastered anything. From cooking to writing, from playing golf to writing code, being an expert at something feels good.

It definitely can make you feel happy most days.

But is happiness equal to success?

Richard Branson said as much in a LinkedIn article called "My Metric for Success? Happiness" (www.linkedin.com/pulse/my-metric-success-happiness-richard-branson): "Too many people measure how successful they are by how much money they make or the people that they associate with. In my opinion, true success should be measured by how happy you are."

There was more to it. He went on to describe what makes him happy. And it wasn't making money or associating with certain people. It wasn't a result of fame or fortune.

Happiness is an emotion. Happiness can be a state of mind. Happiness should help us know if we're on the right track, but it's not success. Like winning, happiness is transitory. It's not long-term. We can be extremely happy today and depressed tomorrow. Happiness is a reaction.

Although we can do things to make ourselves happier and to maintain a state of happiness, it's highly probable that there will be occasions where we will not be happy. If we measure our success based on our degree of happiness, we allow outside factors to determine our success.

We'll come back to Mr. Branson's measure of success, because as I mentioned—he gave some great insights into what made him happy, and that's where we'll find a good example of what success truly is. The key, as with most things, is the underlying *why*. What makes you happy—and more importantly, *why* does it make you happy?

All of These Things May Be Indicators of Success, but They Are Not Predictive

Winning, expertise, and happiness are not the right answers, but they all help with understanding how to measure success. You can win and not be successful. Be it the lottery or a basketball game—winning doesn't in itself lead to success. Of course, you may say you were successful at the specific effort or endeavor. But that doesn't mean *you are a success*.

If you are the best at what you do, if you are *the* expert in your field, if you are the most sought-after person in your profession—this does not mean you are a success.

Even if you are happy or content, there is a good chance you would not consider yourself a success. If you are a *success*, chances are you will be happy—but happiness is not a determining factor in your level of success.

Success is based on something more.

Success has to stand a test of time. You can't determine from a single data point, or a single point in time, whether you are successful. You can't judge it on one action.

When you look back on your life or the life of your organization—how will you see it? Will you look back with contentment and a peacefulness that you did what you were supposed to do and did it as well as you were supposed to do it? Were you effective and efficient in life?

Remember the self-help books and teachers that had you write your own eulogy? They wanted you to capture how you wanted to be remembered. They were on the right track. They were helping you to determine what success meant to you.

But remember, we have to start at the end.

So, we've gone over a lot of examples of what success isn't. But what is it?

Defining Success Through Achievement

Defining success by your level of achievement may be the most common way of thinking of success. This can include everything from winning your fifth-grade spelling bee to being awarded a meritorious service medal.

By Goal Attainment

This would be the simplest way to measure a success. Did we do what we set out to do? If my goal is to write a book on measuring success, did I get it done? Easy enough.

But, that's still very simplistic—actually too simplistic. If I write that book, but it is never published, was I successful? Well, technically yes, if I measure success only by the attainment of a goal. The goal was to write the book—and I did. But therein also lies the problem with poor measurements: if we don't define the root question properly, we end up measuring the wrong things.

If you want to know whether you are a successful writer, we already know it isn't a measure of how good you are. And this should be apparent—if you are the best writer the world has never seen, you are likely not successful. I think of the writers whose works have never seen the light of day. Or those whose works were discovered long after they passed. Were they successful?

Is the goal of writing a book a good goal?

I deal with organizations and individuals who would say yes. It's a good start. It's an attainable goal. It's a SMART goal. In fact, I know some who would argue that better goals would be ones of even a smaller nature. Writing a chapter every ten days would be a better goal.

Breaking down a task or goal into subtasks (and subgoals) is a great tool for figuring out how to "eat the elephant."

But subtasks and subgoals are not great measures of success. No, you have to push back and push up to the higher-level goals. You have to get to the root need, the root goal. You have to ask those *five whys* so you can find out what the end goal is. Remember: start at the beginning but measure based on the end game.

You can feel good about writing a book. You should feel good about finishing the task! Not many people have the discipline or will to write an entire book. You can even be happy with yourself and hopefully happy with the book.

But that's a lower level of success.

To be successful, we need to look at why you're writing the book. What's the bigger goal? Is it to be published? To sell copies? To share your knowledge, expertise, insights, and ideas?

Although achieving the steps along the way may help make you successful, accomplishing those steps is not what you should be measuring against. It has to be the final goal, the root goal.

HOW SMART ARE SMART GOALS?

SMART goals have been around for a while now, but I keep getting confused by the acronym (see Figure 1-1). The idea was that a SMART goal is a well-written goal. One that you can use to build a plan for. But I truly believe that someone decided that SMART made a catchy acronym and then worked to find a way to make the terms fit.

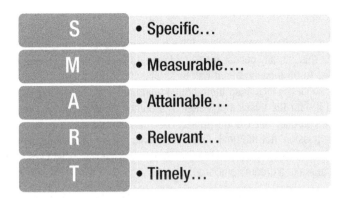

Figure 1-1. One version of a SMART goal

A quick search on the Internet will get you varying definitions:

S—specific

M—measurable or motivational

A—attainable, active, assignable, accountable, aggressive, achievable, or ambitious

R—relevant, realistic, or responsible

T—time-bound, timed, timely, or touchable

And that's only from a cursory inspection. I'm sure there are many more. Notice that only one of the words is consistent? Seems that everyone agrees that *specific* is a criterion for a well-written goal, but the rest are up for debate.

Let's look at each of the terms.

Specific

I totally agree. Any well-written goal should be specific. Specificity allows you to know exactly needs to be done. And to be fully specific, I believe it has to include what has to be done and when it has to be done by. The when isn't so much an exact date or time as it is a clear indication of relationships. Does this goal have to be completed before another goal can be accomplished? Is there a prerequisite effort to this one?

For specificity, I like clear and plain English. It should be simple enough that someone outside your organization (I love using in-laws for this) can understand what needs to get done.

I like specific a lot. If you are specific, I should be able to easily determine how to measure if you have achieved the goal. So, if it's specific, it will be measurable.

Measurable

Yup. Being an admitted metrics geek, I like this one. And if it's specific, it will be. So, I don't think this is really necessary. But if I were to include any of the others, I'd say measurable. To be measurable, it has to be specific. So I'm not sure which should come first, so I'll say let's keep them both. I found only one instance of *motivational*. And I liked it—for the mission or vision. The author thought a good goal should be emotionally charged, but I don't agree. The mission and vision behind the goals provide the passion, not the goal. And many goals are very mundane. It's very hard to get motivated to accomplish many of the tedious goals, objectives, and tasks necessary to make a dream come true.

So I have to disagree with motivational. That's trying to make goals more than they need to be.

Attainable

This is where we really get to the forced acronym conspiracy theory. The ones who use *attainable* or *achievable* realize that R can't then be realistic, because the words are too much alike. So, if they use *attainable* or *achievable*, they have a different R word. If they use *realistic*, they have a different A. I'll address the major two I found for the A in SMART.

I don't really care if you believe your goal is attainable, achievable, or the R equivalent of realistic. Especially if we're looking at the very long-range goals needed to achieve our vision. I don't want a vision you believe is attainable, achievable, or realistic. I want a vision that seems as close to impossible as possible. It should require a serious change in the world to come true. It only has to be desired, hopefully highly desirable. But I never want people to say, "Oh yeah, we can do that."

So if I don't want these to describe the vision, I don't want them to describe the long-range goals that we've identified to get us to the vision.

The closer we get to the operational level, the more these adjectives become acceptable. I want the really short-range goals, objectives, and tasks to be doable. But because the SMART acronym should work for all goals (not only operational ones), I can't agree with these definitions.

The other options for A, *aggressive* and *ambitious*, are almost the opposite. And staying true to the logic for saying no to *attainable*, I also can't agree with these. These work better for the vision, but they don't hold true for the tactical items.

The only other A's were *accountable* and *assignable*. These don't work for me either. Because we know that goals are the *what*—and not the *how*—I don't need a well-written goal to define who should be responsible for seeing it come true. I want it to be wide open where anyone with passion, talent, or the resources to accomplish can take it on. I want to pull more people in, not shut them out. So no, I don't need to assign goals nor do I need to be able to hold someone accountable. And even if I did, if I write the goal with specificity and it's measurable, that should more than cover the need to be able to track progress and accomplishment.

Realistic

The most popular R word is the one I already addressed under *attainable* and *achievable*. The other two I found were *relevant* and *responsible*. *Responsible* harkens back to *accountable* and *assignable* (remember, R and A flip back and forth).

Relevant is new, though. Obvious, but that shouldn't be a reason to kill it. I think *specific* and *measurable* should be obvious too. I teach that goals in a strategic plan have to be aligned and comprehensive to the mission or vision. So I actually like this one. But I think *aligned* and *comprehensive* are much more important. A goal has to help achieve the bigger, parent goal and eventually the mission and/or vision. And when I take all the goals together, I have to have a high level of confidence that the mission will be fulfilled or the vision achieved.

So before I rewrite the acronym, let's just say the majority of the R terms are not necessary. We'll come back to *relevant* in a second.

Time-bound

Except for the very far stretch (and singular) attempt to make it *touchable*, all the T terms are about time. *Timely, time-bound, time-based*, or *timed*. I discussed this under *measurable* a little already. The problems with requiring a good goal to have a estimated completion date are many.

The simplest problem is that the guesstimate of when a goal should, could, or would be done is rarely right. In the rare cases where the goal has to be achieved by a certain date—it makes the goal less of a goal and more of a task or requirement. A *goal* is normally something you're trying to achieve—not a task that must be done, and not one that has to be done by a certain date.

But goals may easily be prerequisites for other goals, or require that other goals be achieved first. It's useful to put a date to our goals because they help us plan. But it's not necessary. This is proven in how many times we're so far off from the original guess for when it will be done.

So I'm down to two of the five terms: S & M. Unfortunate. Perhaps that's why the originator kept going.

Well, I can add *Aligned* and *Comprehensive*. So, SMAC.

You may be wondering why the *why* isn't part of the SMART model. I'm actually happy with it not being there. I don't believe it needs to be. You still have to know the *why* behind the *what*, but you don't need it to be part of the goal. That's what *aligned* and *comprehensive* would do for you. They would assure that your goals are the right goals (in the case of strategic planning, the *why* should be the mission or vision).

To create a well-written goal, it should be Specific and Measurable.

To create a meaningful goal, it should be Aligned and Comprehensive. What good is it to have a well-crafted goal if it's the wrong thing to do?

By Progress to a Plan

I work with many organizations on strategic plans because it's a great way to work toward a vision. I used to help them come up with goals and subgoals, objectives and tasks. But that was a waste of time for me and for them.

Really.

I helped create numerous strategic plans that ended up literally gathering dust on a shelf.

One of the participants asked me if I could help her create a personal strategic plan. I saw no reason not to, so we embarked on a new journey. New to both of us. Luckily, we started by finding her vision, her ultimate dream for the future. She is still today, more than five years later, working toward that vision and making great progress.

Her plan never gathered dust.

When she was able to tick off a goal as achieved or a task as done, it wasn't by accident. Too many goals in strategic plans are achieved without any purposeful direction. The organization looks back at the end of the year to see what they've achieved. It's the first time they pull out the strategic plan they wrote the previous year. They then see what they've achieved "according" to the plan. But anything they accomplished was done with absolutely no directed intention.

But Carmen has been a poster child for doing it right. And it has not gone unnoticed. I now refuse to create a strategic plan with, or for, anyone without first identifying the vision that will guide and define that strategic plan.

Oh, it's okay *not* to have a vision. I like to say, "Anyone can be a visionary, but not everyone." A strategic plan is designed to get you from where you are to where you want to be. And where you want to be needs to be far away from where you are—or you wouldn't need a plan! If I'm only going to walk down to the library, I don't need a map.

Strategic means *long-range*. It means that you have to think more than operationally.

Of course, we can measure success against a plan without that plan being strategic. Just as we can measure success against accomplishing a task or set of tasks—but that's not big enough. We can succeed at all the tasks, objectives, and goals within an operational plan. We can be extremely effective and efficient in our day-to-day efforts. We can also go out of business. Our organization can fail spectacularly while doing really well at the day-to-day because we totally missed the big picture.

If we have a strategic view, a strategic plan we're following, we can measure our progress to that plan. And as with measuring goal attainment, we have to ask the simple one-word question: why? Because there are many steps along the journey, success has to be measured by where we end up, not just how we got there.

Progress to the plan is important. The journey is important. We have to stay true to our values and beliefs. We have to do the right things, the right ways. These are definitely factors in the measurement of success. But the critical measure is our progress toward the end we have envisioned. If you stay on the right path and are working toward your purpose, but you are taken from this life before you finish, you may or may not have been a success. Unfortunately, the definition of success requires that you made progress, not just that you were on the right path.

The *right path* means (hopefully) that you were a good person. That you not only were working toward your singular purpose, but did so while staying true to your values, beliefs, and principles. You can be a *good* person and still not be a success. Success requires more than living a *good* life. It requires that you live the *right* life.

Carmen taught me that we can be successful at two levels: individually and organizationally. If we can have strategic plans and visions at each level, we can also achieve success at each level.

Three Ways to Look at Success

We've looked at success based on what we've done and how others recognize what we've done. Another way to look at success is by who is doing the judging. I guess we could look at it from your boss's point of view, a preacher delivering your eulogy, or Saint Peter deciding whether to allow you through the pearly gates—but I mean at the individual, team, and organization levels. We'll look at success based on the viewpoint of who is successful.

Success at the Individual Level

At its core, how to define success is a very personal question. Each of us defines success based on our own perspective and perception of the world around us. That's because for each of us, success is based on achieving our own personal goals. More importantly than achieving our goals is what drives those goals in the first place.

We have to start at the end.

So what is success to you? How do you determine whether you are a success personally? Is it based on your accumulated worth? Is the foundation of your success a matter of prestige and status? Is it determined by the car you drive? The size of your home? Or your stock portfolio?

Is your success a factor of how many LinkedIn connections or Facebook friends you have?

You may think I'm joking—but why else do people collect connections and contacts like trophies? Too many people measure their success on how others see them. These same people will judge their self-worth based on the opinions others have of them—which, logically, is in direct contrast to the concept of *self*-worth.

What does success mean to you?

At an early stage we are asked, "What do you want to be when you grow up?" We spend many years trying to find an answer to this innocuous question. We end up defining who we are by what we do. Doctor, lawyer, bartender, cook, artist, programmer, or teacher. When we focus on our livelihood, we define success based on our acclaim and status in that position.

Are you a doctor? Are you the head of a hospital? Are you a renowned surgeon?

A teacher? Have you climbed the educational ladder to principal yet? Or are you a professor? Have you earned tenure at a prestigious university?

A cook? Have you become the head cook? Better yet, are you a head chef at a well-known restaurant?

All of these are examples of how others measure your success. If you have a profession, then you are successful if you are at the "top of your profession." Have you perfected your craft? Are you famous yet? Have you written books on your field of expertise? Have others written about you? Better yet, have they named something after you yet?

What does success really mean to you?

You can't judge true success by how others look at you. Their view is clouded by selfishness, jealousy, and a skewed perspective based on how they see themselves. No, you shouldn't define success based on how others judge you. You will never find a sense of accomplishment, self-worth, or peace if you let others define your success.

Only you can determine what success means for you.

Success at the Group/Team Level

The key to defining personal success is not letting others define it for you. Each person has to find their own definition for success. And this is also true of any group or team.

Coaches will readily confess that their job is to help the team define their own goals and vision. The team has to determine what success will mean at the team level.

In *Players First: Coaching from the Inside Out*, by John Calipari and Michael Sokolove (Penguin Books, 2015), Calipari writes that one of his first (and most important) steps in building his team each year is to ask them, "What is your 'why?' Why are you playing basketball for the University of Kentucky, and what do you hope to achieve?" The team has a purpose. It probably has a vision. Finding out what that is is the job of the leader. Not to define it, but to facilitate its identification.

Your work groups have to do the same. Of course, the group leader can determine what she sees as a successful group—but that projection may not hold true with the members of the group. If the group doesn't see it the same way, chances are what the leader wants the group to do and to become will not come to fruition.

Of course, the leader can define what success as the leader of the group means—in fact, *only* she can. But the group has to do much more than "buy in" to a definition of success. The group has to create that definition. And it won't be based on other groups or teams.

Being better than other groups in the organization or even the competition does not define success. You can know this because if a team's success is judged by its status compared to other teams, one path to success would be to work really hard to make the other teams fail. It would only require that your team be a little better than everyone else. Your team could range from outstanding down to mediocre, but as long as it was better than everyone else, it would be judged a success.

This is obviously not a valid way to measure success—unless that is your only goal. Even then, I think that definition of success would fail to pass the gut check.

LISTEN TO YOUR GUT

For all measures, I tell leadership that the data and measures they look at should either confirm their suspicions or provide a surprise.

Most leaders (especially the good ones) already know whatever the measures tell them. They are rarely surprised because one of the things that make them good is that they understand the organization. A good leader can read the pulse of the organization. Any objective measures only serve to confirm their subjective read on the organization. Occasionally the measures provide a surprise because the leader was looking in the wrong direction, and the measures serve to bring the leader's gaze back in focus to what is important.

I tell leaders that their "gut" is probably right. They already know what the measures tell them. That doesn't mean they don't need the measures, because the measures give them tools for sharing their story and gaining support. They also identify small fluctuations, helping the leader calibrate his gut.

Tell a leader that his team is a success because it's the best team out there—and his gut will tell him whether it's because his team is stellar or because the bar is so low that mediocrity is king.

Success at the Organizational Level

If it's hard to get a small group or team together and agree on what success means, imagine the level of difficulty when you are dealing with an organization of 50, 100, or 150. It's hard to come to any consensus, much less actual agreement on anything. How do we get them to agree on what success means for the organization?

Again, the leader (CEO, president, manager) can define what success means for her position in relation to the organization, but she can't define it for the organization as a whole. And I'll grant you, it's not going to be easy or even possible to get everyone together and work through the complexity of determining a common definition of success.

Especially if we seek consensus or buy-in.

The good news? Having a large organization, as a body, agree on what success means is not only possible—it's much easier than it sounds. And it's essential.

What Success Is

I've shared some ways success should not be measured (winning, expertise, happiness) and different ways we currently define success (goal attainment, progress to a plan). We spent a little time looking at how success can be applied to individuals, teams, and large organizations.

Your values and beliefs will play an important role in defining your success. But there is an underlying premise to how we measure success that will help us move forward, and it's based on just two things.

The foundation to measuring success is based on your purpose and your vision. Why these two things? Because these are the highest view you can have of your goals in life. We have to measure success based on the end. The root goal. That root goal, the thing we all want to achieve, is to find the meaning of life. Not life in general, but at a very personal level. What is the meaning of *our* lives? What is *our* purpose? What is *our* calling? This is the at the core of all human beings—we want to fulfill a purpose. Our purpose.

At the individual or organizational level. To be truly successful we have to rise to the highest vantage point possible. This is the "be all" and "end all." It's our full measure of success. All other measures, as we'll learn, are subsets of true success:

1. *Your calling*: Success is defined by the reason you exist. How well are you fulfilling your purpose in life? How well are you answering your calling? Is your organization fulfilling its purpose? Is it meeting its mission?

2. *Your vision*: Not everyone has a vision. Being a visionary is not for everyone. Anyone can be a visionary, but not everyone. If you have a vision, a massively large, scary, world-changing goal for the future, how well you move the world toward that vision is the other definition of success. And organizations are great for this.

Yes, it's that simple.

Don't worry, we'll return to these two pillars throughout the book, so you will not only understand how to measure success based on these definitions, but you will learn how to make them the basis for all your measures of success.

Let's dig deeper!

HOW DO YOU MEASURE SUCCESS (PERSONALLY, PROFESSIONALLY, AND FOR THE ORGANIZATION)?

Lisa, Chief Executive Officer (from her official biography)

Lisa is the CEO of a provider of global financial business solutions. Her company is based in 23 locations worldwide, with more than 4,000 employees. Her customers include financial advisors, broker-dealers, family offices, fund managers, registered investment advisor firms, and wealth managers.

She is a passionate advocate for developing talent and bringing diversity and multiple voices to build the best teams.

Lisa has been with her organization for more than 25 years and brings rich experience to this role. She was most recently the chief operating officer of the firm, responsible for ensuring that the firm had the operational controls, administrative and reporting procedures, and people and systems in place to effectively grow and maintain financial strength and operating efficiency.

Among her many accolades, Lisa was named one of the 50 Most Influential Women in Private Wealth by *Private Asset Management* magazine (2016).

The point I'm trying to make is that Lisa would have to be considered a leader in the financial industry. Most of us would assume that her focus and her measures of success would be centered around profits. Her company definitely has a reason to care about turning a profit and helping its customers do the same. But is that how she measures success for herself, or for her company?

Lisa agreed to a telephone interview, for which I am extremely grateful. While we're talking about money, you can imagine how much her time is worth. So taking time out of her busy schedule to talk to me about how to measures success was a very generous gift.

I really enjoyed interviewing Lisa. She was very genuine and open.

Lisa explained that she knew the norm for being deemed successful was the quarterly performance reports—basically the financial reports.

"It's the traditional way that everyone is measured, but the financial results are actually a result of everything else we do. It's an indicator that the things we do are effective."

Lisa's core or key measure of success was focused on her employees. Were her employees engaged? Were they invested? Were they working as a team? How was employee morale? Were they happy to be working for her company? Were they focused in the same direction? Did they want to "win"?

Looking back at my book *Metrics: How to Improve Key Business Results*, I was happy to hear that she was focused on the Employee Viewpoint. It's a great way to improve the organization and determine how well her organization is functioning.

Per the Answer Key, the choices were Customer, Management, Employee, or Leadership viewpoints. As happy as I was that she wasn't looking at the Management Viewpoint, efficiency measures, I was not surprised that she wasn't using the Leadership Viewpoint: program, project, and strategic goal attainment measures.

I wasn't surprised because from everything I had heard about Lisa before our interview, I knew she cared more about her employees than about tracking strategic plan completion. So I had to ask her why she didn't include profits in her success measures.

"The profit will take care of itself if we take care of our employees."

I would definitely like working for this person.

She measured her personal success (as a CEO) and the success of her organization on her employee's perception of the organization's health.

And not only did she use the Employee Viewpoint, but she believes in sharing those success measures with them.

"Sharing the measures with employees helps them to know that what they do matters. They can see their results and know they're doing well.

"Employee engagement, when employees are happy to be a part of the organization, flows into the customers' view of the organization. We should be viewed as a partner with our customers. We can ask, 'Are we attracting new clients? Are we keeping our current clients?'

"But the basis for it all is our employees and how they're performing. We can look at engagement feedback, upward feedback, turnover rates, and participation rates."

I was very happy with her thoughts on success measures. Not because they were a good way to measure success but because they were a very healthy way at looking at her organization's health.

But I still had to get to success measures. I had to know whether Lisa considered the measures of employee engagement equal to organizational success. So, as I found myself doing with all my interviews, after they shared, I shared.

I explained my views of measuring success with Lisa.

In reply, she offered a story.

Whatever you measure you can improve.

A few years ago, they wanted to improve their service to their clients, so they created performance measurements with the intent of sharing with their clients.

But if they measured performance, how should they deal with the expectation that employees would likely feel as if they were being put under a microscope? They decided to provide the measures of each employee's performance to the employee first using a runway of six months before clients would see them.

Month one, the employee would be the only one to see the measures. Lisa knew that employees were much harder on themselves than any of their management ever were. And true to form, the employees, when reviewing their feedback, were dissatisfied with the results. Employees conducted self-evaluations, listening to tapes of their customer service calls. They wanted to improve their own performance. In the second month their direct supervisors were added to the review process. The employee reviewed the results with the supervisor, discussing the quality of performance, what should be improved, and how that might happen. Month three, the supervisor's supervisor was added. This continued until the most important person was added: the customer. This worked very well, increasing performance to the highest levels up to that point. Besides the runway process, each employee was provided a coach to help them through the process. Employees created the solution and were vested in its success.

By the time the performance reviews reached the customer, many of the employee, process, and organizational issues had been eliminated. But the clients almost didn't need to see the performance report because they were experiencing the improvements in service all along the journey.

This worked great, and the organization saw excellent results.

When I asked about the organization's purpose, Lisa offered, "Every step [the organization takes] should advance you toward your mission and vision. We're immature by these standards [measuring success in this way]."

She added, "We need employees walking on the same path. Leadership has to motivate all of its (more and more limited) resources toward the mission and vision. We can't afford to have any outliers, resources not dedicated to achieving the vision and fulfilling our mission. Everyone has to work together, 'heave ho,' together.

"Our goal is to give our customers what they need by providing the most vibrant and comprehensive solutions in our industry. [To be] the 'Apple' of the financial industry."

So whereas her focus was currently on the employees' contribution to the mission and vision, she agreed that it wasn't enough. There was more that needed to be done.

It's interesting that of all the leaders I interviewed, Lisa seemed to be the most familiar with the topic. Even then, it didn't seem to be something she spent a lot of time mulling over. It wasn't something she was currently or constantly gathering, working on, or using. Success measures seem to be something that leaders and organizations aren't using. And I think I understand why.

If you aren't measuring the right things, you intuitively know. I tell my clients all the time that their gut is a great barometer of the accuracy of their measures. It's also a great indicator if you have found your mission, your vision, and your measures of success. I think they know that the performance measures aren't the answer. They also know that goal-attainment metrics don't tell the whole story. So why spend a lot of time and energy on things that won't really tell you whether you're successful? I'm hoping that this book will help change that. If we have the right success measures, true measures of success that tell the whole story, the right story—I think they will be in high use and high demand.

Summary

What is success?

It's important to understand what we mean by success before we dig deeper into measuring it.

There are different ways of looking at success—traditionally we look at winning vs. losing, being the best at something, or being happy. There are other possible ways to define success: attaining goals or progressing along a plan. We can also look at success differently based on our point of view—individual success vs. team, department, or organization success. But none of these gives us the higher-level view of success that we're addressing in this book. We're looking for the ultimate measures of success because all other measures will grow from there.

This is why we start at the end. You can think of *The End* if it makes it easier for you. At The End (of your life or your organization's existence), how will you judge success? When you look back at your life, a retrospective if you will, how will you decide whether you were a success, an also-ran, or a failure? Not by any of the awards or accolades you received along the way—those are temporary and fleeting. We're looking for a longer-lasting, deeper definition of success.

Why You Should Measure Success Before Performance

If you currently have measures for your organization, chances are they are performance measures. Even if you're doing metrics right, chances are you're not measuring success. If you aren't measuring anything—great! You have an opportunity to start at the end. If you're currently measuring performance, I'm asking you to stop. Not stop using the ones you have, just don't create any new ones, yet. Don't build any new KPIs. Don't develop a program around your performance measures. Instead, take the time to find measures of success first.

The Answer Key

In my book *Metrics: How to Improve Key Business Results* (Apress, 2011), I introduced a tool, the Answer Key, for simplifying how you look at organizational metrics. We need to look at how the Answer Key fits with measuring overall success.

© Martin Klubeck 2017
M. Klubeck, *Success Metrics*, DOI 10.1007/978-1-4842-2586-8_2

Customer Viewpoint measures are also known as *Effectiveness* measures. These measures define how well you (or your organization) are doing from the customer's vantage point. It's made up of things like customer satisfaction, usage, availability, and speed of delivery. But these don't equal success.

What Effectiveness measures tell you is how well the organization is doing—the health of the organization. But good health doesn't equate to success. Granted, you'll probably be a relatively healthy organization if you *are* successful, but health isn't a precursor or predictor of success.

In *Metrics*, I spent a decent amount of ink trying to convince readers to start with Customer Viewpoint measures. The reasons were (and still are) simple. Looking at the organization from the customer's point of view is a "safe" way to introduce the organization to metrics.

No matter what story the metrics end up telling you, it's not a reflection of a team's or an individual worker's abilities, attitude, or effort. It is solely an indication of how the customer thinks the organization is doing.

And it's a necessity.

Every organization, regardless of type, has customers. And customers should be king.

According to the Answer Key, there are four Viewpoints for Organizational Health: Customer, Manager, Employee, and Leadership (Figure 2-1).

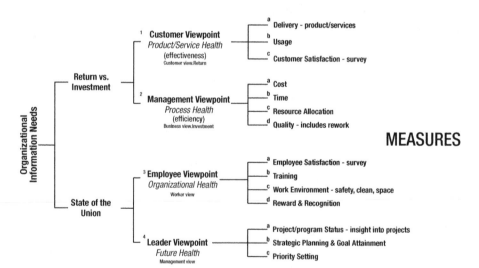

Figure 2-1. The Answer Key

Three of these four choices avoid the fear, uncertainty, and doubt that accompany metrics programs. These insipid, morale killers will fester and grow until they erode the organization's culture from the inside. Management Viewpoint metrics are the only ones that point a finger at the employee. These normally include time to perform, error rates, cost, and resource allocation.

So, I consistently preach against basing a metrics program on the manager's perspectitve. Actually I encourage organizations to only measure with this viewpoint as a tool for improving specific areas identified in the Effectiveness metrics needing greater focus.

I always recommend the Customer Viewpoint.

The other two areas are also safe: Employee and Leadership Viewpoints. I expect most employees would be happy with viewing and analyzing employee satisfaction, training effectiveness, work environment, and reward and recognition programs. But leadership normally balks at these because they don't directly show a return on the investment they require. They also run the risk of exposing poor management and bad leadership. Who wants to put themselves in the spotlight when they can instead start with the customer's view?

When I'm talking to leadership about instituting a metrics program, they invariably want Management Viewpoint measures. If I weren't so cynical, I'd be surprised how often leadership fights me on this. To be fair, I had my optimism beaten out of me—too many trips into the fire. Those in leadership want to work on efficiencies because they think that's their job—to improve the profit margin and manage their people.

In our book *Don't Manage…Coach!* (CreateSpace, 2015), Michael Langthorne and I try to debunk this myopic view of how to lead an organization. We shouldn't manage people. We "manage" things, not people. We work with, build relationships, lead, and coach people. Not manage.

I know a department head who believes he is doing a good job of managing his area. He uses measures to define performance. Each performance evaluation is based on these data points. How fast tasks are completed—you have to be in the average to get a good grade. The tasks can't be done too quickly (it shows you're not spending enough time with the customer) or too long (it shows you're not getting the problems resolved fast enough).

It's data-driven decision making at its worst.

Hopefully, you see how ridiculous this is.

Efficiency measures should never be used for performance evaluations. Besides the ludicrousness of determining the quality of performance by impersonal data points that don't reflect the work done, these measures encourage (loud and clear) workers to focus on the wrong things.

Rather than focus on the customer and the problem at hand, the worker is being trained to focus on the length of the interaction.

Sorry. True story.

So, I spend a lot of time consulting with leadership, teaching them not to start with Efficiency measures. I work really hard to get leadership to stay as far away from them as possible, for as long as possible. Besides training the workforce to focus on the measures instead of the customer, it also feeds the *fear, uncertainty, and doubt* (FUD) that are born of being watched, measured, and judged.

This same FUD exists within all of us. None of us wants to be watched and measured. We want to be consulted, coached, and led. We want to have a relationship with our supervisors, not with our data. The same managers who want to use performance measures to evaluate their people will do everything possible not to be judged by data themselves.

So when we offer up employee measures as a choice to managers, they quickly begin to feel the FUD factor. Even though they'd be the ones receiving the results, they realize that the workers and their bosses will also see these measures and will likely judge their ability to lead based on them. They claim that disgruntled workers will skew the data against them. They fear that their leadership mistakes will be laid bare in front of everyone. Of course they don't want to start with Employee Viewpoint measures!

And Leadership Viewpoint measures aren't any better!

How well projects and programs are progressing, how well the organization is following the strategic plans, and whether the organization is adhering to its own priority setting are all great indicators of how well leadership is doing their job of leading.

The same leadership who wants data on their workers so they can "see" and "know" how well they're doing do everything possible to not measure how well they themselves are doing. Using the Leadership Viewpoint feels like a blame game to leaders—and the fingers are pointed squarely at themselves.

That's a shame because if leaders were to start with themselves and show through example how indicators of performance can be used properly, it could go a long way toward helping the organization mature to a point where metrics are accepted. Imagine if leaders were to be fully transparent with their progress on their strategic plans, prioritization, and programs. If they would show the results without judgment and use the data to identify anomalies so they can find improvements, they'd begin to build trust in measures. More importantly, they would gain experience in using measures properly. Adding to that the experience of dealing with FUD from a first-person perspective should allow them to be more in tune with their workforce's fears, uncertainty, and doubts.

Of course, I've never had leaders actually admit this was the problem. Instead, the reasons usually circle around the lack of immediacy. The leadership measures won't lead to quick improvements. A less common (but more honest) excuse is that the organization frequently lacks a solid strategic plan, has poorly defined goals, and offers no documented priorities. Of course, this is a negative reflection on leadership by itself, and the measures would only highlight these deficiencies.

The metrics would quickly point these out, putting leadership in a poor light. It would also require leaders to work on the missing pieces. Rarely have I found leaders who want to use metrics to identify their own failings or faults.

And in each of these cases—Management, Employee, and Leadership Viewpoints—the common refrain is raised: "But we can't control these measures, and we can't control the outcome, so we shouldn't use them!" That should be enough evidence that FUD is reigning supreme.

Bottom line? Start with the Customer Viewpoint—it works on all levels and avoids the risks of destroying the culture.

That was then.

Now, there's a new sheriff in town.

After working for the last two years helping organizations and individuals define their visions for the future, I've adjusted my position. I won't go as far as to say I was wrong, but out of the four metrics for Organizational Health, you should address them in this order:

1. Definitely start with Customer Viewpoint (effectiveness) and use efficiency only as a tool to improve specific Effectiveness areas.

2. Then go to Employee Viewpoint measures.

3. Followed by Leadership Viewpoint measures.

4. And only go to Management Viewpoint (efficiency) metrics when the organization has matured.

No, the right answer out of the Answer Key is still Customer Viewpoint. The reasons why I developed the Answer Key are twofold.

Leadership Wants an Easy Answer, and Organizational Health is a Valid Place to Start

I've done my best to fight against leadership's penchant for finding an easy answer to the metrics problem, but I can only go so far. I tell this to those I consult with also. Falling on your sword can be admirable, but this is a battle that doesn't warrant it.

A colleague of mine from another university recently sent out a request for benchmark information on helpdesk measures. Actually, she needed to find comparisons for her "scorecard."

"What my supervisor wants is a set of benchmarks for things like percentage of calls resolved at first contact, ticket time to completion, wait time, number of escalations, and number of tickets meeting Service Level Agreement (SLA), etc. We have a scorecard we've developed, and my task is to develop a set of benchmarks that would compare our scorecard to the scorecards of others."

So I gave it a shot.

After apologizing in advance for what I was sure was going to be too much information, I offered the following.

> You likely won't be able to compare your "scorecard" to others' scorecards. Mostly because to find someone else who is tracking all of the same measures in the same form is unlikely. And if you found someone with a similar scorecard, how do you know if that unit's results are typical?
>
> The idea of a benchmark is to find the "norm" for the measures. The idea of comparing to the norm is NOT to determine if you're doing well or not. This is broken thinking. Instead you want to compare to the norm to find out if your results are "anomalies." If your results are far from the norm ("good" or "bad") this gives you a point to start investigating to see if there is:
>
> something you need to improve/change
>
> something you need to continue/encourage
>
> You'll have a much better chance of comparing each measure to as many others as you can find (vs. trying to match them all). You can take all of the others and determine their mean values to see how you fair...BUT that's still broken thinking.
>
> What you really need to do first is:
>
> Develop longitudinal data on your own measures
>
> Identify your own norms
>
> Be able to identify anomalies against your own norms
>
> This will make it possible for you to identify, explain (after investigation), and learn from your own anomalies ("good" and "bad").
>
> The idea that you should compare to others and make changes/decisions based on how you fare against others is broken and lazy. You may want to say that in a much more politically correct way. The point is, comparing

*to others doesn't help if the ones you're comparing to are not almost
identical to you AND you have determined if they are exceptional, good,
fair, poor, or terrible. And you can't determine that by comparing.*

Marty

She was actually thankful for the clarity and thoroughness of the answer. But I
knew this wasn't how her supervisor would take it. Management doesn't want
to hear this. Management wants an easy answer, and unfortunately when we're
talking about using metrics, it's never easy.

So, of course I came up with an answer that at least can start leadership down
the right path with as little risk (and work) as possible. The Answer Key was
this answer. It forced leadership to focus on Effectiveness and gave a repeat-
able, generic answer to a root question that is valid for anyone: What is the
health of our organization? I would still prefer that the leader instead focus on
actual problems and questions, but if you can't get your leadership to invest
this level of effort, the Answer Key will at least minimize your risk.

Root Questions Are Best

Besides the Answer Key, the other types of metrics I suggested were ones in
direct answer to any root questions you had. And that still holds true. It's the
best way to do metrics. The more immature your organization, the better this
is. Rather than try to develop canned measures, benchmark against others,
or measure overall organizational health—it is best to find out what the pain
points are and address those. If you are developing a metrics program for the
sake of having one, you're already in trouble.

An accurate sign of organizational immaturity is developing a metrics program for the sake of
having one.

The best way to start using metrics is to answer a root question. Find out
what it is you need to know and develop metrics to answer that question.
The metrics only exist as long as you need to answer the question and the
results have a clear and understandable purpose. It's fully transparent. No
blame game, no personal attacks, and *no* performance evaluations. Instead, the
information gathered, analyzed, and visually presented is used to answer the
root question.

But most won't listen. They want a metrics program. They want to be able to
say they are "data-driven."

In 2014 I was honored by the Rocky Mountain Association of Institutional Researchers. They invited me to deliver the keynote for their annual conference. My family and I went out to beautiful Coeur d'Alene, Idaho, for the conference. It was one of the best experiences in my life.

When I give presentations, I have a habit of taking some risks. This was no different.

I started off the keynote with a picture representing institutional researchers. And followed it quickly with the statement "I Hate You." Then I showed a picture representing business intelligence, the IT experts who make it possible to access all of your previously hard-to-get-at data. I followed that with "I Hate Them Too."

There were some snickers and giggles, but they weren't sure if they should laugh or be offended.

I think we were both relieved when I explained that I hated these two groups of professionals because they both worked really hard (and most times really well) at making all that data available to management. Big Data is now a reality because of these types of people. Because almost everything is computerized now, there is tons of data to accompany our technology-rich environment. Your car has tons of information about your driving, gas consumption, speed, mileage, and maintenance. When you take your car in for a checkup, the mechanic runs computer diagnostics, pulling data from the car's hard drive.

The simplest survey can tell where the respondent was when they filled it out.

Some of the strongest current software titles advertise how easy they make it to "explore your data." It's all about making Big Data available in a big way.

Data is all over the place, and now we have highly skilled IT professionals pulling that data out of the systems, platforms, and software we use. They are providing that data for our consumption.

The problem, and it *is* a problem, is that we don't have anywhere near the expertise in actually analyzing and using that data properly. Our organization's business intelligence team is still growing, and they have their favorite tool for "playing with the data." This visualization tool makes it easy to make charts and graphs and tables. You can play with the data and see what it might tell you.

I'm getting physically ill thinking about it.

We're handing tons of data to play with to people who have no idea how to use data, measures, and information the right way.

I hate sounding like Chicken Little, but I can see a serious train wreck coming for these managers and their workforce.

I hate institutional research and business intelligence units. Not because of what they do (providing data to the owners of the information). I hate them because we're handing managers poison and sharp instruments with no instructions or directions on how to safely use them.

Add to this the perceived need by management to make "data-driven decisions," and we have already torn up the train tracks. We're just waiting for the locomotive to come around the bend and derail in spectacular fashion.

This fear is well justified.

I still get e-mails and phone calls from staff who have been assigned the task of "pulling together" data so that the manager can make decisions. They are told to find benchmarks with competitors (and peers) so management can decide how well their own organization is performing.

I do my best to talk the callers off the ledge, but unfortunately, the boss keeps trying to push them off of it.

So, I haven't changed my mind. Leadership needs to avoid Efficiency measures like the plague. And when they won't, we have to do everything we can to help them move toward Effectiveness measures instead.

Where I *have* changed my opinion is in starting with Organizational Health at all. If you have root questions, that's still the best place to introduce your organization to metrics. But you're not reading this book because you're looking for a way to introduce your organization to metrics. You're looking to measure success. And that's a great place to start.

But I didn't come to this realization easily.

Four years after helping a nonprofit child development center create a strategic plan, they wanted me back. They told me how impressed they were with my previous work for them, and when it came time to revisit their plan, they knew they had to have me back.

I was feeling pretty proud. I knew we had created a solid plan with long-range, mid-range, and short-range goals. I liked the idea of coming back and basking in the glow of success while helping the organization make any necessary adjustments. I knew no plan totally survived first contact with the enemy (and time is the enemy of all strategic plans), so I expected it to need change.

I told the new board president that I would love to facilitate their revisions. He was very happy, and so was I. For about five minutes.

"I'd like to review the progress you've made so far so we can build off of that for the revision," I started.

"What do you mean?" His earnest reply sent warning bells off in my head.

"I'd like to see what you've accomplished in the last four years, so we can see where we need to go next. We should be able to look at the strategic plan and review which goals were achieved, which failed, and which no longer make sense. Then we can start working on a new set of goals and adjust any that we should keep. It'll make our planning session much more productive."

I was still smiling a stupid grin. I was still proud.

"Oh, well, we haven't used the plan." The warning bells were getting louder.

I'm sure the look on my face told him all he needed to know. He spent the next ten minutes finding a copy of the plan. The one that was bequeathed to him by his predecessor.

It was literally covered with dust. Clang! Clang! Clang!

"Wait. So you didn't use the plan?"

No, they hadn't. Of the 14 goals, they had achieved one, without realizing it. By accident.

So, our first session ran the real risk of being our last. The board and the executive director set aside an hour after their next board meeting for me to have a chat with all of them. I didn't want to waste their time (or mine) with a full-day retreat unless we came to an agreement first.

"How many of you were on the board four years ago when I was here last? How many of you helped develop the last strategic plan?"

About half the board raised their hands.

"So, to the rest of you, I have to apologize. We failed. Miserably." Okay, it may not have been the best way to start a session, but it was honest.

"We created a dead plan. It was stillborn." I had used the terms *living plan* many times with them four years ago.

"Out of the 14 goals we identified, only one was achieved, and that was by accident." There was nervous laughter.

"It's okay that you find it funny. But I don't. I find it sad." I let it sink in.

"We spent a lot of time and effort developing a plan that wasn't used. We created shelfware. And now you've asked me to come back and waste your time again."

And this was probably not the way to secure a job.

"So, here's the deal. If you still want me to lead your strategic planning session, we have to start with a vision." I spent the rest of the hour explaining the need for a very large, very scary, world-changing goal. This vision for the future would provide direction and guidance for everything we put in the strategic plan.

Happily, they agreed. We spent the next five meetings (one hour each) defining their vision for not only the early childhood center, but for early childhood development throughout the geographical region. This vision allowed the board to focus on the *bigger picture*—a place that few are able to work. Leadership is the only component of an organization equipped to do so.

Executive directors, management, and staff are by necessity focused on the operational aspects of the organization. CEOs, boards of directors, and top leaders have to define, articulate, and work toward a larger encompassing vision.

Since that awakening, I demand that any organization developing a strategic plan first define a true vision.

Anyone can be a visionary, but not everyone.

All organizations do *not* have to have a vision—but they also don't need a strategic plan. Many organizations survive happily with just operational plans and a few short- to mid-range goals. For the ones that want long-range goals and a true strategic plan, a vision is a must.

You can't have a strategic plan without a vision.

If you have a driving vision consuming you, awesome! But whether you do or not, every organization and every person has a purpose. I truly believe this. There is a reason for our existence. Without this belief, life is pretty sad. Without a purpose, without a calling, our lives become a series of events with no rhyme or reason.

One good reason to believe we have a purpose is that it makes life exciting. It makes getting up in the morning worth it. It makes it all worth fighting for. And it makes it worth fighting for others.

If we should start by measuring from the highest level possible, we have to look at mission and vision. *Success*—true success—is realized only when we achieve at the highest level possible.

For an organization, success is not topping the Fortune 500, having the highest customer satisfaction ratings, or even dominating its corner of the market.

For individuals, success is not simply amassing wealth, obtaining prestige, or becoming famous.

Success is a result of achieving (or progressing toward) your vision or fulfilling your calling. This should be the very first thing you focus your measurement energies on.

You can't start at the bottom—you can't start with short-, mid-, or long-range goal attainment. Not with "small wins" or low-hanging fruit. Nope. Your first measures should be of success, at the highest level. Your foundational measures should be Measures of Success (MoS).

And you definitely should not start with performance, although most of you will.

Why?

Why, after reading all this, would you still start with measuring performance and not start with finding your overall Measures of Success?

Because it's easier. You can start right now. No thinking required. No introspection, soul searching, or future seeking. All you have to do is use the Answer Key and start measuring your organization's health from the customer's point of view.

And at least you'd be doing some good.

Chances are you won't start with the Answer Key. You'll jump totally off the rails and start by measuring efficiencies. Or you'll dig into that mountain of Big Data you've been handed. You'll demand charts and graphs. You'll not seek root questions. You won't even do the work to figure out the measures you need for seeing your organization from the customer's viewpoint. You'll settle for what's easiest and fastest. You'll not want to put in the effort to do it right.

Why?

Because very few people actually want to do metrics. Very few want to find out where their faults lie. They'd much rather find out what *others* are doing wrong. Introspection is a hard thing to do, at any level or at any time.

The best answer? Find your own root questions and use metrics to improve your business. But if you want to do less work and get right to it—start with Measures of Success.

Start by measuring success. It will be the best barometer of your future.

GETTING IT RIGHT

I met Nathan through my first book with Apress, *Metrics: How to Improve Key Business Results*. A member of his leadership team had read the book and wanted to discuss it with me and her CEO (Nathan). I was happy to. So we set up a teleconference.

After our phone conversation, a subsequent lunch meeting, and more phone conversations, I came to see Nathan as a very strong, kindred spirit. But instead of metrics, Nathan and I are singing in the same choir when it comes to vision setting and defining a greater purpose for an organization. So I was confident that interviewing Nathan would produce very few surprises.

I knew he was someone who got it.

Nathan is the founder and CEO of a young company (launched in 2012) with a special (rare) mission: to help all people [businesses] thrive. And the way to do this is to have something that looks like *Conscious Capitalism* become the norm for how business is done.

"How do you measure success?"

My standard question. And it took no extra prompting to get right to where I want everyone to be.

"How well we are fulfilling our purpose—to have something that looks like conscious capitalism become the norm for how business is done. It's all about how much we move the needle toward the adoption of Conscious Capitalism by mainstream business.

"Conscious Capitalism requires that businesses have a 'higher purpose,' but we have a more specific, rigorous definition. We're moving toward a *Conscious Business model*—which encompasses Conscious Capitalism as a theory/principle. We're currently hashing out how to actually implement it."

I didn't have great, probing questions. Just my standard. "Why?"

"Moral value—we believe that human life is inherently valuable, and the quality of that life is something we should all strive to improve. Businesses (capitalism) should be a major part of that effort.

"Unfortunately, there is persistent inequity within business."

I kept at it. This was the easiest interview I ever had. "What are you doing today to measure success?"

"We're establishing a baseline metric to figure out how many business leaders actually understand the concepts [of Conscious Business]. Currently we have them self-report on whether they are implementing the concepts. We don't think this is reliable. We need to come up with methods for objectively measuring whether they are actually implementing the concepts. We can use your help on that.

"We find that there are many times that our beliefs don't match our actions. Perhaps we can commission someone to create a report on this.

"There are some efforts already in place that try to measure this, a certification program to be designated a *Benefit Corporation* [B Corporation]. For the most part, though, it's highly rigorous, very thorough, and possibly too tough to obtain the legal designation of a B Corporation. To get the B Corporation designation, everything gets checked—from your environmental impact (what cleaning equipment you use) to your community impact (hiring practices) and lots more. I'm proud to say, though, that we've eaten our own cooking. We are certified. It may surprise you to learn that over 1,500 companies are certified."

It did surprise me. I thought their focus was still a small niche. I was very happy to hear that it was spreading.

"We also measure normal stuff—how many companies have we reached? How many companies are we talking to?

"Survival matters. So we need to get the message out, but we also need clients. The good news is that our mission and vision are aligned with our means of making an income."

Nathan's vision was far bigger than his consulting company could accomplish, as it should be.

"In terms of impact, there's a scope issue…it seems ridiculous to believe that all people can thrive. Is a universal scope too large? We could have chosen to focus on one city, like Traverse City. The scope would have been *so* much easier. But we have a universal mission and vision. We fully recognize that there's no way we'll be *the* company that can do it all. No company is large enough to do it on its own.

"We have to be collaborative. We even have to help our competitors! We have to share the vision to make it even remotely possible. We want to make a run on systems that can make it happen…we don't know the answer, but we're trying to do it through Chambers of Commerce in the state of Michigan. And if they take it on as their goal, we all win! Even if they don't use our company, as long as they adopt the Conscious Business model.

"There are five specific domains that create "business as usual," and these domains need to come over to the Conscious Business model if we're going to be successful at changing the paradigm. They are: business schools, professional associations, capital providers (venture capital firms, Wall Street, banks, and so on), Business media (*Conscious Company*, *Fast Company*, and *Inc.* magazines, as well as television), and consultants.

"We want to get all of these five domains to adopt, believe in, and use Conscious Business to change the way all businesses run. We can measure whether those things are changing. We've started by focusing on professional associations, but we are ready, willing, and able to take advantage of any opportunity to work on the other domains."

So, you can see why this was the easiest interview I had. Nathan's company is actually built on helping businesses find their mission and vision—and the definition of each matches mine. The Conscious Business model works for me without modification.

And if you have defined your mission and vision, we can find the right Success Metrics for you. I was very happy that Nathan's company was "eating its own cooking" and wanted to measure success based on how well they fulfilled their mission and moved the needle toward their vision.

Summary

Performance measures can provide value to an organization (or individual). My first book on metrics provided a guide for developing, collecting, analyzing, and using meaningful performance metrics. My biggest concern at that time was to ensure leaders dipped their toes into the hot water first to make sure no one got burned. From years of experience dealing with leaders who had dived in head-first and come out with third-degree burns, I knew it was a much-needed manual.

I still stand by the Answer Key with its four viewpoints: Customer, Management, Employee, and Leadership. I also stand by my conviction that if you are going to measure performance, you should start with the Customer Viewpoint and stay there until your organization matures.

Although I still consult and teach on how to build these performance metrics, I have found another type of metric altogether—which should be your entry-level effort in metrics. If you are already using meaningful performance measures, you should continue. But before you create any new ones, you should learn about and use Success Metrics.

Measuring success provides a special view of your progress—as an individual, team, or organization. It should be the foundation for any measurement program you create. It will help keep you focused on why you do what you do. One of the ways to determine your success is dependent on measuring how well you are fulfilling your calling—and that requires that you know who you are. Each team has to understand its purpose. Every organization has to know its mission.

If you don't have a metrics program in place, I highly recommend you start here. Although performance measures are viable for any organization (or individual), it's better to start with success measures.

Know Yourself

In the preceding chapter I touched on the power of vision and how it can help you define success. I also introduced the universal existence of purpose. We all have a reason for being—we all have a calling. Every team, unit, department, division, and organization *has* a purpose.

Some of us ignore it. We hide from it. We may even actively run from it. And although we have to dig deep inside to determine our personal calling—the mission of your organization should be a lot easier to find.

A Mission Statement

I'll use different terms for this, but most organizations have at least developed a concept of a mission.

I've seen some horrendous ones, even from well-established, top companies.

Here are a few (some good, some really, really bad) from a list of Fortune 500 companies (check some out yourself at www.missionstatements.com/fortune_500_mission_statements.html). If you want to make it a little fun, try to guess the company from the mission statement:

> *Guided by relentless focus on our five imperatives, we will constantly strive to implement the critical initiatives required to achieve our vision. In doing this, we will deliver operational excellence in every corner of the Company and meet or exceed our commitments to the many constituencies we serve. All of our long-term strategies and short-term actions will be molded by a set of core values that are shared by each and every associate.*
>
> —Albertsons

© Martin Klubeck 2017
M. Klubeck, *Success Metrics*, DOI 10.1007/978-1-4842-2586-8_3

Ugh! I had to read it twice just to understand the words—but even then, I don't have a clue to why Albertsons exists. Let's try another:

We strive to be the acknowledged global leader and preferred partner in helping our clients succeed in the world's rapidly evolving financial markets.

—The Bank of New York

Notice that The Bank of New York's isn't really a purpose statement. It's more of a goal. "We strive to be" and then the *what* is more of a measure: "acknowledged global leader and preferred partner."

A few more. This next one is educational on a number of levels:

Our mission is to operate the best specialty retail business in America, regardless of the product we sell. Because the product we sell is books, our aspirations must be consistent with the promise and the ideals of the volumes which line our shelves. To say that our mission exists independent of the product we sell is to demean the importance and the distinction of being booksellers. As booksellers we are determined to be the very best in our business, regardless of the size, pedigree or inclinations of our competitors. We will continue to bring our industry nuances of style and approaches to bookselling which are consistent with our evolving aspirations. Above all, we expect to be a credit to the communities we serve, a valuable resource to our customers, and a place where our dedicated booksellers can grow and prosper. Toward this end we will not only listen to our customers and booksellers but embrace the idea that the Company is at their service.

—Barnes & Noble, Inc.

Let's break it down. The first sentence, the lead, which should be the strongest part of the statement, declares that the product they sell is not "important." *Our mission is to operate the best specialty retail business in America, regardless of the product we sell.* The next four sentences seem to work really hard to argue against that statement. *To say that our mission exists independent of the product we sell is to demean the importance and the distinction of being booksellers.* Very strange.

Later, we get to a much better explanation of B & N's purpose: *Above all, we expect to be a credit to the communities we serve, a valuable resource to our customers, and a place where our dedicated booksellers can grow and prosper.* If it's "above all"—it probably should have been the first sentence in the mission statement.

Our goal is to be the leader in every market we serve, to the benefit of our customers and our shareholders.

—Dover Corporation

Huh? Goal? Is this why Dover Corporation exists? To be the best?

> To constantly improve what is essential to human progress by mastering science and technology.
>
> —The Dow Chemical Company

Okay, I kind of like this one. It's not one of the "good" ones I alluded to, but it's close. I'd like it a whole lot more if I knew what *what* is in their statement. "To constantly improve *what* is essential to human progress…" leaves me with questions. A lot of questions.

I won't torture you with Avon Products, Inc.'s 240-word mission statement. Suffice it to say, it was more advertising copy than a description of the company's purpose.

Here's a good one. Mattel, Inc. gives away the name of the company throughout the mission statement, so no guessing necessary.

> Mattel makes a difference in the global community by effectively serving children in need. Partnering with charitable organizations dedicated to directly serving children, Mattel creates joy through the Mattel Children's Foundation, product donations, grant making and the work of employee volunteers. We also enrich the lives of Mattel employees by identifying diverse volunteer opportunities and supporting their personal contributions through the matching gifts program.

Granted, this one is also mostly a marketing tool. It's all about Mattel, Inc.'s altruistic endeavors. But it still seems to have the essence of their purpose. If given the license to do so, I might start with "Mattel creates joy for children." And though that wouldn't be enough, it's pretty close. Think of it this way, any employee—from a receptionist to the CEO—can determine whether an action fits under this purpose. You wouldn't expect Mattel to create adult games. Or strictly educational games. Or anything else that doesn't help them create joy for children. But it may decide to add product lines that are not games or toys. It could publish children's books.

The idea is not to pitch a slogan or create a wordsmithed testament to your organization.

Word counts aren't prescriptive, but they can help. If a mission is too short, chances are you have a slogan (like my rewrite of Mattel Inc.'s). If the mission is too long, the actual purpose may be buried beneath a blanket of words.

What we're looking for is an unabashed, simple rendering of the reason your organization exists.

Yesterday

What is your history?

Sometimes the best way to understand our present is to look at our past. How'd we get here?

It's important to know where your organization started and where it came from. It's a simple question, which in today's environment, few staff can answer. And that's a shame. Worse, though, is when the leadership of the organization doesn't know the history.

Understanding the history of an organization is essential when we're trying to determine its present-day purpose. The purpose, the mission, could have changed over time. Usually not drastically, but it can and does change over time. A lot of times, this change is what foretells the fall of an otherwise strong company.

When the leadership loses sight of the organization's underlying purpose, trouble is on its way. Decisions made at the highest levels may well go against the actual mission of the organization. When you start making decisions in opposition to your purpose, the organization will erode from within. It will literally implode.

You have to know the purpose. A great place to start is asking, "Why was the organization founded? What was the driving need it filled?"

You have to determine its founding purpose. It's not enough to try to ascertain why it exists today (we will do that shortly). You have to know why it was created, because if its purpose has changed, you have to know why! Whatever caused the organization to change its purpose (if it did), those same influencers may push another change in your future, and you should be aware of that possibility.

So, research the history of your organization. Remember Big Data? Chances are the history is captured somewhere (maybe even on paper). Search it out. And not just the motto or mission statement that was created for business cards or advertising (below the logo). You want to dig deeper and determine the actual *why* behind its creation.

You may be able to find out through original incorporation papers. Perhaps it's buried in an ancient copy of the business plan. If possible, find someone who was around back then. Wherever you can find it, find it. It's an essential part of your organization's story.

For the last five years I've been a member of the board of directors for our district library. Last year I became the president of the board. One of my first edicts as president was to have the executive director present to the board the library's mission. We have a neat catchphrase; "Inform, Entertain, and Enrich." But that's not clear enough.

So, she worked with her staff and developed clear explanations of not only what they do, but why they do it. How does our library inform? Whom do they inform? Whom do they entertain? How do they entertain? Whom do they enrich? How do they go about enriching them?

And most important to all of these was *why*. Why does our library inform, entertain, and enrich? And that's when we started getting to the mission.

It would be very logical to think the sole purpose of the library was to provide books to the public. Of course, that was a *how*, not the *why*. The purpose wasn't simply to provide books! Today we provide much more: computer labs, electronic reading devices, audio books, and video. But that still isn't our purpose—providing these items.

To find out the mission it helps to examine why it was founded

The library was founded in 1904, supporting the work of the Ladies' Library Association, thanks to a grant from Andrew Carnegie. Over 1,400 communities around the country started libraries during the early 1900s, and most of the libraries were made possible as a result of funding provided by Dale Carnegie. Carnegie usually required that cities agreed to fund the work of the library, and he provided the monies for the building.

Although I could not find a documented purpose for the Niles City Library (which later became a district library), we do know about the philanthropist who made the library possible. In 1903 Andrew Carnegie donated the funds to build Washington, D.C.'s oldest library. This building was "dedicated to the diffusion of knowledge."

There's no reason to believe the Niles library had a different purpose at its founding. Understanding this foundational reason for existing helps to calibrate the library's current mission.

Notice that the purpose didn't include any reference to "books."

At the time, books were the best way to diffuse knowledge. Carnegie improved his personal lot in life by educating himself—you guessed it, at the library. He had to "fight" for his right to use the facility, as at the time you had to pay a fee he could not afford. Winning that battle was only one of his accomplishments—but I like to think of it as one of his best examples of championing those who help themselves. He wrote a letter to the administrator of the library and was summarily turned away. "So 17-year-old Andy got the letter published in the *Pittsburgh Dispatch*. He made his case so well that the administrator backed off immediately," explains Carnegie biographer David Nasaw. "And the library was opened to working men as well as apprentices." (From "How Andrew Carnegie Turned His Fortune into a Library Legacy" by Susan Stamberg (www.npr.org/2013/08/01/207272849/how-andrew-carnegie-turned-his-fortune-into-a-library-legacy).

So the *how* for Carnegie's mission to diffuse knowledge was realized in funding libraries in America and abroad. Libraries that would be public and free. Libraries where everyone could go and gain access to knowledge.

"Knowledge is power" (usually attributed to Francis Bacon) is a great and true saying. Andrew Carnegie sought to make that power available to everyone. Carnegie's vision for educating the masses drove him to provide institutions for diffusing knowledge.

It takes time to see a vision fully realized. One of the roadblocks is society's standards. In the case of Carnegie's vision, society was a problem. When he funded libraries, children weren't an area of focus. Libraries didn't reach out to children until nearly 40 years later.

Sometimes our visions push society along. In 1903, the Washington, D.C. library was one of the few desegregated public buildings.

If we look at the library today, what is its mission? You would think all libraries, being a specific type of institution, would have very similar (if not exactly the same) missions.

> *The mission of the Niles District Library is to provide our community with access and guidance to resources that inform, entertain, and enrich.*

We can find this easily enough because the library makes this very public. So, today the library believes its mission is still to diffuse knowledge to the public, its community. If you think I'm trying to force fit it, let's check. To understand a mission we have to dissect its language:

- *"Provide our community"*: So, yes, the mission is still about giving to the public.

- *"Access and guidance to resources"*: *Diffuse* means to spread out over an area.

- *"That inform, entertain, and enrich"*: Which is what knowledge does.

The wording has definitely changed, as it will with every person who explains the mission. This "official" statement has equal weight with any description a librarian, board member, or patron would give. Our purpose is a calling. It's what we are destined to do, who we are destined to be. Not surprisingly, the essential mission of a library has not changed since the first public library opened its doors over 100 years ago!

How we fulfill that mission has changed—in some ways drastically. We still have books (thank goodness), but we now also have microfiche, electronic books, audio books, video, and the Internet with all of its resources living in the "cloud."

Andrew Carnegie couldn't have imagined the many diverse and exciting new *hows* available to libraries for fulfilling their purpose. And still the mission is the same.

Our library's vision is built on its mission. "…we see our library as building a community of life-long learners who will make Niles their life-long home." If we shorten that to the core, "to create a community of life-long learners," we find a logical vision from the purpose of providing the resources to those life-long learners. Rather than simply diffusing knowledge to all those who enters its doors, the Niles District Library also seeks to encourage and grow lifelong learning. And now with technology, the library can work toward its vision even if you can't walk between the shelves of books. Now those resources can be made available to the community through technology, becoming truly fully inclusive. *There should be nothing* keeping knowledge from everyone. Notice how the vision aligns with Carnegie's vision?

These examples are intended to help you see the benefits and reasons for learning your organization's past.

Today

Besides the past, we need to take a hard look at why your organization continues to exist today. Is it for the same reason it was created? Has it changed drastically? Many times, the tools and equipment of an industry change—but the purpose doesn't. The industrial revolution changed the way we did things in extreme and drastic ways. Rather than organic-driven power, the world was introduced to steam-powered engines. Later we saw fossil fuels take the forefront. And in our time we've reaped the benefits of a rapidly growing technological revolution.

In all of these massive world-changes, manufacturers and those organizations that use manufactured goods changed too. These changes were sometimes extreme—from the Pony Express to the telegraph to the telephone, and now to cellular communications, changes have been felt at all levels in all places.

But while some businesses became obsolete, others morphed with the changes. AT&T is still in the telecommunications business, still providing its same purpose even though the means of fulfilling that purpose has evolved. Missions can change, but not easily or quickly.

If the purpose changes, the organization is no longer the same. It's a new organization—perhaps with the same name, but essentially it's a different entity. Just as if our individual callings change, we will also change. We are *not* who we were then. We will be someone different in the future.

It's important for you to know what your organization's original purpose was and what its purpose is today.

Has it changed?

Why did it change?

If it hasn't changed, why not?

If the mission of your organization is to fulfill a need, why does the need still exist? How will that change in the future? How has it changed in the past? These are important questions for you to ask. This will also help you to ensure that you're looking at the real calling of your organization. Remember our library?

I mentioned how you could easily mistake the mission of the library to be "provide books" to patrons. But that wouldn't even scratch the surface. Even today you might think the mission was to provide information—but that sells it a little short too because it's more than information. It's knowledge. And knowledge implies learning. If we understand the history of libraries, how they were funded, and why, we have a much better understanding of the purpose behind their existence.

Hopefully this all makes sense.

We've talked about understanding the history of an organization, but this can also be used at the individual level. We want to know what success means to us personally. I can remember spending many days, weeks, and months trying to figure out why I existed. I think this is a normal experience for most teenagers. It's called "finding yourself."

I remember reading *Spider-Man* comic books and identifying with Peter Parker's struggles to find his place in the world. I wasn't bitten by a radioactive spider and I had no superpowers. I also didn't have writers providing me with dialogue and solutions to my problems.

It took me much longer to get a handle on my purpose than it took me to read those comics. I'm talking years. Many years. But the internal inquisition started back then, when everything seemed life changing.

This is also known as *finding your calling*. For some it's a spiritual journey, with a spiritual awakening at the end. And a good portion of us don't find what our calling is until much later in life, if at all. Like an organization, an individual's calling can change. But also like an organization, it doesn't happen easily.

Just as the industrial and technological revolutions affected organizations, the significant emotional events in our lives can affect, or outright change, our calling. And as with an organization, it's useful to spend time looking inside and determining whether your calling in life has changed.

Why? For the same reasons an organization should. It tells you a lot about who you were, who you are, and who you are likely to become.

You may believe that your calling as a youth was very different than what it is today—but chances are the change (if it exists at all) is minimal. I found my calling relatively late in life. At about 33, I came to the realization that who I was wasn't equal to what I was doing.

I was an Air Force officer. I had found my way to the officer corps via the long road. I had started as an enlisted member, with only a year of college. I failed at my first job, unable to fulfill the requirements of the specialty they had assigned me after basic training. But in that failure I was blessed to find my wife. We fell in love, married, and had a child. So I thought perhaps that was my calling—to be a parent.

I think all mothers and fathers believe at some point that being a good parent is their calling. But it wasn't my calling any more than being an airman was. My calling wasn't being a student, either, although I attended night school and attained an associate's degree, then a bachelor's, and finally a master's degree. I spent over 20 years serving my country as an airman, and yet that wasn't my calling either.

What we do isn't our calling.

Who we are is.

I realized that my calling was to help others. I was able to keep my actions (and jobs) in line with this purpose without fully understanding that calling. And for the most part, having a clear understanding of your calling isn't that important, unless you want to be a success. Being able to articulate it isn't critical to your success...it's only critical to *measuring your success*.

And my calling wasn't just to help others—it was to help others using the talents and gifts I'd been given. The way I help others isn't the same as you would. I teach, and I coach, and I preach. I write books. I give presentations and keynotes. I deliver seminars. But these are hows, and they can change. My calling is to help others realize and succeed in their role as visionaries.

This drives me to provide a free weekly (at least I try to get it out weekly) newsletter for visionaries. I created a company and published a website.

The years I spent finding my purpose wasn't wasted time.

I can see how, throughout my life, I've helped others to believe in themselves and in their dreams. I've always done this. I just didn't know that it was at the core of my calling. So the good news is that I have always worked toward my calling—and most of us can say the same. But also, as for most of us, I did it without intentionality. I was drawn to it instinctively.

You may know your calling and choose to ignore it. I find if you ignore your calling and turn your back on your purpose, you will be an unhappy person. If this is you, it's highly likely that you are a miserable person, dealing with depression.

If your calling is to make music that enriches people's lives, but instead you've spent most of your life writing computer software programs, you will likely be a very unhappy person. Because you have not only denied your inherent talents, you have turned your back on your true purpose.

This is one of the reasons that you can use happiness as an indicator (though not a complete measure) of success. Other things can make you happy. Lots of other things. But the euphoric, endorphin high you get when you are going about fulfilling your calling is unique and pretty awesome.

When you're making music, when you see the listener's reaction and know that you are doing what you are meant to do—there's nothing like it in the world. It's exhilarating.

If you find that you are unhappy for a good portion of your life, chances are you are on the wrong path.

But you have to remember happiness is *not* the goal, endpoint, or even a complete measure of success. It's only an indicator, and it's a better negative one than a positive. The absence of happiness is a good indicator that you are on the wrong path, but the presence of happiness is not necessarily an indicator that you are on the right road to success.

Richard Branson argued in his LinkedIn article "My Metric for Success? Happiness" (April 20, 2016) that money is not a good measure of success, that happiness is the measure he uses and that other entrepreneurs should use. And I agree, except that happiness, as I've stated, isn't a positive measure of success.

Remember, Branson is what many of us consider to be a successful business-man. But we would be judging his success on his financial portfolio, and he's telling us that we'd be wrong to use that. Instead he says we should look at how happy he is.

I can hear a lot of you saying, "Sure he's happy—he's rich!"

Let's set that aside for a moment because although the article's title says his metric for success is happiness, and he does his best to sell us on that, the truth is hidden just beneath the surface.

If we read between the lines we find the things that he says make him happy. Let me pull those out of the article:

- Every Virgin product and service has been made into a reality *to make a positive difference in people's lives.*
- *My family* are my greatest achievement. When they are happy, I am happy...
- ...it's all *living and learning.*
- One of the things that makes me happiest is *being able to give back.*
- ...our not-for-profit foundation...to...*create real lasting change in the world.*

So although Branson says, "Happiness should be everyone's goal," I think it's critical to point out that happiness, true happiness, is founded on fulfilling your calling. Branson is doing more than being generous—he is fulfilling his calling.

His abilities and talents may be centered around an entrepreneurial spirit, but his true happiness isn't in creating new businesses, selling those businesses for wealth, or making money. His happiness is rooted in living out his purpose fully. It's why he can be happy.

Being true to yourself is the most essential ingredient to being happy. When we deny our calling, we lock ourselves into a life of missteps and lies.

So, yes. You need to know your history. You need to know how you came to be where you are today. This is true for an individual and for an organization.

You must find out your purpose—why you exist.

To be truly successful, you must know what your calling is.

And then fulfill it.

Granted, you can fulfill your calling at different levels (from barely doing what you are called to do, to living it fully every day), and some do it better than others. Some fail to do it at all. You can have different levels of success, and that's where the measuring comes in.

It's not a go-no-go proposition.

We've covered a 100-year-old institution (libraries) and an individual's calling. But what about a new startup? What about a business you are only *thinking* about creating?

From Scratch

If you're just starting your organization, you're in luck! You have all the corporate knowledge you'll need at your fingertips. Instead of researching back through archives to see what your original purpose was, you get to define it right now.

I was asked to join the board of a nonprofit startup, Michiana Chess. I was impressed with the three young founders, who also acted as the board members, organization officers, and volunteers. But before I agreed, I needed to ensure it would be worth my time. I had to ensure that this was an organization I wanted to invest in. Being a board member requires time and energy. It requires an investment of my limited resources.

So I had to find out.

One of the first questions I asked them was, "Why does Michiana Chess exist?"

This was over dinner at a favorite Mexican restaurant. No pressure or stress. I wasn't quizzing or testing them. I needed to know.

The answers came back in a flurry.

"Get chess in the schools."

"Make chess accessible to youth in the area."

"Make chess fun for everyone."

"Hold tournaments everyone can afford."

They were all things that the organization wanted to do. Things they wanted to achieve. To their credit, their answers were insightful. They could have told me things like "Start a chess team at the local high school," which is something they *are* doing. They kept their answers at a higher level than tasks.

I let them go on for a while before I brought them back to the question.

"That's what you want to do, but not why you exist. Why does Michiana Chess exist? Why do you want to do those great things?"

"It'll help students with their grades. It will teach them new skills, how to analyze, think things out, and make plans."

"It will give a way for different generations to connect."

"It will…"

I still didn't get the *why*. Instead I got a list of benefits that the things they wanted to do would bring.

So I stopped them again.

This was an organization in its infancy. There were little more than good intentions in place. This fundamental question should have been easy to answer. *Why* do you want to create this organization?

It took a while, but finally we did get to the root need, the underlying mission of the organization. The funny thing is, they already had a mission (purpose) documented in the bylaws they had drafted. I was happy to hear that it wasn't finalized and they were willing to tweak it.

"Michiana Chess's purpose is to promote the use of chess as an educational tool" was the official version in the bylaws. Remember, I don't care about wordsmithing. It does not have to be an "awesome" statement. It's not going to be engraved over a doorframe or on a statue. It should be something every member of the organization can articulate in their own way, using their own words.

I think (even if you don't know anything about the game of chess) you can see that there's a bigger *why* beneath that mission statement. Why does Michiana Chess want to promote the use of chess as an educational tool? It probably has something to do with changing or improving the lives of those whom the organization influences through that promotion. Granted, we want to keep "chess" in the mission because it is the preferred tool, but we have to know why. And the *why* is to positively affect the lives of those touched by the organization's efforts. And this is critical.

No one that I know would give any money to this nonprofit based on the purpose of promoting chess as an educational tool. That's not very inspiring. I wouldn't even be excited to help or join the board. No, after our two-hour session, we all knew there was something much bigger behind the foundation of the organization. There was a more important purpose.

Michiana Chess wasn't founded to simply promote chess in any form or for any use. It was still just a tool and means of fulfilling the purpose. This team of young men believed in the power chess had to change lives. To help youth who might be headed down a wrong road. To help youth with learning disabilities. To help those who weren't sports superstars to have an outlet. To bring male, female, old, and young together in a common adventure.

Chess can be a tool for changing lives. And Michiana Chess is really about changing lives and changing the region we live in.

That's a purpose I can get excited about. That's a mission that can convince me to invest my time, money, and intellect. And it's a purpose that has to stay in the spotlight. It has to be front and center at all times.

Show Me the Money!

I recently had a lively discussion with a friend about the mission of for-profit businesses. He, with extreme sincerity, explained to me his position that all businesses have the same purpose—to make money.

Is that the whole story?

As businesses age, many times they lose sight of their purpose. He agreed that industrial and technology pioneers had other reasons behind their efforts. Steve Jobs, Bill Gates, Thomas Edison, and Henry Ford can all be said to have had a mission far beyond making a buck. But he argued that the businesses that they founded, *these* had the sole purpose of making money. "Otherwise, they'd have given the stuff away."

That is, of course, an extreme that supports the underlying belief that if you're in business, you're in the business of making money. We have come to believe that is what *business* means. We think that's the essence of capitalism.

But is that the whole story?

We need to know our history because we may lose sight of the purpose. When I took over as the president of the Niles District Library board of directors, the only thing we focused on was our fiduciary responsibilities. It was all about the money. Were we in the black or red? Where could we cut costs? And it sickened my stomach because we, the organization dedicated to enriching the lives of others through knowledge, had been degraded to being bean counters. I don't want mean to besmirch accountants, but we had lost focus on what the library was about.

As a board of trustees, we should have been setting and championing the long-term vision for the library: creating a community of life-long learners. We should be the keepers of the torch—the light that burns within the community to provide resources that inform, entertain, and enrich everyone.

When enough time goes by, and we worry about making a living or sustaining income, we lose sight of the real purpose for our organization's existence. Disney seemed to lose its way after Walt Disney passed. Apple also seemed to falter after Steve Jobs's death. That's not because their companies were only about making a buck—just the opposite. The visionaries behind the businesses were no longer providing the constant direction required to move the ships forward. It's now the mission of their replacements to pick up the torch and continue the race.

If those leaders are misguided and don't pay attention to the true purpose for their organizations, they will falter. They will trip, stumble, and maybe fall.

If it were only about making money, they could do that without doing things "right." They could make money without upholding the quality and service their companies have come to be known for. They could sell off assets, lower salaries (why pay a dime more than you have to if your purpose is to make money?), and stop any altruistic ventures.

No, it's critical that the new leadership of these powerhouses understand the reason their companies exist. And it's not the shareholders that will define that for them, it's the stakeholders.

Shareholders are those who invest money in your organization and hope that the value of your company increases so their stock value increases. These are betting people. They are betting that your organization will continue to grow (in revenue especially) and therefore give them a high return for their investment. Why are they buying stock in your company? Well, to make money!

There are those cases where people invest in a company because they believe in the company's mission or vision. They believe in what the company is trying to accomplish. When dreamers are trying to raise capital for their venture and pitch their stock, rarely do people "buy in" because they think they'll get rich. Many of these businesses are housed in the founder's parent's garage. No, it's usually a donation to help a friend or to encourage a young dreamer. Even then, you want to believe you're possibly part of something special. You invest because you believe in the dream.

But if you invest in an established company (or commodities, for that matter), you normally do so to make a profit. There are still exceptions where you may invest in a company because you really like what it stands for or its mission—but ostensibly you do so with the express hope of making a profit.

That makes you a shareholder.

And that's okay. No shame in trying to make a profit. You can do so much more for yourself, your family, and others if you have enough wealth to give.

But there is a much larger contingent of people who are touched by the company. There are employees who have to decide whether they will be loyal to the company or start looking for a better paying position as soon as time allows. There are collaborators within and outside the organization. There are those who benefit from the altruistic efforts of the organization, and, of course, there are the all-important customers.

I'm not considering the suppliers and vendors that sell to your company. I'm talking about those we call *stakeholders*. They have a stake in your organization—not for monetary gain. They have a stake in your organization's mission. Employees actually can be both. They can see their job only as a means for earning a paycheck. You know people like this…they're in your organization right now. And they are usually the most miserable people in the company. The best (and happiest) employees believe in the company's mission and therefore feel good about themselves and about their organization.

This has been true in every organization I've worked for. Even in the Air Force we had young men and women who were there for a paycheck. Some were there for the educational opportunities. Others wanted a little job security. And every one of the airmen I've ever met for whom I knew this to be true did not enjoy their time in the Air Force. In contrast, if you believed in the Air Force mission, you loved being an airman.

The new adage goes: "If you don't like where you work, stop working there." We're not in a depression, where you have to take any job you can find to feed your family. We are not currently struggling en masse to satisfy Maslow's survival needs. But those needs are important. They are required for us to survive. And therefore we will take jobs that aren't about being a stake-holder—they're a way to feed the family.

I'm not suggesting that every employee has to love their organization or quit their job if they don't. But believing in your organization's mission makes it a much better existence.

Stakeholders are those who are affected by your organization's fulfillment of its mission. Stakeholders care deeply about why your organization was founded and continue to believe in its mission. They buy stock in your company to help fund your mission—any profit they make is a bonus. Stakeholders take pride in being associated with your business. Stakeholders promote your business to others. Many times, your best (and most loyal) customers are also stakeholders.

You don't get stakeholders based on how much money you make.

You don't keep stakeholders if your purpose is to make money.

Your company has to be about more than the almighty dollar. It has to have a purpose.

HOW TO WRITE A MISSION STATEMENT

Remember that the mission is your purpose, the *why* behind your *what*. It's why your organization exists. Not what you do or how you do it.

So we start with the simple question: Why does your organization exist?

What we usually get as an answer is a high-level view of what the organization does. Things like "Provide X for Y" or "Distribute N for M." But these are *whats*. We have to ask, "Why?"

There is a reason for what your organization does. And it's *not* make money. Why do you make money? Why do you do it the way you do it?

If there weren't a reason for your organization to exist, it would likely cease to exist. It definitely shouldn't show growth. I can say this because regardless of what you do, there must be a need you are filling. Without a perceived need by your customer base, you would fail to make sustained profit and therefore fail to keep your doors open.

McDonald's, Burger King, and KFC all do the same thing—sell fast food. They do it differently, but the *whats* are essentially the same. When we look at other fast food chains, we may find that they also have different values and principles they function under. Chick-Fil-A, Pizza Hut, Domino's, and Rally's all still do the same *what*.

Are all of these organizations functioning under the same mission?

Why do they provide fast food? What is the need they are filling?

Find Your Why

Ensure it's not a *what* or a *how*. Start your sentence with "My organization exists because _____." Most statements start with "to provide…"—which is all right, but many times it turns out that these are high level *whats* and not a *why*. It's harder to start with "because" and give a *what*. You don't have to leave that language in your finished statement, but it's a good way to build it.

Don't Wordsmith Your Mission

Nobody cares if it has the perfect set of words, number of syllables, and punctuation. This has to be the most common error and biggest waste of time when an organization is trying to document its mission statement. It's why I avoid even calling it a *statement* when I can. Don't waste time and effort trying to find the perfect words. You can't. And more importantly, you shouldn't. We want every employee in our organization to feel comfortable and confident in sharing the mission. The best way to do that is to have them express it in their own terms.

I recently conducted an exit interview for a worker who was taking a leadership position at another company. He told me he was going to miss his current organization because his coworkers were great and made a great team. Out of curiosity, I asked him whether he knew the new organization's mission or vision. He didn't. I suggested he find out what it is as soon as possible. Then I asked him what the mission/vision was for the organization he was leaving. I knew they had a good mission and vision (I had worked with them on it). He gave an embarrassed laugh and said he couldn't remember it…it was right there on his tongue, but he couldn't remember it.

When I led him a little, reminding him of the slogan on the website, he was able to finish it. And he was also able to express the vision. What this told me was that the leader of the organization had failed to communicate the requirement for the workers to be able to express it in their own words. Because he couldn't remember the coined, documented phrase, he thought that he didn't remember it. But in reality he could have shared it—easily, in his own words.

So, don't worry about the exact wording. Instead make sure all members of your organization feel comfortable and confident in expressing the purpose and aspirations of your organization in their own words.

Keep It Short

Although I definitely am not, in any way whatsoever, concerned about your having a well-worded statement, I know that organizations want something they can post on their websites. And for me, that's a good place to start evaluating the clarity of the mission.

I'm much happier when I find a documented mission statement that's actually a slogan or catchphrase then I am with the mission statement that's a run-on sentence that doesn't even get close to a purpose.

Usually I can look at a mission statement and get an idea of what the real purpose is, but the more words there are, the less clear the statement is. So keep yours short.

Use Passion

Find words that express the reason why the organization exists. Find words that express this with passion. If you want to spend time trying to get "just the right words," spend that time finding passion-filled words. "I believe" is a great way to start a discussion of your purpose or dreams. As Simon Sinek said in a Ted Talk, "Martin Luther King Jr. said, 'I have a dream,' not, 'I have a plan.'"

Your purpose should create passion in those who hear it. You should have passion when you share it. An organization's purpose for existing should be inspiring. I know the reason I exist in the world creates passion in me. If my purpose only encouraged yawning, I think my life would be depressing. I want my purpose to keep me up at night and make me want to jump out of bed in the morning.

I'm told I'm a morning person, but I'm pretty sure a lot of my being "up" is due to my feeling that I have great things to accomplish every day.

Employees Should Be Able to Express This Purpose in Their Own Words

This works directly with using passion and avoiding wordsmithing. Employees have to express the mission and vision in their own words. It has to be simple and direct. It has to be clear to anyone who hears it. Every member of the organization has to be able to express it in their own words. And leadership has to ensure that the workforce knows that this is more than acceptable. It's expected.

It's not just that they *should* be able to, but they *have* to express the mission in their own words. If they can't or won't—you haven't engaged your workforce yet. The employees have to take ownership of the mission, of their organization's purpose. And the first step to them owning the mission is to recite it...in their own words. It's in this expression of the purpose that the workforce takes the first step toward full engagement in the organization.

Develop a Version for Your Marketing

This includes your website, correspondence, and even business cards if you like. But don't try to make it perfect. Actually, go with sharing a catchphrase or slogan before you wordsmith a mission statement. This tag line should help remind people of your mission. It should be a good starting point for expressing the mission.

This is a critical step in measuring success and strategic planning. You have to have a very clear understanding of the purpose for your organization's existence. It used to amaze me how many organizations didn't have a clear understanding of their purpose. I say it "used to" amaze me because by now I've found that, by far, most don't know what their mission is. I am now surprised when I find an organization that has a clear definition of its mission.

HOW TO WRITE A VISION STATEMENT

A vision is a Very Big Hairy Scary Audacious Goal. It's something you want to achieve in the future. Visions have specific attributes that make them stand out from a goal. In a newly formed organization, many times the organization's purpose is to achieve the vision.

No Wordsmithing Here Either

Yup. I disdain efforts to elicit elegant descriptions that communicate the precise interpretation…

Oh, you get the idea. Don't waste your time trying to find perfect words to explain your vision. The vision, like the mission, should be stated as simply as possible. And it must be readily shared by everyone in the organization. Leadership must share the vision, but everyone should know what the overall goal for the organization is. Everyone should be able to explain how their jobs help move the organization toward that vision or how they help fulfill the mission.

Sometimes your work efforts will do both.

There are simple tests we can use to determine whether your goal is a vision or not.

It's Too Large for You to Achieve It on Your Own

You have to enlist help. You have to find collaborators to make it come true. This is one of the basic rules to defining a real vision. If you (or your organization) can achieve the vision on your own, then it may be a worthy goal, but it's not a vision. It's not world-changing. It's not big enough or scary enough. A true vision cannot be achieved in isolation.

Don't believe me? Think of any of the world-changing visions you know of. Our history books are full of visionaries and visions that either came true or are still in process. Putting a man on the moon and bringing him back safely, a free South Africa, or a professional women's basketball league. None of these visions was achievable without the collaboration of many people and many organizations.

One of my favorite examples of a vision is Dr. Martin Luther King Jr.'s dream. He said he dreamt of a nation where his children would be judged not by the color of their skin but by their character. This dream has already changed the world, although it has not been fully realized yet. Whole organizations have been founded because of this vision. Federal laws, policies, and regulations have changed. The way we talk, act, and work has changed. And none of these changes could have been brought about by any single organization or person.

Your Vision Will Attract Enemies

Oh, you'll also attract believers, disciples, and apostles. But you'll like that—the enemies are the part that will surprise (and annoy) you. It will also worry you if you don't realize that this is natural and should be expected. If you encounter no "naysayers," your vision isn't big enough.

Think of any of the visions I already listed. Think of the visionaries who championed the dreams. They all had enemies. You will too. Hopefully your enemies won't be violent or threaten your life. Hopefully your enemies will be loud naysayers rather than assassins. But one of the constants with a true vision is that it will attract enemies. But that's okay. Expect it. Welcome it.

If you have no enemies, if everyone that hears your vision thinks it's a great idea and wants to join you, something is wrong. It's either not big enough or not scary enough. It's not world-changing enough.

Attracting enemies is just one indicator that you have a real vision on your hands.

It Will Take a Long Time

Chances are good that your vision will actually outlive you. That's because visions take a long time to come true. You might argue that in the short list I provided, the ones that didn't live to see their visions come true were killed before their dreams could come true. And that's true for a few, but also realize that most of those visions weren't born with their most famous visionaries. Nelson Mandela wasn't the first to dream of an apartheid-free South Africa. Martin Luther King Jr. wasn't the first to dream of a world without prejudice and bigotry. John F. Kennedy wasn't the first to promote visiting the moon.

From the time the vision was born to its achievement is a long-term endeavor.

Sometimes it takes a long time because the technology hasn't been created yet to make it possible. Sometimes it's because the human race isn't ready for it.

But regardless, a vision will take a very long time to achieve.

It Is Selfless

Not only is it not just about you or your organization, a vision (a good one) is selfless. It's something that will change the world for the better. It's in no way selfish.

This is extra tough when you're talking about a for-profit organization. Remember, you can have some long-range goals that you can achieve on your own, or that are about your organization. But to have a world-changing vision—one that will excite your organization (and others)—it needs to be bigger than your organization. Not only will you need help, but it can't be selfish.

Think about John F. Kennedy's vision of putting a man on the moon and bringing him back safely. This might seem like it was only for our country—a selfish endeavor. But space travel, and specifically reaching the moon, was much bigger than just a patriotic shot in the arm. It was more than a Cold War competition. The world watched, learned, and cheered (except for our enemies). And what was learned from it wasn't hoarded by our country. The world gained knowledge from it.

Anyone, but Not Everyone, Can Be a Visionary

Anyone can share the vision. Each vision can be championed by more than one visionary.

Anyone who passionately believes in the vision can be a visionary. A visionary's primary responsibility is to share the vision early and often. A visionary champions the vision to everyone possible. But logically, everyone can't be a visionary. If everyone were a visionary, no one would be working to make it actually come true. A vision needs many "doers." Only a few visionaries, but many, many doers.

Summary

Knowing thyself is one of the most basic tenets of philosophy and personal growth. It should also be the basis for an organization of any size, from a sports team to a multinational conglomerate. If you want to measure real success, you have to understand where you came from, where you are, and where you're going.

I usually don't encounter any resistance to this notion of introspection from individuals I coach or mentor. But when you're talking to a business leader about their organization, this is a little harder sale to make. Many people, especially ones who work in a free-market or capitalist society, believe that their purpose is simple: to make money. The more profit, the more successful they are.

This is not only a bad way to look at success for businesses, it's wrong. Businesses that thrive and have a chance at true success understand that their profit margin is a means to an end—it's not the ultimate goal. Just like any of its assets, income is something the business needs. It's not the reason for being.

No matter which name you use, mission, purpose, or calling, it is important to know the reason your organization exists. It's at the core of why you do what you do. Without it, you may find yourself working diligently and repeatedly on the wrong things.

The good news is that you already have a reason for being. You just have to find it.

The How Matters

Values play a large part in our overall success because values are important to defining who we are. Our calling is essential, but values help define us in a special way. We determine what is acceptable in how we behave mostly based on our values. Values define us so well that you can easily mistake them for your vision or mission.

Values are the tint on our glasses. How we see the world is through our own value-tinted glasses. It flavors and colors how we see others and ourselves. We find this in some of the best companies. Disney has values that it adheres to. Apple has values. The U.S. military has values.

Core Values

One of the best parts of being in the Air Force is the core values that link each and every airman. I lived by them for over 20 years. I still live by them over a decade later. They aren't the mission, they're not the reason the military exists—but they define how the military functions.

The University of Notre Dame (my current employer) also has a set of values. Those values are one of the reasons I feel at home here.

Each year I have the privilege of sharing presentations to alumni. Occasionally I get asked about how I was able to "adapt" to civilian life, specifically to an academic environment. Especially since many people think of a university

© Martin Klubeck 2017
M. Klubeck, *Success Metrics*, DOI 10.1007/978-1-4842-2586-8_4

as existing at the opposite end of an imaginary spectrum from the military: academia, then non-for-profits, small businesses, larger businesses, corporate America, and then the military.

I enjoy explaining why I don't have a problem with working for the university. It's not at the opposite end of the spectrum. In many ways it's the same. Military installations are cities unto themselves. There are fire departments, military police, shopping centers, supermarkets, bowling alleys, gymnasiums, chow halls, barracks, and even movie theatres. The university has pretty much the same facilities (I believe the bowling alleys were removed a few years back). Both are gated communities. Both serve the public, but both also have stringent participation rules. And that's familiar. It makes it feel good to be on campus. (I still call the dining halls "chow halls").

But what really makes it comfortable working at Notre Dame is the compatibility of our values. The Air Force's core values are

- Excellence in all we do

- Service before self

- Integrity first

Excellence in all we do just means that we always do our best. We give it our all. My mother used to say, "If a job is worth doing, it's worth doing right." And that's the essence of "excellence in all we do." Do your best. Notre Dame strives for this too. They want the best ("The Few, The Proud..."), but they also expect the best. In all things. It's one of the reasons recruiting athletes to the university is a challenge. Notre Dame doesn't only want the best athletes—they want athletes who will strive to excel at all things, especially their education.

Service before self also works with the university's values. The military teaches us to put others before ourselves. We commit our lives to protecting our country, our fellow Americans, and our way of life from all enemies—foreign and domestic. When others run from danger, we run toward it. That isn't bravery. It's selflessness. It's putting others before yourself. Notre Dame develops this in every student—you can see it in the requirements to get into the school. You can see it in the continued dedication to community service while students attend classes. You can see it in the graduates and the support the university gives to others.

When people ask me how I can "make it" at an academic institution, I tell them "when the academic institution is the University of Notre Dame? Easily. Very easily."

Integrity first doesn't mean that integrity is more important than other traits. It doesn't mean that it's actually first in comparison to the other values. All it means is that you have to put integrity above all else. And integrity simply means doing the right thing—always. Honesty, yes. But more simply, when there are choices, you always do the right thing. It doesn't matter what others are doing—you do what's right. It doesn't matter if anyone is watching or anyone would know. Remember the philosophical question (test really); If no one would ever know, if you could do anything you want and no one in the world would know—what would you do? What wouldn't you do?

Integrity first makes that answer pretty easy. And you find the same values at Notre Dame. I would be shocked if the NCAA ever had to sanction Notre Dame for anything. And if there were integrity violations, I would be even more shocked if the university hadn't already meted out worse punishment and sanctions than the NCAA would or could. I'm not implying that every member of the Notre Dame family is honest, forthright, and always chooses to do right. No more than I would try to say that every military member has those traits. Not every military member believes in or follows the core values or even believes in the oath they took. Remember? Some airmen are just in it for the job and don't believe in the mission, vision, or values. And the same is true for Notre Dame. In both cases I am happy to see them go. Some last out their commitment, be it four years in the military or four years to get a degree, but they aren't *lifers*. We call those who make it a career, being an airman for life, *lifers*. Notre Dame has the same thing—they call them *Domers*. Oh, technically any graduate is a Domer. But a real Domer is easily recognized from the imposters.

Real Domers live by the university's values. Real Domers don't have to even be alumni. They can be staff or faculty.

How can I make it at an academic institution?

Easily.

I love the Air Force—and always will. I also love Notre Dame. This strong emotion is elicited because of those values. And although I love these institutions, what makes me dedicate decades of my life to them isn't the values—it's the mission and vision.

Faith

In the military we were taught not to talk about religion or politics—because we had to be above the potential arguments that ensue from these two things. Why? Because people are not ancient Greek philosophers. We can't discuss or debate religion or politics rationally. We get wrapped up in emotion and have no willingness to listen to dissenting views.

This lack of reasonable discourse is not conducive to "good order and discipline."

But I'm not in the military anymore, and one of the benefits of being at an institute of higher learning is that it encourages discourse. So I'll have a short say about religion.

Religion is another tint. Our faith plays a large part in what we believe our calling is. But what a sad way to live if we think there is no greater purpose. Or that we all have the same exact purpose! Then most, if not everything we do, is unimportant or meaningful. If there is no greater purpose, whatever we do doesn't really matter. You may have a set of values that dictate how you think people should treat each other and how we should behave, but if there is no greater purpose—does it matter? Do sociopaths have it right?

What are your values? Your beliefs? It's hard to be a success if you don't adhere to a set of values. They define how you should go about the task of being successful.

The *how* does matter.

Values also show all those who care to look what type of organization you have. Is it an honorable one? Is it a money-grabbing, environment-killing, scheming, selfish organization? Is it all about taking as much as possible? Or is your organization one that cares?

Remember my friend, the cynic? He felt that we were only fooling ourselves if we thought that a business's mission was anything other than making money, turning a profit. And the more profit, the better. He argued this was the only true measure of success for a business.

And yet he also promoted the importance of values. He surmised that we support or invest in organizations because of their values. And as you can see, I don't agree. Values play a role, but if you have morally strong values—yet your mission and vision are askew—you won't have supporters. If you have no mission or vision except making money—again, you won't have supporters.

Values help define how we fulfill our mission. Values give us borders and guide-lines. There are some lines we're meant to stay within—otherwise the drawing becomes a mess. Coloring outside the lines is a nice visual for trying to get people to think "outside the box." But when we're talking about our values, coloring outside the lines is not a good thing. Coloring outside the lines of our values means going against what we know to be right. It means we don't have to follow any rules—not even the ones we've adopted for ourselves.

There are organizations that fit this model. There are organizations that will do everything they can to build more wealth and hold onto what they've col-lected. Even if it means going way outside those lines. That said, I don't even know if that's true. We've seen CEOs, organizational leaders who have lost their way...but whole organizations?

Well, that's what happened in late 2016 when it came to the public's attention that over 5,000 Wells Fargo employees were fired for unscrupulous practices. These fraudulent activities were carried out because the organization was chasing numbers instead of a vision. "Wells Fargo employees secretly opened unauthorized accounts to hit sales targets and receive bonuses," said Richard Cordray, director of the Consumer Financial Protection Bureau (http://money.cnn.com/2016/09/08/investing/wells-fargo-created-phony-accounts-bank-fees/). Shameful? Of course. But when you have convinced your workforce that the mission of your organization is making money, such behavior should not be fully unexpected. Just the sheer magnitude of the number of employees involved should throw up a gigantic red flag that something is wrong with the organization's focus.

Here's an exciting futuristic fictional drama for you.

The Future Is Now

A super conglomerate of chemical companies have cornered the market on a means of killing off the insects that are eating the crops we need to survive. These companies have a chemical that they spray over our crops, and it's awesome. It destroys the bugs and leaves the crop. Farmers and the government are happily paying these companies ugly money to protect crops. This means everyone makes more money. Farmers don't lose any crop to insects. The chemical companies rake in the dough.

We need a protagonist. And we have one, a woman, an author, an activist who is claiming that the chemical companies are being negligent. They are greedy. They are ignoring the damage their chemicals are doing to the environment. They are killing more than bugs. They are destroying the ecosystem and their chemicals are even threatening human lives.

Now we have our conflict. These companies that have forgotten their reason for existing, who believe their purpose is to make money, are at war with one woman. Censorship is the tool at hand. Fahrenheit 451 in our modern age. It's time to shut her up. The chemical companies send legions of lawyers to block the publication of her writing.

They fail.

So they send out their publicists to discredit her. Do whatever it takes to make her look like a nut case. Make sure no one will listen to her nonsense.

They fail again.

How about a live debate on national television? A small team of agents against one demure woman who was simultaneously struggling to fight cancer.

They fail one more time.

We have a tale of two cities. One being the companies who believe their purpose is making money. They ignore any values of integrity. They lie. They fabricate. They try to mislead and misinform. The other city is a woman with a purpose and a vision. She sees the wrong being waged against not only herself, her family, and her friends. She sees the wrong for what it is. Greed. Selfishness. All of the world will pay for this evil.

Pretty exciting, huh?

Well, it's not fiction. It's history. And it's not the history of some third-world country or far-off foreign nation. It's our history. It's part of America's legacy. After War World II, companies were haphazardly using dangerous chemicals—DDT being the most famous. We lived through more than a decade of greed-born risk.

I'm happy to tell you the heroine won! Rachel Carson won her battle against the chemical companies (and the public's apathy), though like many visionaries, she didn't live to see her vision come to fruition. Rachel Carson died of cancer in 1964. Within the next decade, DDT had been banned, the Environmental Protection Agency had been created, and crucial laws—the Endangered Species Act, the Clean Air Act, the Clean Water Act—had been passed.

So which one lived out their purpose? Rachel Carson or the chemical companies? Which one had a vision worthy of fighting and dying for?

Sixteen years after her death, Rachel Carson was awarded our nation's highest civilian honor—the Presidential Medal of Freedom. That didn't make her a success, though. No, the posthumous award was our way of acknowledging her success. She fulfilled her purpose! She made significant progress toward her vision. And most of us don't have a clue who she was. We don't remember her war against our willingness to destroy ourselves. We aren't taught about her in school.

She was fighting a lonely, uphill battle. Everyone seemed to be against her. Yet she persevered. A vision does that for you. It gives you strength to battle against the majority. There are many people who are likewise successful but who don't get an award from our government. In truth, no one may ever hear their stories. At least Rachel Carson's success was captured by *Life* magazine and then shared again in its *100 People Who Changed the World* pictorial history (Life Books, Vol. 10, No. 3, May 2010).

And now you should be wondering about those other successful people that you've never heard about. But you may also be wondering about those chemical companies. If they had succeeded at blocking the publication of

Carson's book *Silent Spring* (Houghton Mifflin, 1962), if they had succeeded at their attempts to discredit her, if their passionate but dishonest arguments on national TV had worked—would they have been a success? Would they have been "successful?" Would their measures of success be how much money they continued to make? Or would their measure of success be the destruction of Rachel Carson's reputation? Would their measure of success be the continued destruction of our environment, nature, and human lives?

Of course not. Even if they had won the battles, they would have to be judged unsuccessful. Of course, society and history may have seen it differently. But by our measures of success—did the chemical companies fulfill their purpose?

No.

I don't care how much money they made. If they are coloring so far outside the lines that they've destroyed the picture, they are not seen as a success. Oh, they might win the battle, but they are working against their own mission. Even if they had beaten Carson, they would have imploded eventually. Others would have risen up and taken up the fight.

Regardless of your religious beliefs, only sociopaths believe there is no right or wrong. Only antisocial personalities believe that they can and should be able to do whatever they want.

No, most of us realize there are values that we have to adhere to.

We should also realize that there are other things in life than making a buck. Even for businesses. The chemical companies in the early 60s would have agreed with my friend. They lost sight of their true purpose. They believed that their only mission was to fill their own pockets and those of their shareholders.

But credit to my friend for recognizing the importance of values. Although he may have agreed to the misconception that profits were the companies' mission, he would have fought tooth and nail against their lack of moral fiber and character.

Unfortunately, this is not an isolated story. Today we still have companies that have lost their way. Some believe their only purpose is making money. They think Jobs, Carnegie, Edison, Ford, and their ilk are misguided dinosaurs. Make as much money as you can, as fast as you can, and move on. There is no need for loyalty to employees, collaborators, or customers. It's all about selfishness.

This is not a path to success. It's a path to destruction.

THE HOW MATTERS

I really like a set of commercials currently airing for a smoking cessation patch. The part I like is how the commercial starts with the *why*. One commercial has a young man talking about wanting to play with his newborn child for years to come. The line he uses is "For a great *why*, you need a great *how*." Of course, they're selling their *how* as great, but I love that they start with the *why*. And those *whys* should be the company's *why*. The reason the company exists should be to make those *whys* come true.

RUTH

I've known Ruth since 2000, when I came to the University of Notre Dame as an Air Force Reserve Officer Training Corps instructor. She was on the varsity women's basketball team, and they were building a strong following on campus.

Of course, the fact that I'd played basketball my whole life (although not organized) didn't hurt. But what made Ruth special in my mind was her kindness to others. As a superstar on campus, she treated others with respect. When I had the pleasure to play with her during noontime basketball, we got into a conversation. When I told her about my unfortunate habit of twisting an ankle, she noted that I should be wearing braces to support my ankles. She then handed me a spare pair from her bag. I wore those braces every time I've played since. I'm a little embarrassed to say, I was rubbing them for luck while I watched Ruth and the Fighting Irish win their first (and to date, only) Women's NCAA Championship title over Purdue the next year.

Ruth went on to also win a gold medal at the 2004 Olympics, and two WNBA Championships. I've followed her career through TV and the Internet. It wasn't easy, though. Many times I had to do some serious web searching to find out where she was (what team she was on), what she was doing, and her stats. Why was it so hard to follow one of my sports heroes?

You'll see that this issue has something to do with how Ruth measures success.

I started the interview like every other interview. I asked her: How do you measure success?

"I think I've measured it by my ability to fulfill my potential, while living out my priorities and values. I can't measure success by someone else's standards. I have to be really careful not to sacrifice my values and priorities for what other people consider success.

"You need to think of success in a holistic view—not just achievements. I take into consideration my faith, my family, and whatever I'm currently defining as my job.

"Success should not be measured by my championships or accolades, but rather by going beyond the achievements and considering how I have been able to leverage them to positively impact the world around me."

I let her keep thinking through the question.

This has proven to be a common theme with all of my interviews. It doesn't matter if the interviewee is a CIO, CEO, small business owner, entrepreneur, chess master, or general manager—they all have to take time to think about how they would measure success. Being a metrics guy, that tells me that they aren't currently collecting, analyzing, or using any measures of success.

This should be a critical tool for every leader. Every organization should have a metrics program built on measures of success. I'm not even talking about getting them right— just that all organizations should be trying to measure success.

This lack of Success Metrics isn't surprising, though. After more than 25 years of working with metrics, I know they aren't a favorite tool for anyone. In my book *Metrics: How to Improve Key Business Results* (Apress, 2009), I cover in detail the reasons organizations and individuals work diligently to avoid metrics. I won't repeat that here. But even with that knowledge, I thought I'd find that a small percentage of the leaders I interviewed would be actively measuring success.

Yes, I thought they'd be doing it wrong—but I still thought they'd be doing it. Zero percent is a little smaller than I thought the number would be.

Although I was surprised, I was secretly okay with it. I've said many times that it's better to have no metrics than to have the wrong metrics. This may seem illogical. You may think that having any metrics would be a good start.

You'd be wrong.

Metrics is a dangerous tool. If you use it improperly, you can do serious damage to your organization and make it nearly impossible to do metrics right later. So, although I'd be happily surprised to find that my interviewees were actively trying to measure success, I'm actually happier because they aren't using the wrong metrics.

When it comes to metrics, it's much easier to get it right the first time.

Like all of my interviewees, Ruth did a good job of thinking it through.

"There are so many different ways to look at it—as an individual and as a team.

"As a team, the dynamic changes. Players contribute at different levels—I don't know if you can have an exhaustive definition—it should include betterment of everyone. Many times players need to be selfless.

"For me, I ask myself, am I truly putting faith and family first? It's important to me to have those priorities ahead of my work. And through my work I have a platform to make a positive influence and to make a difference in the world.

"So for me, a key to measuring success is 'how am I impacting the world?' Not only immediately, (like my humanitarian work), but there is a factor of influencing and mentoring others. A legacy is based on how you influence others to reach their potential."

A lot of what Ruth shared fit my views of success, but it was time to share my definition of success metrics.

When I did, her response was simple and straightforward: *"Makes sense to me."*

I also explained that I saw values (and priorities) as the *how* to accompany the *whys* and *whats*.

Her reply made me smile.

"Values are the lens I use to look at the world. I use them to determine how I operate in the world."

No, I had not told Ruth about my description of values as the colored lenses we use in our glasses when looking at the world.

"For me now, in San Antonio, I'm focused on building a championship culture. A culture where players are able to reach their potential as a collective unit and do it in a way that positively impacts the San Antonio community. This is how you truly win in sports."

So, how would you measure success for the San Antonio Stars or even the WNBA as a whole?

"The WNBA has a vision and mission to empower women as we continue to fight for equality. It would be a strong, positive message to have a professional women's sports league that's successful. I didn't grow up with that dream—a professional women's basketball league didn't exist when I was young. We're providing a platform for younger generations of girls to dream.

"We have lots of room to grow in trying to gain true equality, and that's with the WNBA being the most successful women's professional team sports league.

"For me, personally, my priorities align well with the WNBA's. I understand that being paid the same as the men isn't a realistic measure of equality, because it's pure economics. WNBA players can't expect to be paid the same if they don't have the same attendance, sponsorship, or paid advertising. There are other [better] measures of success for attaining equality for women's sports.

"Did you know that only three percent of ESPN's coverage goes to women's sports?

"It's not just the amount of coverage, but the level of respect given to women's sports. The coverage by the media [not just ESPN] has been lethargic and apathetic at best. Respect has been earned and demanded, yet we are still waiting for it to be granted. I can't wait for the day when these conscious and unconscious gender biases are eliminated from how female athletes are covered in the sports world. When that happens, equality will grow organically and we'll be successful."

Now that's a clear Success Metric!

Summary

Values, mission, and vision are the trifecta of measuring success. Adhering to our values is essential to happiness and contentment in life. Even if you fail miserably at all else, you can hold your head up with pride if you never wavered in living by your values. You can fail at fulfilling your purpose in life or working toward your vision, and still hold your head up.

In other words, you can be a failure in life, but still have self-esteem and pride in how you lived your life. This is why I don't consider living by your values equal to being successful.

To be successful you have to achieve your ultimate goals—to fulfill your purpose and work toward achieving your vision. You have to do these while adhering to your principles. If you are honorable, you will not consider yourself successful if you fulfill your purpose through dishonest means. If your faith dictates that you cherish all life, you won't consider yourself successful if you achieve your vision while harming others.

Your values provide the guardrails for your journey. You can live up to your values and fail your calling. You can fulfill your mission and go against your morals. Living consistently by your values doesn't make you successful—but you can't be a true success if you go against who you really are.

"Why?" Is a Great Place to Start

There are two main, foundational points to start building our measures of success: mission and vision. These are universal concepts, applicable to all organizations. Every organization has a core reason for existing—a purpose—although it may manifest itself in different forms.

The easiest examples are those organizations that have the clearest mission and vision.

Nonprofits

Nonprofit organizations, by their definition and nature, have a clear purpose. This purpose is likely to be one that serves the community, the city, state, or nation. Some serve society as a whole—or even all of mankind. It's usually a reaction to a current perceived injustice or wrong. Nonprofits that I have helped include education alliances, churches, the Salvation Army, early childhood development centers, and recently a new startup that seeks to bring true peace to the world by teaching inclusiveness through storytelling. But I've also helped chambers of commerce, libraries, and economic development organizations.

© Martin Klubeck 2017
M. Klubeck, *Success Metrics*, DOI 10.1007/978-1-4842-2586-8_5

They all had clear missions and, more importantly, strong visions.

Each mission was formed on a similar foundation of helping others. They all served others far before themselves. The only difference was the tools they chose. Their destinations were alike, but the paths they were choosing to take were very different. And this was true of their visions also.

One chose to provide information and knowledge to help produce life-long learners. Why? To make their community a great place to live, work, and play.

Another's purpose was to provide quality education to at-risk children. But when pressed for a vision, it expanded. They wanted to see all children in the community have a quality early education. This was their way of breaking the cycles of despair and pain.

And the beat goes on.

Saving children. Helping those who need it to find their self-esteem and dignity. Providing a focal point for change. Everywhere I turned there were individuals, small nonprofits, ambitious nonprofits, and even some for-profit organizations that had the vision of changing the world for the better. This was (and continues to be) extremely heartening. To know that young and old alike are seeking to make the world a better place gives me hope and happiness.

In a time when the newest generation of workers is seen to be selfish and imbued with an unearned sense of entitlement, it's nice to see that people still want to make a difference. Newly graduated alumni of the University of Notre Dame are staying in the South Bend, Indiana, area and creating startups with the express purpose of making the world a better place. Their desire to help and serve others was encouraged and nurtured at the university—something I had never given institutions of higher education credit for doing.

Nonprofit organizations should measure success based on how well they fulfill their mission, first and foremost. This was made obvious to me when I was working with the Salvation Army.

I agreed to work with its leaders and board to develop a viable, useful strategic plan. My role was to facilitate the creation of the strategic plan. I started by having the board review their past accomplishments. I did this for a couple of reasons: One was to celebrate their successes (they hadn't done so and didn't produce an annual report); the other was to make a point.

Using their collective memories, we documented on a large sheet of paper, all the good things they had accomplished over the past year. This included feeding the hungry (Thanksgiving Day was a special event each year), raising money over Christmas (they are well-known for their bell ringers), and providing a family with a much-needed major appliance. They had a very long list of good deeds they had done for those in need. It was impressive.

And it wasn't an abnormal year. Each and every year they did good works, like they did the year before, and the year before that. After affirming this and reminding them of all the good they do, I asked them *the* question.

"Taking into account all of these good works, how much of a real difference do you think you made?" After letting that sink in a little, I rephrased it. "If your purpose and mission is to change your city for the better, to bring God's Kingdom to earth, how far would you say you moved the needle?"

The answer was disheartening...to them. I saw it as a great opportunity. Without the realization that they were failing to fulfill their mission, they would never succeed.

Without understanding what their vision was and that they were not progressing toward its achievement in any significant way, they would not embrace a strategic plan.

You have to know what your vision is and want to measure progress toward it to embrace strategic planning.

It would be a grave error to consider their organization successful based on the good deeds they had performed year after year. Their mission and vision were much larger than what they were producing on a daily basis. They were confusing *what* they did with *why* they did it.

And it's the same for all nonprofits. Not all have clearly defined their mission or vision, but that's the only way to truly measure their success.

Nonprofits are the easiest because usually their mission was the foundational reason the organization was created. The new ones are young enough that someone on the board remembers the reason they came into existence, and because few succeed at completely eradicating the problem, their purpose usually hasn't changed.

Even so, most nonprofit organizations have trouble identifying their underlying purpose. When I peruse the Internet, the posted mission statements I find, even for nonprofits, are poorly written. Not because they use "weak" words, but because they don't get to the *why*. Most list the bigger, more impressive *whats* and sometimes *hows*.

If the organizations that should have it the easiest get it wrong, you won't be surprised to find that the others miss the boat too.

Now that we've covered the easiest one, let's look at the other categories of organization, from smallest to largest.

Individual Success

You may be reading this book because you want to measure your personal success. That makes a lot of sense. I have a friend, Justin, who is making a living by helping people define their legacy. People want to know they've made a difference, that their lives were meaningful.

This innate desire is in line with the concept of measuring success through your calling and vision.

Leaving a legacy is something many of us want to do. From the billionaire to the single parent living on welfare—we all want to have our lives mean something.

At the individual level, our mission is our calling. *Who* are we called to be. Not *what*—that's a job description. I taught a class for our human resources department on goal setting. In it, I offered that in order to set meaningful career goals, you had to know what your calling was.

The best career you could ever have is to fill a job that didn't previously exist.

If you can find the perfect job, the one that allows you to fully realize your purpose in life, chances are that you will be creating a job just for you. Don't laugh—this is very possible. My good friend Brian did it, and he's one of the most contented people I know. He had a vision and a calling to transform his hometown through education. From cradle to grave. He loves his community and he loves education. So he did the research, laid the foundation, and helped create a nonprofit organization to fulfill his calling. Then he got hired as the executive director of the organization and is currently working every day toward his vision while fulfilling his calling.

Brian is one of the most successful people I know.

Many times it can seem to be too hard to find your personal calling.

I have met my fair share of people who have given up. They are tired of struggling to survive. They are disenchanted with their jobs and have no desire to continue with their current career paths. But worse, they don't feel their lives have meaning. They can't imagine a purpose for their lives. And if they can't see a purpose, they rarely find a vision.

It's hard to be selfless when you believe your life has no purpose.

And yes, you may have guessed it—evil takes advantage of these lost people.

I truly believe that we all have a calling. Some of us have been distracted and misguided so far from that calling that we can't find our way back. Some of us have been lied to and intentionally misled away from our calling. Some of us are too afraid to follow what we know is our purpose.

Living in alignment with your calling is not easy. It requires faith and fortitude. It requires perseverance and self-discipline.

Many things fight against us when it comes to living up to our calling. Addictions, temptations, and peer pressure are just three things that can push us down the wrong path—and usually off the cliff.

When we fall away from our purpose, it can be a simple stumble. We can even catch ourselves before we fall. Other times, though, we may have climbed so far out on the ledge, so far away from our calling, that when we fall we fall a long way—sometimes so far, we don't think we can make it back up again.

"I've fallen and can't get up" can be a refrain we tell ourselves. It's a lie, of course, but we tell ourselves anyway.

The main reason (besides all of the things that are against us) we fail is simply that we try to go it alone. It's our calling—so no one else can help us, right?

Wrong.

It *is* your calling. No one else will know what it is better than you will. But that doesn't mean you should take the journey alone. There are many others on the same path as you, perhaps even working toward the same, or a very similar, calling. You will also find those (like me) who are happy to help you find the right path. You'll find mentors, coaches, and accountability partners. They may be your supervisor, manager, spouse, parent, or friend. Even your children may help you find your true calling.

But in the end, you have to be willing to listen and then believe your eyes and ears. You have to listen to your heart and believe it when it tells you which path to take.

You have to be open to finding your calling.

CARMEN

Carmen is my first individual visionary. She helped me realize that a strategic plan will only live if there is a vision behind it. I like to think that I helped her a little too.

Carmen is my poster child for personal mission and vision. She changed her trajectory from one where she was existing—doing what was necessary to put food on the table for her family and herself. She changed from working to dreaming. She took the leap of faith and is chasing her vision for the future and fulfilling her calling. It has drastically changed her life.

I'm extremely proud of her. I am in awe of her resolve and determination. She tries to thank me for helping her find her calling, but all I did was turn on the lights. She has done all the heavy lifting. She is an inspiration to me and I'm so grateful that she asked me to be a part of her awakening.

In the early 2000s, I was working with Carmen's organization on their strategic plan. She came to me at a break and asked if I could do my "magic" for an individual. I had never thought about it. It made total sense to me that the process I was following should work for an individual, so I agreed to give it a shot. I mostly listened while Carmen found her calling among her passion and talents. It was a great experience for me—and I thank her for introducing me to a part of my own calling I had been neglecting. I now eagerly help individuals as well as organizations with finding their purpose and vision.

Group/Team Viewpoint

Small groups and teams can be divided by their permanency.

Some teams exist for a short duration. In business, teams can be formed for specific efforts—for projects or programs. This can be confusing and misleading to an organization trying to measure success.

We sometimes (incorrectly) think that if a team has a definite (and usually highly focused) purpose, the measures of success will be easy to define. The error is in thinking the effectiveness and efficiency of the team will equate to success. You may argue that the team in isolation was a large success, and that we should measure that as such. But that would be creating a selfish and myopic view of the whole. This is the same problem we run into when we choose to use measures as our goal instead of indicators of success.

Any time I hear a leader (or organization) using a number as a goal, I cringe. It almost always means that they've taken a possible measure of performance and made it into a target. For example, instead of looking at the number of people who attended the opening of the event to see how well the marketing team is doing, that number becomes the goal. The marketing department is told that they have to sell out the house on the first night to be successful. You might as well not count the attendance any longer because it won't let you know how well the marketing department is doing (it was always only one indicator out of many). Now the number is seen as a pass/fail criteria. And the marketing team will do whatever is necessary to pass.

This is the same problem that drove more than 5,000 Wells Fargo employees to engage in illegal activities—to reach numbers that the organization was chasing. The measures of performance were distorted into targets and pseudo-goals.

If a measure is supposed to tell you how well you perform, you can't turn around and make that measurement the goal to achieve. Measures are supposed to tell you whether you're achieving the goal—not be the goal itself. Chasing data is a sure way of losing focus and heading down the wrong road.

If you were to build a metric around your employee integration program, what would you use as measures? If we look to determine how effective our program was, we'd want to look at things like the following:

- Number of workers indoctrinated
- How comfortable the new workers were in the organization
- How fast the workers felt part of the organization
- How loyal the workers were to the organization

Using just these as a starting point, we may be able to get a good feeling for how well the integration program was functioning. But sometimes we fall into the trap of making these measures more important than they truly are. We start chasing the numbers instead of using them as indicators. Say the message has been passed down the chain that leadership expects good numbers in the four measures they've defined, and rewards or punishment will be doled out based on those numbers.

This is a misguided and destructive use of measures.

Workers, especially those responsible for the program, will start making the numbers more important than the workers' integration. We start making the numbers the goal instead of using the measures as an indicator of how well things are working.

The mistake is simple (and unfortunately very common): Leadership put expectations on the measures, so they morphed from an indicator to a target. Indicators aren't something to achieve; they are information.

When we look at the success of a team toward achieving a subgoal, objective, or task, we make that effort more important than it is. Instead of using the team's effort as an indicator for how well you are progressing to the overall purpose, we make these mini-efforts the new goals.

The problem is simple: Teams, in and of themselves, are normally part of a smaller *how*. They are tasked with accomplishing a subgoal, objective, or even a complex task. Therefore, these are part of a bigger picture. Even if the team is successful (or even highly successful) at their task, that task may not do what we thought it would. The smaller effort may not get you closer to the bigger picture—our true destination that we're trying to reach.

So, although a team may be very effective and efficient at what they are tasked to do, what they are doing may not have been the right choice. You can definitely reward and recognize the team for their work, but you can't say that the team is a success. Even if every team you form works at peak levels, if they are working on the wrong things, the organization will not be successful.

Some teams and groups are more permanent in nature. Rather than being created to work on a specific project or problem, they are meant to perform a specific function. Again, these teams can perform well, but if the function they are providing isn't the total of the organization's mission or vision (and likely it is not), then progress at the team level won't equal overall success.

Some of the products I manage for the university have outstanding customer service call centers. Part of the mission of the company is to provide a certain type of experience. In the case of a survey/form application provider, the experience includes ease of use and a self-service functionality. They also want the experience to serve varying needs. The customer service call center helps the organization fulfill its mission by providing assistance to its customer base.

If the Service Desk does its job well, it should translate to helping the organization fulfill its mission, and therefore become successful. This is logical, but it doesn't always work that way. If the Service Desk doesn't "remember" its purpose and the mission of the organization, it can lose focus.

The joke "This would be a great job if it weren't for the customers" unfortunately reflects reality. Many people who intend to do their job well lose focus on the purpose behind their work and therefore work against success instead of toward it.

It's critical that every level of the organization—from leadership to divisions, departments, groups, teams, and individuals—stays in tune with the organization's purpose and vision.

Department/Division Success

As with groups and teams, success has to be predicated on helping the organization achieve success...not on any success at the departmental or division level.

Imagine the department or division that wins awards for their innovative approach to marketing. If they win awards but forget the mission of the organization—forget that they are part of the whole—the organization can end up being an abject failure.

Don't believe me? How about departments that exceed quotas just in time to see the organization go bankrupt? This happens more often than you might think. How about where the department heads across the organization compete with each other for resources? Instead of teaming together to help the organization achieve its purpose, they only see their own department's goals and performance.

This is not a new story or a unique observation. Most large organizations that have multiple departments or divisions have competition between them. This is not just "friendly" competition, as leadership may like to think (and hope). Along with this competitive spirit comes a level of mistrust. And although such departments won't openly fight against each other, they also won't work as a cohesive team across functional lines. It becomes an "us vs. them" mentality. Resources are hoarded, information is leveraged, and directors behave more like adversaries than teammates.

Why?

Because they have lost sight of the mission of the organization. Their performance is not measured by the fulfillment of the mission—instead they are judged by how well their individual departments are performing. If their people are winning awards or if they are functioning at high effectiveness and efficiency levels, they are recognized. If the department is saving money or earning money, they are rewarded. They are not judged by the overall success of the organization. This is another example of misusing the measures we have on hand. Rather than blend the results for each department together, we reward, recognize, and punish based on each department's segregated performance.

That's akin to rewarding players on a team for their individual performance while ignoring the overall results. In our book *Don't Manage…Coach!* (CreateSpace, 2015), Michael Langthorne and I tackle this problem from a different direction. Rather than discuss how the measures of success can be misconstrued and lead to disharmony, we champion the concepts of having organizational goals and a focus on the big picture. For example, team chemistry is much more important than individual performance.

Imagine a basketball point guard, the one with the ball in her hands the majority of the time, who loses sight of the overall mission and vision for the team. Imagine that instead of trying to make her teammates better and finding ways to win, she only thinks of her own performance and the big contract she hopes to earn at the end of the season. Rather than help, push, or encourage teammates, she stays on her own. Instead of passing the ball, she shoots more. She seeks to pad her own statistics and win games single-handedly. She seeks to be a superstar first and a team player second (if at all).

If the head coach, general manager, and owner also lose sight of the overall success of the organization, they will reward her with a large contract to keep their "star" player. You may say her selfishness should be obvious, and they should correct the behavior or get rid of her. And you would be right—except that same star player may be bringing in the crowds. She may be a draw for ticket buyers. The fans like to see her score over 40 points in a game, even if their team loses by 20. So, the leadership of the organization may look only at her statistics and the increased revenue (her memorabilia—shirts, basketballs with her name on them, and posters—are their best-selling merchandise) might blind them to the truth. They forget why they have the team in the first place.

But the bottom line is the same. If you make the bottom line your measure of success, you will miss the mark and end up risking true progress. Any department's performance is secondary to that of the organization. If one department is a shining star in the darkness, you have deep problems. And rewarding that super star by promoting, rewarding, or recognizing that department leader only encourages more dysfunction.

When we turn measures into goals, we change our indicators into targets. What was supposed to tell us how well we're doing becomes a catalyst for dysfunction and selfishness.

Measures of success cannot be relegated down to the department or division level. They have to be elevated to the organizational level. We have to stop looking at measures at the lower levels of the organization independently of the larger, overarching measures for the organization.

Leadership's View of Success

By now, you may think you could write this section—and if you've read each section up to here, you're probably right. But I know many people skim and skip around, looking for the parts that relate to them. I won't go into the power of finding wisdom in unexpected places.

Most times, leaders have an incorrect view of success. And this invariably causes problems. Top-level leaders are judged by some things that just don't make sense when we look at the organization's overall success. I know a lot of people that look at the leadership of their organization and want to know how much money they make. How much do the CEO, CIO, COO, and CFO make? How much do directors make? As if their income can be used to define success. Another error of this type is the questions around stock holdings, control, and power. How much autonomy does each leader have in making decisions? Can they fire people on the spot?

"You're fired" garnered Donald Trump more mileage than any campaign slogans his speechwriters could have come up with during his presidential candidacy.

We're fascinated with power. We're afraid of power.

Dictators make good press for a reason.

But none of this relates to success. Being in charge isn't success in and of itself. Power isn't any better than fame or fortune—and top leaders can have all three. And these traits can mislead them into thinking they're successful. They think they've achieved the highest pinnacle they can.

But it's a falsehood. It's a lie.

There's more to being successful. You still have to fulfill your calling. If you ignore what you're called to do, and instead you spend your life and energy chasing fame, fortune, or power, you very likely will miss the boat. The lament of "top dogs" is more common than we want to believe. They sacrifice their families, their loved ones, their children. They exchange human relationships for the trifecta of the ego. And then they lament not having spent more time with their family. They don't regret not spending time with friends because they don't have too many. Not real friends. Not people that don't see them as a stepping-stone to their own efforts toward feeding their ego.

Nope. Fame, fortune, and power do not define success. And the best leaders are not confused by their status. They stay focused on their purpose and enjoy the fruits of their labor. They don't lose sight of their calling.

I interviewed leaders to get their take on how they measure success. The CIO of a 250-person information technology division helped me understand what the leader's viewpoint could (and should) be.

RON'S VIEWPOINT

Ron has seen success. But it wouldn't be what most people think.

His organization has continued to climb the ranks each year of nationally recognized organizations. Ranked 35th, then 25th, then 9th, and most recently at 6th among the best places to work. Of course, there are qualifiers: Large Organization, Information Technology, or Higher Education Institute, but the accolades are still impressive.

But that's not what Ron uses to measure success.

The organization has found ways to save its parent organization significant amounts of money: streamlining processes, selecting better tools, changing platforms, and training the customer base.

But that's not what Ron uses to measure success.

The first thing that strikes you is that his measures of success are not about himself. Regardless of whether Ron was someone who enjoyed the limelight or preferred anonymity, his measure of success looks outward at the organization, not inward. To that end, the organization has a strategic framework to guide it.

Deliver Value, Drive Innovation, and Develop Talent. These provide a structure for change and improvement. But this is more of a tool for focusing effort toward the things that will help create their customers' experience than a means of measuring success.

"It's about creating experiences. Our job is to help students learn and develop themselves so they can get great jobs, contribute to society and potentially make remarkable differences in the world. We help faculty be more effective teachers and conduct research that can solve some of the world's most confounding challenges. We improve efficiency so we can run a world-class university in which the focus can be on teaching, learning, research, and scholarship."

Ron's definition of success is not a quick off-the-cuff answer. He is very specific about how he measures success for himself and for the organization. And neither is predicated on recognition or awards. Ron makes it very clear (he corrected me more than once during our interview to make sure I had it right) that he measures success at the organizational level—not at the individual level (especially not himself). But that's not quite it either. He went on to explain that the organization's success is measured by "the success of those who use the services we deliver."

"The ultimate measures of success are the experiences we help create for our customers."

Rewards and recognition won by the organization are only *indicators* of how their customers experienced their service. "We're not in the conversation at all—not even 'How well did we serve our customers.' Our success is measured by what the customer experienced."

And this makes total sense. Success is not measured by how hard you tried, but by results. Measures of success are result-oriented indicators. The top-level goal for Ron's organization is the end user's experience, so that's where his measures of success reside.

How great the world would be if all leaders tied their measures of success so clearly and stringently to their mission.

The last viewpoint we're going to look at is the Corporate Viewpoint, because this is the one that has the most likelihood of being misunderstood.

The Corporate Viewpoint

"Show me the money!"

Movies and books are great for offering quotable phrases. Even when talking about measuring success, it's easy to find examples of right and wrong answers to our deepest questions. How to truly measure success is definitely a "deep" question, and we want to look at it in the deepest sense possible.

In the movie *Jerry McGuire*, Cuba Gooding, Jr.'s character, Rod Tidwell, mispresents all Americans with his over-the-top focus on making money. Besides misrepresenting all pro athletes as caring about the paycheck above all else—it has also stood as a descriptor for American business.

Remember my friend? He felt that the definition of "business" meant that the organization's success was measured by the amount of revenue it generated. The more money the business makes, the more successful it is.

Unfortunately, my friend's viewpoint is not unique or even in the minority. Corporate America is seen by many as a vehicle for making the wealthy wealthier. That they put the interests of employees and even customers below income.

And as with the other views of success, this one is wrong. Corporations have to have a larger mission. Making a profit is a means to an end - and the corporation needs to find out what that end is.

Summary

When we're looking at true success, it's imperative that we start with the *why*. Why was your organization founded? Why does it continue to exist? The *why* tells us the purpose, calling, and mission.

That *why* can be hard to find sometimes. If your organization has been around for a while, you may have lost sight of your roots. You may not know what your real purpose is. Whereas nonprofits should have the easiest time of finding their mission, even they fall victim to apathy. There will be times when a clear mission is anything but clear. I've seen organizations and volunteers working diligently to raise enormous sums of money without fully understanding the mission of the organization.

So it should come as no surprise that individuals, teams, groups, departments, divisions, and leadership can work every day with no idea of the actual mission of their organization.

This should scare you.

Do you know why your organization exists? Do you believe in your organization's purpose?

The journey to success, like every journey, has a beginning and an end. The great thing is that to measure success, you should start at the same place you will end—with the *why* behind the *what*.

We don't measure success by what we do—we measure success when we achieve the *why* behind it.

The Fulfillment of Your Purpose

For an individual, the question is "What is your purpose?" or "What is your calling?"

For an organization, we ask, "What is its mission?"

I've touched on these earlier in the book and tried to explain why this is one of the two foundational elements to measuring true success. But what exactly is a calling? What is a mission or purpose? How do you find it?

Purpose

If you know what your purpose is, then measuring how well you fulfill it should be simple. For example, if your purpose in life is to make America a great country (again), you can measure how well you've helped toward that goal. And it would flavor your actions, thoughts, and education. You would want to rise to a position of enough importance to help push change in the right direction. There are many roles you could play to make this happen. From President of the United States, to any of the key cabinet members. You could shoot for being a senator or even Chief Justice of the Supreme Court. But you could also look for a career in the FBI, CIA, or the U.S. military. You could become a teacher or a librarian. There are many paths to travel toward your purpose—a purpose which you will likely share with thousands of others.

© Martin Klubeck 2017
M. Klubeck, *Success Metrics*, DOI 10.1007/978-1-4842-2586-8_6

You will find that you are not the only one with your purpose. The larger your calling, the more colleagues you will find.

If your purpose is very finite, like "Give my children a better life than we had," you'll find fewer colleagues with the same calling. But there will be others! Your spouse, your parents, your children's teachers, and other people in your community who also want the best for your children.

Organizations aren't any different. The larger the mission, the greater the number of potential collaborators because there will be other organizations (and individuals) with the same calling. The more finite the organization's mission, the fewer the number of potential collaborators.

In 2016, I helped an organization define their mission, vision, and strategic plan. They had a mission that was scoped tightly. It focused on "at risk" youth in a specific county. You would think that would make them a niche type of nonprofit (they thought this). But in reality, they shared their purpose with numerous organizations in and outside of their county. There was the Boys and Girls Club, United Way, Big Brothers/Big Sisters, and the Salvation Army. The entire local school system (public and private) could also join in the fight. There were others who also wanted to help "at risk" youth. Others who were pushed to action due to what they called "unacceptable" situations. And there were also national-level organizations with a comparable mission.

By defining and sharing your calling, you will likely help many others who aren't sure what their mission is to find their calling.

What Is Your Personal Calling?

On an individual level, we occasionally confuse our talents with our calling. Granted, our talents may indeed be aligned with our calling, but not always. Of course, you should be able to leverage and use those talents for the purpose of your calling, but to assume that your calling is simply to develop those talents is misguided.

We hear all the time about the "failures" in life who ignored their talents. People who have wasted their "God-given talents." The failures who turned their backs on their talents and let themselves be consumed by drugs, alcohol, or something else.

The ones who "could have been famous," "the best [fill in the job or role of your choice] that no one ever knew about." But we've already established that fame is not the same as success.

Even artists who went unknown during their lifetimes and become famous after death are seen as failures because they didn't reap the praise and recognition during their lifetimes. But were they failures? If they fulfilled their calling in spite of not being publicly or critically acclaimed, were they failures or successes?

"…nothing is more common than unsuccessful men with talent."—Calvin Coolidge

---

Let's say we go with the premise of divine intervention. Each of us has a talent (or talents). And each of us was bequeathed talent by a higher power (which explains prodigies). So is our mission to develop our talents and be the best at our strengths? And if we have multiple talents, do we have to develop each? If we fail to develop them, are we failures?

I don't believe so.

If you and I were given talents, it's highly unlikely that we were given these talents for the purpose of honing them.

No, the question we have to ask is "Why were we given these talents?" If we were given talents as a gift, what is the purpose of them? If I am a good writer (I'm hoping you think so), then why? What am I supposed to do with that talent? I believe my talents of writing, public speaking, coaching, and consulting are all tools for me to use to fulfill my calling, my purpose: to help others.

The same can be said for organizations.

What Is Your Organization's Mission?

What are the talents of each organization? You can look at the talents of the individuals who make up the organization—and think that the organization's capabilities are a conglomeration of these skills—but you'd be wrong.

In our 250-person IT organization, it is fascinating to find how many people have extraordinary talents that are not used in their day-to-day jobs. We have musicians, thespians, teachers, and games makers. We have orators, artists, and writers. We have triathletes, ex-pro football players, and physical trainers.

No, an organization's capabilities are not simply a product of the talents of its people. But organizations do have talents and skills. As a group, the organization's people have (or don't have) strengths in performing certain functions, creating, innovating, and developing.

Our organization (Office of Information Technologies) is exceptional at customer service. Most people at the university see our mission as helping the rest of the university achieve higher heights. They see us as enablers. We deliver the experience they want and need to do their good works, which means that we enable and assist others in fulfilling the university's mission. So we would have to look at the university's mission. Unfortunately, the mission statement for the university is more than 500 words long. I could pare it down, "to pursue and share the truth for its own sake," but obviously that would be taking a lot of literary license. Luckily our CIO has a different understanding of our mission.

But let's keep working on the generic organizational mission. If it's not developing our talent...what is it?

We have to get back to the key question: Why?

Why do we exist?

Why does the organization exist? Chapter 3 discusses using your past to help define your present. If we look at the reason the organization was formed, we should get a good picture of the *why* behind the *what*. This helps us lay the groundwork for helping us find our mission.

Whole Foods, Inc., says it doesn't have a mission statement. Which is fine by me.

> *At Whole Foods Market, "healthy" means a whole lot more. It goes beyond good for you, to also encompass the greater good. Whether you're hungry for better, or simply food-curious, we offer a place for you to shop where value is inseparable from values.*

The company expresses its purpose as a set of values. Eight to be exact:

1. *We sell the highest quality natural and organic products available*
2. *We satisfy, delight and nourish our customers*
3. *We support team member excellence and happiness*
4. *We create wealth through profits and growth*
5. *We serve and support our local and global communities*
6. *We practice and advance environmental stewardship*
7. *We create ongoing win-win partnerships with our suppliers*
8. *We promote the health of our stakeholders through healthy eating education*

Nice.

But.

That doesn't really tell us why they are in business. It doesn't excite or impassion us. These values aren't enough to bring the customers out of their own flood-damaged homes to help recover a local store. And that's what actually happened early in Whole Foods history. No, it took an unspoken understanding of the store's mission.

So, let's look at what the purpose of Whole Foods could be since it chooses not to have a mission statement. I don't think it's at all presumptuous of me. I'm happy for Whole Foods to function without a clear statement of purpose…if the organization and its stakeholders all have a common understanding without a statement to clarify it, I'm very happy with that.

But for the purpose of this book, and for your edification, we have to try to understand it. Whole Foods and the Conscious Capitalism movement may be the best examples of the mission of for-profit organizations.

Let's look at those core values and see if there isn't a purpose hidden in there.

Table 6-1. Core Values May Lead to Purpose

Core Value	Description
We sell the highest quality natural and organic products available	This is definitely a value and principle. A guideline for how the organization functions. It's also their niche market. But it's more than that. It feels like it's more than their niche. I get the impression that if everyone chose to sell only the highest quality natural and organic products, they'd be happy for the competition.
We satisfy, delight and nourish our customers	Is this simply how they try to be profitable? Is this their modus operandi? Satisfying and delighting customers would definitely seem to fit this thought, but "nourish?" Nourishing is different. Satisfying and delighting will encourage customers to come back. It will encourage them to promote the business to their friends and neighbors. But nourish? Let's come back to that one.
We support team member excellence and happiness	Supporting employees. Nothing actually groundbreaking or new here.
We create wealth through profits and growth	Keeping the lights on and reaching more people.
We serve and support our local and global communities	Nice, but not a purpose.
We practice and advance environmental stewardship	Yup, great value and focus.
We create ongoing win-win partnerships with our suppliers	Nice—all stakeholders are covered.
We promote the health of our stakeholders through healthy eating education	Hmmm. Here we go again. Promoting health? A food store? Not taking advantage of the most profitable items we can stock our shelves with but instead choosing to promote health and providing healthy eating education?

So, from my detached, outside-looking-in viewpoint, I'd say the purpose of Whole Foods has a lot more to do with making the human race healthy than with making a buck. Nourishing and educating its customers seems to be at the core. That and perhaps being stewards of the environment. It is in here that I think we'll find an underlying purpose.

Is it to perpetuate the human race? Is it to help the human race reach its potential and not kill itself off prematurely? Who wouldn't want to help make all of our lives healthier? Who wouldn't want vaccines, cures, and preventative medicines? Who wouldn't want to be healthy?

Let's see if we're on target. After wading through the eight values and the rhetoric that Whole Foods doesn't have a mission statement, we finally find nestled between the "declaration of interdependence" and "sustainability and our future" the company's purpose—something like this:

Our Higher Purpose Statement

With great courage, integrity, and love—we embrace our responsibility to co-create a world where each of us, our communities, and our planet can flourish. All the while, celebrating the sheer love and joy of food.

I think we're right on track. And even better, they may have a vision also:

Whole Foods's vision of a sustainable future means our children and grandchildren will be living in a world that values human creativity, diversity, and individual choice.

Not bad. Not bad at all!

No matter the size of your organization (you could be an "army of one"), the question isn't what you do, it's who you are. That's worth repeating.

The question isn't what we do, it's who we are.

In a recent class I taught, we discussed how to make a great first impression. When we meet someone for the first time, a normal question is "What do you do?" It's innocent small talk that may or may not lead to a more in-depth conversation. If we find out the person has a job in an industry that interests us, we'll dig deeper. If the job title sounds compelling, we'll ask follow up questions.

The first time I met an FBI special agent, I had a ton of questions.

But I suggested that when asked "What do you do?" the students answer without stating their job title at all. For example, for the woman who set tables for receptions, rather than "arrange the tables, silverware, glasses, and dishware for a wedding," I suggested she explain the benefit. "I help make the most important day in a newly married couple's lives perfect." This provides the *why* behind the *what*.

And that would be followed up with stories of wedding parties, specific decorations, and special settings she had been tasked with.

It's still not the *what*. It's always the *why*.

For another worker, we suggested that she not say she was a cook, but instead when asked "What do you do?" respond with something along the lines of "I make people's mouths water and bring joy to their taste buds." Or she "makes any event special through culinary feasts of wonder."

The security policemen didn't give their title either. Instead they said that they ensure visitors to our campus have a safe visit. They keep us all safe.

In any and every job, there is a *why* behind the *what* that we do. And describing our careers by what we do—with a job title or even the tasks we perform— bypasses our purpose. The reason for the role's existence isn't the list of tasks performed…it's why those tasks need to be done.

We have to dig deeper under the surface to find our purpose.

The same goes for every organization.

We have a facility called the Wellness Center on campus. It provides immediate care, a pharmacy, and some preventative diagnostics. Those are the services offered, but they're not the reason it exists.

The *why* behind the *what* in this case has to do with employee health and comfort—customer service to the employees of the university. But if we go even deeper, we find that the reason for this convenience is to help our employees be healthier. And that would be a pretty good reason by itself, wouldn't it? There are other benefits, though, that could be at the root. The parent organization benefits from employee good health because the healthier the employees are, the less cost to the university in insurance payouts. Companies across the U.S. are learning that investing in employee health is much cheaper than paying for poor health later.

It turns out that an ounce of prevention really is worth a pound of cure. Prevention is much more economical than dealing with ill health later. But these are benefits. They make a good sales pitch to why we should have a wellness center.

So, what's the mission of the Wellness Center?

The benefits are many, and they have good breadth and depth. The organization as a whole benefits, the workers benefit, and leadership benefits.

But what's the purpose?

Regardless if it exists to keep employees healthier because we care about our employees or because it's economically wise, the bottom line is the same. The mission of the Wellness Center is to improve and maintain the health of our employees.

So, how would you measure the success of the Wellness Center? Here are some possible measures we might find in use:

1. *Usage*: How many employees are using the Wellness Center?
   a. Daily
   b. Weekly
   c. Monthly
   d. Annually
   e. Repeat customers

2. *Expenditures*: How much money does it cost to maintain the wellness center?

3. *Savings*: How much money is it saving the university in insurance claims?
   a. For existing conditions
   b. For new conditions

4. How many sick days are employees taking? Has that number gone down since the Wellness Center was created?

5. Are there special programs?
   a. How many offered?
   b. How well attended?

6. *Customer satisfaction*: Feedback from those using the Wellness Center.

The Wellness Center as an Example

What do you think of the list in the preceding section? Seem logical? I wouldn't be surprised if these were the measures used to create a dashboard for the Wellness Center's success. I wouldn't be surprised if savings were left out—possibly because the organization thought it was too hard to collect. Let's look at that list again:

1. Usage
2. Expenses
3. Savings
4. Special programs
5. Customer satisfaction

What's missing?

If the purpose of the organization is to help our employees improve and maintain their health, where did we measure fulfillment of that? Remember, insurance cost savings is a benefit, not the *why*. Even if the university was convinced to establish the Wellness Center because of the expected savings, that's not the *why* behind it. There are other ways to save money in insurance costs—ones that don't show as much concern for the workforce. But even then, we should ask why we offer insurance. Even if it's regulated and required by government, there's a reason behind the rules that demand it. Our health is important not only to ourselves, but to our community, society, and country.

If we agree that the purpose of the Wellness Center is to improve and maintain the good health of our workforce, how are we measuring that?

Just a reminder: If I asked any of the Wellness Center staff what they did, they could answer with its purpose. "I do my best so you can do your best." That would work. The purpose for our career should align with the purpose of our unit, which should align with the purpose of our department, division, and ultimately our organization. If they don't align, something has to go.

Usage

Has potential as an indicator—we need to see whether we're helping employees, so it's useful to know how many are using our services. But usage by itself is not a good measure. It doesn't tell us how healthy the employees are.

Expenses

This will give us insight into the cost of our efforts—which can tell us if we can "afford" to carry on with our mission. It doesn't tell us whether we're succeeding.

Savings

This is an expected by-product—a benefit. The savings won't tell us whether the employees are maintaining good health, although fewer sick days taken and smaller insurance payouts can be good indicators (like usage).

Special Programs

Like all of the measures identified, special programs is a *how* that may or may not do anything toward fulfilling the mission of the Wellness Center. We may use special programs to encourage good health, to promote our services, and increase awareness—but the number of programs and even attendance at them does nothing to provide measures of success. The programs could be well attended and not result in any improvements to employee health. Then again, it could. But if we measure the wrong things, we'll never know. We'd have to measure whether the special program actually resulted in better employee health (or sustained health).

At best, all the measures so far have a small potential for informing us on how successful we are at fulfilling our mission. Why would we gather and analyze them if they are such poor indicators? Because they are *easy* to collect. Usage only requires counting. Expenses and savings use data that is already collected for accounting purposes. Special programs is a count also. And this ease of collection is the reason almost every organization makes the mistake of putting a high value on customer satisfaction surveys.

Customer Satisfaction

Of course an organization wants feedback from its customers. The Wellness Center would be no exception. But knowing how the customer rates your services isn't the same as success—unless your purpose was to have customers report that they liked your services!

Notice the nuance.

Customer satisfaction surveys do *not* tell you how satisfied the customer was with your service. They only tell you what the customer decided to report. If the customer was in a bad mood or an exceptionally good mood, the feedback will likely reflect that unrelated temperament. Even if the feedback were completely accurate (you have no way of knowing whether it was), the organization's purpose wasn't to garner this feedback.

Of course we want our customers to be satisfied! We want excellent customer service because this will help our cause. It will make it more likely that our customers will use our services and thereby have better health. But these are *hows*. They are a means to the end that we're seeking.

If we measure the means on their own, we miss the point. When we undertake a journey, the most meaningful measures are as follows:

1. Did we reach our destination?
2. How well did the path we chose get us there?
   a. Faster?
   b. More directly?
   c. More accurately?

We make the mistake of measuring the steps we take along the journey—not in relation to how they help us get to the destination, but as standalone efforts. This is akin to measuring how well the car handled, the mileage per gallon we got, and how comfortable the ride was instead of how much closer we got to our destination. If we gathered all the information about the car but ended up going in the wrong direction or getting totally lost, the measures we collected would do nothing for indicating our overall success.

We can't measure the steps independently of the reason we are taking those steps.

Customer satisfaction is important, but if we measure it independently from our achieving the purpose, we'll go astray. At best, we'll celebrate prematurely. At worst, we'll not collect any other measures—the ones we really need—and we won't have any clue whether we're successful or not.

The Biggest Mistake

This is the biggest mistake I see and the most common: We measure the wrong things and then compound that error by refusing to measure anything else. We put the check in the box and call it quits. We never really wanted to do the work required to gather meaningful metrics, so once we have something that looks good and is widely accepted as a viable measure, we quit.

If you presented the measures listed earlier—usage, expenditures, savings, special programs, and customer satisfaction—to your leadership, you'd have a very good chance of gaining acceptance. You may even get accolades for developing such a nicely rounded metrics program. You could even call them Key Process Indicators (KPIs) and make them sound important. There are a lot of books that provide guidance on how to chart and graph your KPIs. Most data-collection software and visualization tools offer dashboards that combine all of your KPIs on one page. That way leadership (and stakeholders) can see how well you're doing at a glance.

And all of this is folly.

The measures are wrong to begin with. They are non-comprehensive. When you put them all together on your dashboard, they don't tell a complete (or accurate) story at all.

They also lack alignment. They don't build up to the answers you need: "Are we successful?" Or "Will we be successful?" None of the measures listed will answer either of these questions.

I'll say it again: The biggest mistake is measuring the wrong things and thinking you've answered the question.

So what should you do? What should you measure?

It's not what you do, it's why you do it.

The *why* is your purpose. In the case of the Wellness Center, we have to measure against the reason the Wellness Center exists. And it exists to "improve and maintain employee good health." It's that simple.

So, our measures have to do the following:

1. Measure employee health (with a range that includes "good health")
   a. Current health
   b. Future health
2. Measure how the Wellness Center affects employee health
   a. Does the Wellness Center improve employee health?
   b. Does it improve it enough to be good?
   c. Does the Wellness Center help employees maintain good health?

That's it! Nothing more. These are the key measures for determining the success of the Wellness Center. You could (and maybe you should) stop there. If you had these metrics in place, you'd be doing a great job. But to do this, you might want to build these with some lower-level measures. There are secondary measures that we can analyze to determine whether the Wellness Center can fulfill its purpose better.

By *better* I mean more effectively or efficiently.

Remember the Answer Key discussed in Chapter 2? The Answer Key will help with lower-level concerns and measures. They don't define success at all, but they help us determine if there may be better ways to do what we do.

Effectiveness

We need to measure whether what we're doing is doing what we intended it to do. Are our special programs satisfying the need we were trying to address? Let's say we're seeing a trend of employee stress rising and we determine that these heightened levels of stress will lead to poorer health. So we develop a special program to make our employees aware of the stress, provide tools for mitigating the stress, and finally a means for eliminating the stress altogether.

We do a pilot run of the program, measuring stress before and after. Did the program reduce the stress? Did it reduce it significantly? If so, we can say that it was effective.

How about the cost and effort involved?

Efficiency

How well we do things are measured under Efficiency. How long did it take? How much did it cost? How many resources were required? These are all things we can measure to tell us whether we're working smarter instead of harder.

I told you earlier that we shouldn't start with Efficiency (ever) or Effectiveness (although it's the best second-choice ever!). Instead I recommended that you start with Measures of Success (MoS). And here we are coming around full circle. If we start where we should—by measuring success—it will lead us unerringly to measuring whether and how well we fulfill our purpose. The difference is that we put the most emphasis and focus on the Measures of Success and only delve into the next tiers of Effectiveness and Efficiency when we need insights into how to be more successful.

All the measures we started with—usage, expenditures, savings, special programs, and customer satisfaction—live at the Effectiveness and Efficiency levels. That's why they were the wrong indicators for measuring success.

Start at the End

What is your organization's purpose? Even if you work in a group below a unit that answers to a department, controlled by a division—you can answer the question "What's your mission?" Even if the hierarchy above you has not clearly defined its mission, you can take a shot at yours. Of course, it's much better (and easier) if the structure above you has already defined its purpose...but don't let the lack of clarity stop you from measuring the right things at your level.

We start at the end (or the top) by first and foremost measuring how well we are fulfilling our mission.

First

By *first* I mean don't bother gathering other data to analyze. Don't create dashboards full of Effectiveness and Efficiency measures. Don't drop down into the weeds before you've surveyed your plot of land. *First* means start at the end. You need to first know the answer to the root questions—are you successful? Will you be successful?

Foremost

By *foremost* I mean that measuring success is the most important measure. Don't ignore it. Don't get wrapped up in the minutia of the weeds. You can spend your whole life pulling up the weeds and thereby miss harvesting your crop. Measures of Success are not only the first measures you should be collecting, they're also the most important ones.

When you review your metrics—what are you looking at?

Efficiency data? Effectiveness measures? Or are you reviewing how successful you truly are?

THE HAMMER, THE NAIL, AND THE WOOD

The hammer was a proud tool. He was multi-purpose (the packaging said so). He could drive nails and remove nails. He could also be used to drive other nail-like things. He was crafted with care and precision. And for every 100,000 nails, there was one hammer.

"You think you're important because you are more unique than me, don't you?" Nail asked the hammer.

"Sure! And I'm also stronger and better made than you" the hammer reminded the nail for the tenth time that day.

"But that's pretty narrow minded...."

"It's just the truth. I can get the job done, unlike you. You need thousands of you because you're flimsy and fickle. If I don't hit you just right, you twist or bend. Then I have to pull you out and throw you away. Thank goodness they finally figured out how to recycle you."

"Just because there's a lot of us doesn't make us less important. And just because sometimes we fail…"

"Sometimes? One out of ten of you gets tossed!"

"Even so, that doesn't mean we're not important. If there were no nails, what would you drive into Wood?"

Hammer thought about Screws and winced. He didn't like Screws or Power Tools.

"What makes you think you're important?"' Hammer asked Nail.

"Well, my purpose of course."

"Hah! Your purpose is to get driven by me! If anyone has an important purpose, it's me."

"Oh really? What is your purpose?"

"To drive you into Wood! And if I don't do it well, things fall apart, literally."

"So you think your purpose is to hit me on the head?" Nail asked.

"Yup! And I know your purpose too," Hammer continued.

"Continue, please."

"All of you guys have the same mission: You hold things together, with my help."

"Hmmm."

"And my purpose is to drive you so you can fulfill your purpose." Hammer smiled.

"So, you're only purpose is to help all of us inferior nails fulfill our purpose?"

Hammer stopped smiling. "What are you trying to say?"

"Just that if your purpose is to drive us into Wood to hold things together, then your whole purpose is to serve us nails."

Hammer frowned. This wasn't going the way he had anticipated.

"Let's ask Wood which of us has the more important mission."

They walked over to Wood, who was piled high, warming in the midday sun.

"Hey, Wood, we need you to settle an argument."

"Sure," Wood answered. "I love solving problems."

"Who has the greater purpose—Nail, who holds things together, or me, Hammer, who makes it possible for Nail to do his job?"

"Well, that depends. Do you know what your purpose is?"

"Sure! I drive nails into Wood," Hammer said, barely hiding his irritation.

"Of course, I allow things to stay together," said Nail.

"That's how you do your job, not why you exist."

Wood liked the silence that followed. Wood was hoping the conversation was over and he could finish sunning in silence.

"So who has the more important job?" Hammer and Nail asked in unison.

Well, if Wood wasn't going to get to enjoy his free time, at least these two were providing some humor.

"It depends on your mission," Wood tried.

"Grrr! What do you think our mission is?"

"Do you think all Wood has the same purpose?"

"Don't you?" asked Nail.

"I don't think so. Some are used for holding up tree houses, some for making houses, and some for heating a home. Some are used for fencing and some for making boxes, cards, and paper."

"Isn't that your job?" Hammer thought he was pretty clever for being able to throw that one back in Wood's face.

"Nope. My job is to stand beside my brothers and create a wall."

"I thought you said your job was to make a house?"

"No, I said that was my purpose. My job is what I do to help make that dream a reality," said Wood. "I can't make a house all by myself. I only do a small part to make that vision come true."

"So which of us is more important?" Hammer tried to get them back on topic.

"Which of us is more critical to the success of the vision? Can they build the house without any of us?" Wood asked.

Again a peaceful silence came to the undeveloped lot. But it didn't last for long.

"So, if driving Nails isn't my purpose, why am I built the way I am? Why am I so talented at it?"

"Because it's how you help fulfill your purpose and how you help make the dream come true."

"Riddles!" Hammer snapped.

Nail had been quietly contemplating what Wood had said and finally felt confident enough to chime in.

"So what's our purpose?" Nail asked.

"Do you mean individually or together?"

Nail looked at Wood. He looked at the plot of land, the trees, the heavy earth-moving equipment, and the construction trailer—and smiled. He got it.

"Thanks!" Nail said as he walked off to tell the news to the other thousands of Nails.

"What? Where are you going? Don't you want to know whose purpose is more important?" Hammer called after Nail.

"Why do you think your purpose is different than Nail's?" asked Wood.

"We have totally different talents. We don't look the same, work the same, or do the same things. He's nothing without me."

"And how good are you at holding boards together without nails?"

"Yeah, yeah, yeah. Now you're sounding like Nail."

"So why do you think your purpose is different than Nail's?"

"Because we're totally different! How could we be made for the same purpose?"

"It takes a lot of different types to make a dream come true. This house is someone's vision. It's destined to be more than a house or structure made of wood, glass, mortar, and metal. It's going to be someone's *home.*"

"Okay. But I do this work all the time, not just for this house. You and the Nails will never do anything else. This is all you'll ever do. That's why I'm more important."

"I'd say *privileged.* We only get to make one dream come true. You have the potential to help make many dreams come true. But even so, our purpose is the same. To make this dream come true."

"Today and until this house is finished, we all have the same purpose in life. And like most good dreams, this one can't come true with only one of us doing our best. We all have to be involved, fully. Engaged, dedicated, and focused. And not focused only on driving Nails. We have to remember the big picture, the real vision. Not even that we're building a house."

Hammer looked truly puzzled.

"The vision is more than to build a house, it's to make a home."

"So we're all equally important?" Hammer asked with a snicker.

"No. The secret is that we aren't important at all. None of us."

"How so?"

"What's important is the vision. We're not important in and of ourselves. The only important thing is the dream."

"Great! So none of us is more important than the other…"

"No, none of us is actually important at all," Wood corrected.

"And we all have the same purpose—to build a house."

"A home."

"Right," Hammer said.

"Right," Wood agreed.

"You're all nuts." Hammer said as he walked back to his toolbox.

Nut and Bolt looked up at Wood and thought about asking what that was all about. But Wood was looking so content and peaceful in the warm sun that they decided not to. Instead they asked, "Does the sun make you so happy?"

Wood smiled at Nut and Bolt. "Nope. I like the warmth, but what makes me really happy is knowing that tomorrow we'll start fulfilling our purpose. Tomorrow the frame goes up on the home."

"Yeah, we're looking forward to that too," Nut and Bolt said as they settled into their bucket for a nap.

Summary

Your potential for success is built on your ability to fulfill your purpose. You have to find your calling—as an individual or an organization. Your personal calling can be much more important to your success than your organization's mission. Based on your personal calling, you may choose to work for a different organization—one that is aligned with your purpose.

The adage *It's better to have a something than nothing* is wrong. The biggest mistake I find in the world of metrics is when we measure the wrong things, or not enough things (to tell the complete story), and then compound these errors by refusing to collect other measures because organizations believe they have done enough.

Finding the right Measures of Success requires that we have a healthy and accurate accounting of our purpose. This is equally important for organizations.

What to Measure: Progress to Your Vision

In our book *Don't Manage...Coach!* (CreateSpace, 2015) Michael Langthorne and I have an explanation of how a vision fits into the realm of goal setting.

Most teams succeed in part because they have and know what their common goals are. Having common goals allows everyone on the team to know why the team exists and it makes it possible for each team member to make role-based decisions. It's why an overarching vision is so valuable. A vision is the goal. It's the top-level goal for the organization. A common, top-level goal provides direction and purpose. A shared direction and purpose.

A vision is a dream for a better tomorrow.

A vision is a very large goal—an immense goal that is so large, it scares you. And it scares others.

© Martin Klubeck 2017
M. Klubeck, *Success Metrics*, DOI 10.1007/978-1-4842-2586-8_7

I love it when I'm helping someone (or a group) create a vision. I love it when we're discussing possible dreams…and that moment comes.

You can feel the tension in the room. The excitement. The emotion.

I get goose bumps every time.

And someone offers a possible vision. Carefully worded. Not too large. Not too small. What they think is just right. And I challenge them. I ask them if that's really as far as they want to go. And they come back with, "Well, I had a different one written down, but it scared me."

I smile and ask them to read it to everyone. Read the dream that was so large that it scared them to share it aloud. I am all ears. They have my total attention, and I expect everyone in the room to also be locked in.

You may have heard that a vision is a Big, Hairy, Audacious Goal or BHAG. But whoever came up with this nifty description left out Scary. Probably because it didn't make for a good acronym. Before you make this an episode of the *Twilight Zone*, let's look at some of the really good things having a vision does for you.

What a Vision Does

Visions are awesome. Seriously!

They get people fired up. They drive change, innovation, and dedication. They inspire. They motivate. Visions drive revolutions. Your organization's vision can do all these things.

Visions provide some measurable benefits: They galvanize believers behind the ultimate common goal, focusing your efforts, projects, programs, and strategic goals.

A vision will provide direction when you find yourself at a fork in the road. It's a lighthouse in the pitch black of a stormy sea. A vision gives hope for a better tomorrow and incites a passionate response.

Galvanizes

Visions are great. They help bring people from all walks of life together to achieve a common goal.

Galvanize is a great word, but it's probably not big enough. Million-man marches or whole countries pulling together to change the world, a vision has the power to make people forget and ignore their differences, personal needs, and even their own safety.

Coaches, the military, and world leaders all know the power of a common goal. Nothing has the power to change the world like a shared clear vision of the future.

Political statements are strong, but they don't get anywhere near the power of a clearly articulated vision for a better tomorrow.

A vision can galvanize a neighborhood to take back their streets from criminals. It can pull together former adversaries to fight against a common foe. It can create alliances between sworn enemies.

A vision can bring together organizations, municipalities, and even entire nations.

It was a common vision that gave birth to the United States. This vision—to have a country where all men are believed to be created equal, where everyone has a right to life, liberty, and the pursuit of happiness—was enough to incite a revolution.

> We hold these truths to be self-evident, that all men are created equal, that they are endowed by their Creator with certain unalienable Rights, that among these are Life, Liberty and the pursuit of Happiness.

And as with most visions, this one still hasn't come totally true. It took many years from that written declaration of independence from an oppressive government to the day when slavery was abolished within our borders. It took longer still for equal rights for people of all races. Along with racial inequality, we have suffered from gender inequality. Our country was not created in perfection. But the ideals behind its creation were near-perfect. The vision of our founding fathers was well stated.

And we are still fighting today for its full adoption.

Not all visions have to ignite a national fervor. You can have a vision on a much smaller scale. So can your organization.

Any common goal can do the same, but a vision does it exponentially better. A vision is so large and audacious that people want to join in. Your passion and enthusiasm toward accomplishing the "impossible" galvanizes others to the cause.

It's held true in the past. It will continue to hold true in the future. We love fighting for a good cause. And a vision is all about a good cause. It's about making the world a better place.

Focuses

Visions provide a clear focus for your attention. Ever notice how you fail to keep New Year's resolutions? It's because you have no focus on the resolutions. They normally aren't inspiring, and you are easily distracted from accomplishing them. A vision, on the other hand, is a focal point. It helps you to focus your attention. *Focus with laser-like intensity* is a common refrain nowadays for accomplishing tasks. If you can focus on one thing, you have a greater chance of accomplishing that one thing.

Whole books have been written on that simple idea. My boss gave all of us *Essentialism: The Disciplined Pursuit of Less* by Greg McKeown (Crown Business, 2014) to help us deal with the numerous (and often conflicting) tasks we deal with each day. I have to confess, I really liked the idea.

If you lose focus and divide your attention among a myriad of ideas, tasks, and hopes—chances are you won't accomplish any of them. A vision provides that focus.

Even when you're working on subgoals beneath the vision, the overarching, really big, scary, audacious goal allows you to focus on the bigger picture. It's why you're doing any of the lower-level tasks or objectives. It benefits you to remind yourself of the *why*. And it's the reason we don't measure at the subtask level. That would put the focus too low and disperse your attention in too wide a swath. No, we measure at the vision level so that we can stay focused on the real prize.

It's a critical factor in true success. Someone in the organization has to keep their focus squarely on that ultimate prize—the reason the organization exists and why stakeholders provide support. And it's always a good idea to revisit the purpose and vision. As a coach, I've learned to set goals at the beginning of the year. We set them as a team so that the players know what we're focusing on. Granted, this isn't a big, hairy, scary, or audacious goal (although it could be—like winning Nationals!), but the concept is no less valid because the top goal is less world-changing.

Each year I coach in a developmental volleyball league for girls in grades 3–6. This year I had a fifth/sixth-grade team. Some girls had never played organized volleyball before, whereas others had played for a year or more. Because the purpose of the league was to introduce girls to volleyball, have them learn the basics, and give them a chance to have some fun—our goals for the year were easy.

But rather than have my goals for the year dictated by the purpose, I gave myself some stretch goals above and beyond fulfilling the mission. At every turn I was able to remind myself of the purpose, though. It allowed me to be more patient and enjoy the experience because the purpose provided me with guidance for how to behave and what to expect. Within that, I set some simple "long-range" goals for the girls. I told each of them that my vision for this (short) season was for each of them to improve perceptibly. I wanted their parents, us their coaches, and they themselves to all recognize a significant improvement in their ability to play the sport.

This mini-vision gave me a focus and helped me know what to do each week at practice. It also allowed me to stay centered during our weekly matches. While other coaches (and parents) were pushing their teams to win, win, win—I was pushing our girls to demonstrate the skills we'd been teaching regardless of whether they won the game.

You might not see the difference. Let me elaborate.

At this age (and actually for many years yet to come) when girls are playing volleyball, the team that serves the best usually wins. That's because their ball control is very weak, and if you can get the ball into the opponent's side of the net more than on yours, you will win easily. So, the first step is whichever team serves better wins. And by *better* I mean *can get serves over the net and into the opponent's side of the court.* It doesn't matter which technique you use. This is so obvious at these younger ages that the league I'm coaching in restricts each girl to only five consecutive scoring serves before the other team gets the ball.

So, some coaches get to the weekly matches, and if they've spent time teaching the girls how to actually play volleyball, all of this instruction is forgotten for the sake of winning. They no longer try to control the ball and execute the normal pass, set, and attack. Instead the coach (and the parents) encourage the girls to get the ball back over the net in any way possible. The faster the better. Because that's how you win. Serve it in when it's your turn to serve and pass the ball back over the net as quickly as you can when it's not.

The problem is that this is not the skill set the girls will need for later. It teaches them to swing wildly at the ball, to be ball hogs, and to rely on their opponent's inability to play rather than to demonstrate good skills.

My teams are different. We practice the basic skills, over and over. We make it fun, but we work to improve each girl's skill set. Then when we play a match we count how many times the girls pass, set, and attack the ball the way we've practiced. We reward the girls based on their success at demonstrating the skills as taught—not based on the game score. We have only won one match (of five so far), and that was because the other team served worse than we did. But my girls have been improving every week. They are all showing progress—from the worse to the best player, they are all improving, and I'm very happy.

Of course, I have to educate my parents that we're not trying to win (they still yell at the volunteer scorekeeper if they miss a point). I have to remind them of the purpose of the league and of our goals for the girls. I want my girls to love the sport—but also to get better. I want them to learn how to play the game, not just win.

And there is a difference.

Provides Direction

Ever wanted to say no to a request but figured it was a good one, so why not add another task to your ever-growing list of commitments?

Want to get something done? Give it to a busy person.

In his book *Essentialism*, Greg McKeown teaches us all about when and how to say no. He also covers the importance of doing just a few things (one thing is even better) and doing them really well. Vision helps us do that. It gives us that *one* thing we should be doing. It keeps us focused on the most important thing.

It provides clear direction. If the request helps you achieve the vision, if it helps move you along the road to the vision, then it's up for consideration. If you don't have enough time to do all the things that may help with the vision, you have to pick the ones that have the most potential to get you the furthest in your journey.

In *Essentialism*, McKeown guides us clearly toward achieving our number one priority—which, I offer, should be the achievement of your vision. We know what direction we want to go and we can even decide which path we prefer: the one that gets us there faster and with the least detours.

I love my GPS. I remember the days of going to AAA and picking up my TripTiks for my vacation. It was kind of fun plotting out our trip and then having my wife play navigator, reading off the upcoming routes we'd be taking. But now I have a GPS.

I don't even plan out a trip anymore. I just plug in the address and go.

One of the best features is the ability to pick various routes. Online trip-mapping tools are really good at this. They give you the option between "fastest" or "avoiding back roads." You can even plan your trip based on the conveniences available on each particular route.

My brother loves Waze, the free, community-based mapping, traffic, and navigation smartphone app. Not only is it a GPS, it allows drivers to share information about the route you are looking at. While we were driving to a Chicago Bears game, Waze let us know that there was an expected slowdown coming up in a mile. We didn't see any slowness. Checking the app it showed there was a car on the shoulder of the expressway. This had been reported by other motorists earlier.

When we reached the spot, the car was no longer there. So we clicked the icon for hazard and updated the app, letting other motorists know that the delay was gone and the car was no longer an issue. What a simple and brilliant idea.

Now motorists can share information about the traffic conditions. And much more.

Wouldn't it be great to have help in determining the right path to take to get to your destination? Community-sourced navigation can work for your vision too. You just have to share it with as many people as you can so they will know your destination and the path you've chosen. Then you need to be open to their inputs.

The key is sharing that vision so that it provides you with clear directions for your day-to-day actions and your longer-range efforts. It will make the trip planning easy for everyone who decides to travel to that destination with you.

To really nail down this metaphor: Your vision *is* your final destination. You can use different planning tools for your trip. You can try to go by the fastest route, or use the one with the least obstructions. But you have to plug in the destination. This is the most important benefit of a vision—you know where you're going.

Gives Hope

Hope may be the most important weapon we have against the "human condition."

Hope is a powerful thing. It keeps people fighting even when defeat is certain. It's kept concentration camp prisoners fighting. It's kept prisoners of war fighting. It can destroy despair. It can obliterate oppression. Hope is one of the things that can never be taken away from you. It can only be willingly given—it cannot be forcibly taken. Tyrants have tried to do that for ages.

Oppressors have as their number one goal to remove their victim's hope.

A vision gives hope. It paints a picture of a better future. When you share your vision, you give hope. Those who hear your vision are not only encouraged by the words but by your courage in sharing them. They know someone else has the same dream. And that dream can be enough to change the world. And the lives of those who hear it.

The fact that your vision is a big, scary, hairy, audacious goal doesn't make it less hope-inspiring. Actually, just the opposite. Because it's so large and so audacious that it's actually scary, that makes it inspiring also. And that you have the courage to share it, to shout it from the rooftops, gives others hope.

If you believe, they can believe also.

No wonder you will make enemies. There are always those who don't want the world to change—even for the better. There are those who don't want the oppressed to have hope.

There are selfish people. Selfish organizations. There are those who would allow hundreds, thousands, or more people suffer so they can gain fame, wealth, or status. There are those who are happy to step on others to climb a ladder of false success.

Your vision gives hope.

An organizational vision gives hope to many people, not just the employees, stockholders, and leadership. It gives hope to all those your organization touches. It gives hope to other organizations.

Your vision gives hope to more people than you will probably ever realize.

Incites Passion

A vision is predicated on passion. You can't have a vision without it. If you have a big, hairy, audacious, scary goal that will change the world but there is no passion involved—you don't have a vision.

If there's no passion, chances are it's not big enough. Or hairy enough. Or audacious or scary enough.

Passion is the number one litmus test I have for a vision and for a visionary.

When I coach people on finding their vision, I spend as long as it takes to find their passion.

I know a vision when I hear it because it gives me goose bumps. It incites passion in me.

When the visionary tells me about the vision, they are full of passion. They can't hide it anymore than a baby can hide its feelings. This is why I don't care for vision statements. You can't email me your vision. Why? Because you can't email me your passion.

Nope. I want to hear it from your lips. I want to see it in your eyes. I want to see your face when you share that vision. I want to hear your voice crack from the excitement. From the unbridled passion. I want to be swept up by your emotions, by your belief in your dream for the future.

When I meet with anyone—individuals or boards of trustees—and demand that we first find a vision before we create a strategic plan, I'm looking for that passion.

You don't have to have a vision. But if you have a vision, you have to be passionate about it. It has to drive you. If your vision is going to change the world, how could you not be passionate about it?

Listen to a recording of Martin Luther King, Jr. telling the world that he had a dream. He had a dream that someday his children would live in a nation where they would be judged only by their character.

In the middle of the speech, you'll hear this:

I have a dream that one day this nation will rise up and live out the true meaning of its creed: We hold these truths to be self-evident that all men are created equal.

I have a dream that one day on the red hills of Georgia the sons of former slaves and the sons of former slave owners will be able to sit down together at the table of brotherhood.

I have a dream that one day even the state of Mississippi, a state sweltering with the heat of injustice, sweltering with the heat of oppression, will be transformed into an oasis of freedom and justice.

I have a dream that my four little children will one day live in a nation where they will not be judged by the color of their skin but by the content of their character. I have a dream today!

And it goes on. Building. But as a believer in his vision, I chose this last paragraph as the essence of the dream. To live in a nation where we are not judged by the color of our skin but by the content of our character.

I extrapolate that to become, "…to live in a nation where we are not judged by our appearance, gender, status, heritage, or infirmities. To live in a nation where we are not judged by our strengths, talents, or skills. To live in a nation where we are judged solely on the content of our character."

Seeking to achieve such a vision will change the world.

How can such a vision not incite passion? How can it not provide focus?

How in the world could it not give hope? It has already given hope to more than one generation of American's still seeking to make our nation live up to its founding fathers' dream.

Too deep for you? Here's a lighter way to look at it.

If I haven't already mentioned it, I love movies. Movies are my guilty pleasure. But because I have a very limited amount of time to watch them, I'm extremely picky. I don't watch movies (knowingly) with unhappy endings. I rarely watch comedies (never in the theater, occasionally at home). I don't watch tragedies, blood and gore, or horror movies. The movies I watch have to meet specific criteria:

1.   They have happy (or at least righteous) endings.

2.   If they are good animated/children movies, I take my ten-year-old to them (and buy a fair amount of them when they get on DVD). Disney rocks!

3.   They have a purpose—preferably teaching a moral.

So as you can imagine, I watch a lot of animated, superhero, and action movies. I'm on a first-name basis with Arnold, Mel, Bruce, and Tom. So when I recommend a movie, it's going to meet most (if not all) of these criteria.

Tomorrowland is a movie I highly recommend. It's all about hope. And it shares the power of hope in a non-preachy, fun, fantastical way. It's clean (I was happy to have my ten-year-old see it). It has a good ending, good morals, and good action. But the reason I'm recommending it in this book is that it inspires hope.

And the way it provides hope to the characters (and the world) in the movie is by encouraging dreaming. No spoilers here (I hate it when a good movie is ruined), but trust me when I say it will emblazon you to share your vision.

A vision gives hope not only to those sharing it, but to those who hear it. That same hope is why some fear it and attack you for it. Some people don't like it when you give hope to those who didn't have it before.

Visions feed our hopes because they remind us that we *can* change the world. They give us a clear picture of a preferred future, a nearly impossible future. They give us a reason to challenge the status quo and to fight for a better tomorrow.

They inspire others to dream. Mother Teresa, a religious woman without wealth, power, or fame was able to found a religious community, win the Nobel Peace Prize (1979), and build homes for orphans, nursing homes for lepers, and hospices for the terminally ill. Visions give hope to those in need and those who want to change the world.

Many of us are looking for our purpose, seeking our place in the world. Many of us are looking for a way to help make the world a better place. A vision provides that direction, focus, and hope necessary to do that.

How Do I Know Whether My Goal Is a Vision?

There are distinct differences between a big goal and a vision. I use some tests to determine whether you actually have a vision. This section covers them. They are, in no particular order.

It Incites Passion in the Sharing

A vision can incite passion in the sharing. Passion is a powerful thing. It can drive people to do things beyond their norm. It can push us to reach and sometimes to exceed our potential.

And passion is a requirement for a vision.

I was helping a young lady find her vision. She had founded an organization (a nonprofit) with great intentions. She had already accomplished great things and a lot of good works. I was very impressed. But she didn't know how to express her vision. She wasn't really sure what her vision for the future was. She knew what she wanted to change in the world, but she didn't know her vision.

So we sat over lunch and chatted. I asked her what her vision was for the future, and she spent the next half an hour telling me about the origin of her organization and the well-deserved accolades the founding efforts had been awarded. These were impressive "wins." But they lacked something essential. There wasn't any passion. I listened without excitement, without awe, without engagement. I was impressed but not impassioned.

So I dug deeper.

I asked her why she had founded the organization. And we got closer.

I asked her why she had resigned from the board of directors for the organization she had founded. Why she took on the position of executive director for little to no pay. She explained why she did so while others her age with similar degrees from a renowned university were pursuing futures of wealth and fame.

She said it was because things weren't happening, at least not as fast as she wanted. She realized someone needed to have their feet on the ground, changing the world. She was a doer. She wasn't so much a visionary—she just wanted to make it happen. Sharing it wasn't enough; she needed to get her hands dirty.

That got us even closer.

She had recently graduated college, had meager savings, and jumped into the executive director role for her organization even though there was little likelihood of making a decent salary in the future.

Finally she told me her story, her personal reason for wanting the world to change. The driving force behind her need, her compulsion to change the world. Her eyes were glassy with moisture. Her voice cracked a little.

In turn my eyes watered up. I had goose bumps. I wasn't just listening attentively...I was hooked. I was caught up in her story, in her passion. I told her, "Yes! That's it! That's what I've been waiting for."

She smiled sheepishly, and tears started streaming down her face.

We laughed.

"That's the passion I was looking for. Up until now I was willing to give you a couple of dollars, maybe even volunteer once or twice to help you. I was impressed, but I didn't really *care*. You didn't give me anything to believe in. You didn't make me impassioned."

She apologized for the tears, and I told her not to. That the tears were evidence. They were what sold me on her vision, on her passion. And in turn it gave me passion for her cause.

It Attracts Naysayers and Enemies

Why in the world would a vision that is supposed to make the world a better place attract enemies and naysayers? Why would people work really hard to convince us to give up on our dreams? Why would people want to discourage us from making a difference?

Is it simply jealousy? Are people so petty that they don't want others to succeed?

Yes.

Are people so scared of change that they want to keep us from making the world a better place? Do they fear change, even change for the better, so much that they'd tell us our vision isn't worth the effort?

Yes.

Remember, your vision is a very large, very scary, nearly impossible, world-changing goal. And for some, that means giving up something. We don't like being scared and we don't like change. So you will attract enemies. Not only those who will tell you you're stupid for trying, that you will definitely fail, but you'll also have those who actively work against you. They may sue you (or your organization). They'll slander you. They'll work really hard (harder than they do at their jobs) to make you fail.

Expect it. This should not be a surprise to you. Don't think that everyone will jump on board and love your vision. Even if you think everyone should—you are forgetting that not everyone wants to the world to improve. Not everyone wants to see the downtrodden lifted up. Not everyone wants to see the underdog win. Although your vision may be a great beacon of hope for many, it will also scare many.

When you rock the boat, people fear drowning in the waves of change.

Some enemies are obvious. Most of the visionaries we've talked about were up against an established power with a lot to lose—from petty politicians to massive chemical companies. But there will be other enemies and naysayers. People close to you. Even family members.

Don't let this shock you and throw you off your path. Realize that it will happen.

For various reasons, even people you think should jump on board because it will directly make their world a better place may fight you.

Embrace it.

Yup. Don't just expect it—embrace the naysayers. Use it like I do, as proof that your vision is worthy of the big, hairy, scary, audacious goal title. It means it's worth fighting for. If everyone readily agrees, it may be a good idea, it may be a worthy effort—but it's likely not world-changing.

Martin Luther King, Jr.'s vision for our world has not been achieved yet. His dream has many disciples and believers. It has been the impetus for the creation of national organizations and global movements. It has also continued to create enemies and naysayers.

And remember, his vision is that the vision of the founding fathers of the United States would come true in all of its glorious meaning. So the dream has been alive long before Dr. King presented it with passion and purpose.

The closer we get to achieving a vision, the louder the naysayers become. They become louder and more violent, but they also grow fewer in number. And because there are fewer and fewer in their ranks, those holdouts become more adamant. They scream against the winds of change until finally their arguments for why the change can't happen are buried under the reality that the change has already come about.

Be heartened. No one remembers the naysayers. At least not without video.

It Scares People

Yes, it scares people, and many of them react to this fear with anger and illogical attacks against you and your vision. But it will also likely scare you too.

Remember: It is a scary goal. That means it scares even the visionary! This fear may make you reluctant to share your vision. You believe you'll be ridiculed and laughed at (you will be). You think others will think you're a fool and a stupid dreamer (they will). And the fear of this, of being thought poorly of, can drive you to turn your back on your vision.

Don't let it. You are right if you think that these things will happen. You're wrong if you think that these occurrences will in some way hurt you. They only hurt the ones who partake in attempts to discourage you.

You may worry that others will think less of you. Perhaps they will. But, they probably don't think much of you now. The only difference is that you will scare them enough that they will tell you how they feel about you. Before this, you weren't even worth their expending the energy to put you down.

Yes, a vision will scare people. Including the visionary. Including those who are working to make the vision come true. Putting the dream into words, putting that vision out in front of you, is scary. Even if you've been doing good works for years toward the vision, once you start talking about changing the world, really changing the world, you scare people.

Every time I work with boards of directors to define a vision, we lose some members. They quit. They say it's because this wasn't what they signed up for. They didn't join the board to work on a utopian folly. They wanted to help others by doing concrete work. They believed in what the organization was doing.

I tell the remaining board members that this is a good sign. If we lose members because the vision scares them away, that means the vision is big enough to warrant our adoption.

What I hear isn't just that they believed in what the organization was doing, but also that they didn't believe in why the organization was doing what it was doing. They didn't believe in the *why* behind the *what*. And now that they see it in front of them, they are scared.

They're scared that it will be too big or too hard to accomplish.

They're scared of failure, and the size of your vision makes it quite likely that there will be a lot of failures along the way.

I not only have the board develop, own, and share the vision. I also teach them that it's their number one responsibility. The executive director's focus is on the day-to-day operations of the organization. They are the supreme doers! And rightfully so.

So if it's not the board, who will own the vision?

The board *is* the leadership of the organization, and that's why I have them develop the vision. Who else will keep the focus of the organization on the guiding vision? In most cases this totally changes the board's role and responsibility to the organization. Though it is still accountable for fiduciary responsibility by regulation and common sense, that's no longer the key focus. The new focus has to be on fulfilling the purpose *and* achieving the vision of the organization.

This requires a change of heart, a change of perspective, and a change in attitude.

Instead of simply providing oversight (looking over the bookkeeping and making sure monies are spent wisely), now the board has to become engaged. The board must be a major catalyst for change.

So, yes, your vision will scare people.

It Cannot Be Achieved Alone

A vision cannot be achieved alone. We don't like relying on others. And we don't like knowing that we have to collaborate with others who before we had a vision may have been our competitors. We like to believe we can succeed without asking for help. But this is impossible with a vision.

By definition, a vision requires more than you can do alone. It requires you to collaborate with others. It requires that you share the vision far and wide and actively work to enlist others to your cause.

You are looking for apostles, disciples, believers, and followers. You're trying to build a super team to achieve a world-changing vision. The good news is that you don't have to be the general manager or even head coach for the team. You just have to get people to sign up (not literally). You won't need to track who is with you and who is against.

Your job is to spread the word and inspire others to join in the fight.

You may choose to bring the players together. You may even choose to facilitate the collaboration. And all of that is fine...but it's not required of you as a visionary.

Don't let your pride or independence keep you from letting others join in on your dream.

Jesus was one of the world's greatest visionaries. His vision for God's kingdom on earth fits all of the criteria. Check as we go through and see if it works for you. One example specifically for this test can be found in the Bible in the books of Luke (9:50) and Mark (9:38).

> "Master," said John, "we saw someone driving out demons in your name and we tried to stop him, because he is not one of us." "Do not stop him," Jesus said, "for whoever is not against you is for you."

You should also not worry over *how* others work toward your vision. As long as their methods fit within your values, other *hows* are other right ways to get it done. Even within your organization, this is true.

Martin Luther King, Jr. wouldn't care how many others took up his vision. He would embrace their intent and efforts to change the world for the better. Of course, if those who were following his vision were to use violence, fear, or abuse to try and force his vision to come true, he would undoubtedly denounce these efforts. You must use your values and beliefs to discern between good and bad. But there are many right paths to the same destination. As long as others are heading to the same place and taking an acceptable path, you don't have to micromanage their journey.

In your organization if some of the departments under you take innovative approaches to your vision, celebrate their journey. If they take approaches that you would never consider—but don't find unacceptable—celebrate their journey. Even if you think the path selected won't work, if it's not against your values or principles (you just think it will fail), swallow your tongue and cheer them on. Oh, feel free to give constructive criticism, but don't get in their way.

There are many paths to achieving the vision. Don't be so arrogant as to believe your preferred path is the only one that will work.

One thing that may help you is to remember that your vision isn't yours. It's a higher calling you've been impassioned to share. It's not about you. It's way bigger than you. You have a role to play, but so do many other people. You may not even be able to imagine how your vision will be realized. The technology may not exist today. The change you seek in the world may not be possible yet. Don't think that you are more important than the vision.

By the way, you'll also find naysayers and enemies. The difference is you won't have to actively seek them out.

It Is Likely to Outlive the Visionary

Chances are you won't see your vision achieved in your lifetime. As I've mentioned many times, one of my favorite visionaries is Martin Luther King, Jr. In my youth I was excited to realize that my initials matched Dr. King's. I always thought it sad that his dream for the future outlived him. Actually, it probably would have outlived him even if he had not been taken from us by an assassin. We are *still* struggling to achieve his vision.

Some of my contemporaries like to use President Kennedy's vision of putting a man on the moon and bringing him back safely before the end of the decade as an example of a vision come true. They would have to argue that his vision would be an exception to this test! He set it for less than a ten-year period! It was an awesome goal. A scary one. One with its fair share of naysayers... but also there was stiff competition from other nations try to do the same. It changed the world, created our nation's space program, pushed other nations around the world to create programs of their own, and changed our childhood occupation dreams from just firefighters, police, and circus performers to include astronauts.

But was it truly a ten-year goal?

The "space race" had been going on for decades. The Soviet Union was getting close. President Kennedy decided to light the final fire under our country to finish what many had been working on for years. The journey started long before.

But when was the vision first shared? How long had the dream of sending someone to the moon been around? President Kennedy may have simply finalized the last steps in the vision. When was it first dreamed? When was it so close to impossible that no one believed it would ever occur?

Although traveling to the moon was written into fiction as early as 79 A.D., these science fiction works couldn't be called a vision because they weren't shared with the intent of seeing the dream come true. They, like *Star Trek* and *Star Wars* today, were simply fantasy in the form of space travel.

We may want to use Jules Verne's book *From the Earth to the Moon* (1865) as the first declaration of the vision. Verne's works (like *Star Trek*'s communicators and universal translators) seemed to be working plans for what would later become reality (submarines, planes, and space shuttles). If you claimed that his vision was the advance of technology to allow human exploration and travel in magnificent ways, I may have to agree.

But a specific vision for traveling to the moon? Not so sure.

Submarines, space travel, and air travel all became common reality after Jules Vernes shared the dream. And at the time it was all seen as fantasy or fiction. The same as when I used to watch Captain Kirk call up to the Enterprise with his (now-antiquated) flip phone. We used to look at it and think, wouldn't that be neat?

The same for the universal translator that allowed you to hear the words of someone speaking in Vulcan in your ears in English.

But are these visions or just inventions? Vision or imagination?

MAN ON THE MOON VISION

I use JFK's "vision" of putting a man on the moon and bringing him back safely as an example of a vision. The last time I did (for a master's class on leadership), a student challenged my criteria that it should be over ten years out. I explained that the vision had been around long before President Kennedy focused our efforts on getting it finished.

A trip to the moon was first conceived during Dwight D. Eisenhower's administration as a three-man spacecraft to follow the one-man Project Mercury that put the first Americans in space. Landing men on the moon by the end of 1969 required a burst of technological creativity and the largest commitment of resources ($24 billion) ever made by any nation in peacetime. At its peak, the Apollo program employed 400,000 people and required the support of more than 20,000 industrial firms and universities.

Perhaps you'll also be lucky enough to see your vision come about. Perhaps it will be because you joined the battle near the finish line. There is no reason to hesitate sharing your vision even if most of the journey has already been traveled. When the day comes that America is the great nation it was meant to be, there will be visionaries ushering it in. Dr. King is recognized as a visionary, as was the country's founding fathers, as others will be.

It Will Change the World for the Better

Actually a vision can be the product of an evil mind. Hitler had a vision for the world—one in which he ruled, where the "Aryan" race dominated and all others were subjugated. In his vision for the world, inferior classes and races of people would be exterminated so only the "pure" race would walk the face of the earth. This was a vision by all of the criteria except this one: His vision would change the world, but not for the better.

His vision incited riots. It attracted countless enemies. It scared a lot of people. It could not be achieved alone (he even acquiesced to collaborating with peoples he would rather exterminate). He did his best to see it come to fruition in his lifetime, but it wasn't going to happen that fast. It definitely would change the world—with most visions, the earnest attempt to make it come true changes the world along the way. Just trying to achieve the vision changes the world. Hitler's vision definitely changed the world. Not as he foresaw it, thankfully.

Nothing I've ever read said a vision had to be born of goodness. For my purposes though, it does. I refuse to work with people who have a vision which I believe will not change the world for the better. This may be a tough call to make—who am I to decide what will and won't make the world a better place?

Well, like you, I'm a member of the human race. So I have to discern, in my view, whether a vision is "good" or "evil." And act accordingly. We all have to make these choices in our lives. It's our responsibility to do what's right. It defines who we are. It's an expression of our values.

So far, I've only turned away one visionary because of this. I count myself lucky. Her vision was born of righteous indignation, which I have no problem with. Many visions come about because of perceived injustices in the world. But her response to the injustice was more injustice. To fight against prejudice, bigotry, and ignorance she wanted to create her own culture of hate. She wanted to have people go back to their roots, literally. To up and move away from the country their ancestors had chosen and return to a perceived birthplace. Of course, this was rife with issues, but the kicker for me was that she wasn't seeking healing. I couldn't help her. Well, that's not accurate. I *wouldn't* help her.

Nope. We have to discern right from wrong.

For me, a vision has to be one that helps others, one that will change the world *for the better*. Yes, any world-changing dream can be a vision, but not necessarily one I will assist with—nor one I plan to use as an example in this book.

A vision will change the world, but it doesn't have to be directed at global change. If your dream is for your small community, that can qualify. Because if you succeed and drastically change your community for the better, it will end up changing the world—for those in your town, but also those who visit your town. Some people from your community will move and take your vision with them. It will spread. It will affect other communities. You can't have a vision come true and have it remain an isolated incident. It will change the world if it is big enough.

Anything that is big enough to change the world will require a long time to succeed. It's the nature of change. We, as a people, change slowly. Countries, nations, and peoples change slowly. Cultures change slowly. Even with significant emotional events, change is still slow. We may change policies and laws quickly in reaction to threats, but deep, cultural change takes time.

Each of the tests for a vision intertwines with the others. This is why the order of presentation really doesn't matter. But the tests are very useful for helping you determine whether you've dug deep enough to find the root, the dream, the ultimate *why* behind the *what*.

A vision is the ultimate *why* behind the *what*.

How do you know if it's a vision?

- It incites passion in the sharing.
- It attracts naysayers and enemies.
- It scares people.
- It cannot be achieved alone.
- It is likely to outlive the visionary (it's a very long-range goal).
- It will change the world, for the better.

What should you get from having one? What does a vision do?

- It galvanizes.
- It provides a clear focus.
- It provides direction.

- It gives hope.
- It incites passion.

Do You Need to Have a Vision?

Do companies need to have a world-changing, large, long-range, audacious, scary vision?

Nope.

Seriously. I know you were expecting me to say you do, but you don't. And actually, everyone *can't* have a vision. If everyone did, nothing would get accomplished.

Nope.

Although *anyone* can be a visionary, *not everyone* can be.

Besides logic, the other thing keeping everyone from being a visionary is simple. Not everyone has the personality or drive to be a visionary. It takes a certain type of person to be one. Just as it takes a special type of person to lead, and another to follow.

But if you do have a vision, a dream for a better future, it will be a foundation for your measures of success. Fulfilling your purpose is one of the two pillars to being successful. The other is fighting for, working toward, and seeking your dreams.

You don't have to have one of your own. You can work to achieve someone else's vision. Visions, like many things in life, are not unique things. If you have a dream for a better future, chances are others have had (and still have) the same dream. If you don't have a dream of your own, you will likely find yourself working to make someone else's vision come true.

Why?

Because dreams are compelling. They give us hope for a better tomorrow.

Many took up the dream of Martin Luther King, Jr.

His dream was one of the best visions you'll ever find. It was clear and simple. But you shouldn't take it only at face value. Look just a little deeper and you'll see that the real dream is to have all of our children, all generations to come, be judged only by their character. By what they do and say, by how they treat each other. Not by the color of their skin, by the size of their bodies, not by the color of their hair or the shape of their eyes. Not by their height or weight. Not by their gender or sexual preference. Not by their accent, or their oratory skills. Not by anything other than their character.

What a great world we'd have if everyone judged each other only by what they did and said—by their actions, by their character. By who they are—not what they are.

This is a vision.

What Is Your Vision?

Do you have a vision? Is there something that is driving you or your organization? Something more than your purpose? Something that is pushing you to be better, stronger, or more effective? Is there a problem in the world that is eating away at you? Do you find yourself raging against the storm?

Is there a cause that you can't let go of?

You may have a vision.

For nonprofit organizations, I find that a vision is mandatory. I know I said not everyone can be a visionary, but every nonprofit should be.

If your purpose is altruistic, if your calling as an organization (or individual) is to improve the world—you almost have to have a vision. You have to do more than just good deeds.

Doing good isn't enough.

Feeding the hungry is a good deed. Thank you for that.

Clothing the naked and giving shelter to those who are homeless are good deeds. Thank you.

Healing the sick of body, mind, and soul is nothing less than awesome. Thanks.

But all of these good deeds are not enough.

If you do nothing to change the plight of those you help, you're not doing enough.

You might rightly say, "We can't help everyone. We can't give every homeless person a home. We can't change the lives of every drug addict, alcoholic, and wayward child. We can't help everyone.

"We can't change the world."

And I would answer, "Of course not." At least not alone. Not by yourself. And not tomorrow.

But it doesn't mean that you shouldn't be seeking to do exactly what you say can't be done.

Every person who achieved true greatness, every person who was truly successful, started by tilting at windmills. Every organization that has changed the world for the better did what was at one time impossible.

Do you have a vision?

Does your organization have a vision for the future? Or does it just have some goals? Some milestones it would like to achieve? I've spoken with many startups, entrepreneurs, and businesses. They all like to talk about achieving milestones.

The funny thing about milestones are that they are markers along a road. They literally are stones that mark mileage along a path. And the reason we normally celebrate reaching a new milestone, a marker of progress, is that we are closer to our destination. Imagine the milestone on the circular path around your block.

My wife has taken to walking almost every day. And I'm happy to encourage her. It's her main source of exercise. She used to walk one of three routes she had mapped out. She knew each milestone along the path. But she stumbled upon the simplicity of walking around our city block. It's a set distance—and if she does five laps, she does a little over three miles. This is perfect for her because she can trust our young daughter at home for the short time it takes to do a lap, so even if Grace doesn't want to walk, my wife still can. And most times, she can convince Grace to walk with her, because it's "only a block."

But the thing is—she's not going anywhere. I don't think this is the intent of tracking milestones achieved by an organization. In reality, her journey isn't around the block—it's a journey to good (and better) health. The *how* is the walking she does. Each milestone is a marker along the way to improved health.

Your organization's milestones are the same. They are markers along a path to something. What is it you are trying to reach? What is that destination?

Are you setting, achieving, and celebrating milestones that don't lead to a destination? Are they visionless goals?

Many times I find that like a mission, organizations already have a vision—but most haven't clearly articulated it yet. We have a calling, we have a purpose. We may also have a destination, something great we are working toward. Our purpose may be to move the world closer to that improvement. But if we don't know where we're going, we can't measure how well we're doing at getting there.

Measuring milestones as indicators of success only works if we know where we're going.

If we don't know where we're going, then how far we travel, how fast we go, and how much gas we use are meaningless to our success. We may be traveling in the wrong direction, taking the longest, most ineffective, and most inefficient route. It would be like opening up your mapping program on the computer and clicking the option for "worst route."

Your GPS can purposefully find every detour, delay, and road construction possible. You would never pick these routes on purpose, but if you don't know where you're going and all you're measuring is distance traveled—you may very well be picking the "worst route" option.

It's worth your time to find out whether you have a vision and what it is. It will guide your path for decades to come. It's the ultimate *why* behind the *what*.

DENNIS

Dennis was one of my most interesting interviews, mostly because of his occupations: chess teacher, coach, and professional player.

I'll admit a love for the Royal Game. I've played chess since I was eight years old, when my father taught me the game. It's the most inclusive activity/game/sport I've ever played. It doesn't matter your age, gender, background, physical prowess, height, weight, or academic status. Anyone can play and be competitive. There is a U.S. National Chess Federation and an International Chess Federation. There is a national championship in most countries, and a World Championship.

Bobby Fischer became famous (and made chess a popular game) in the 1970s when he became the first American to win the World Championship in the modern era. And he did it by beating the dominating Russians. This coincided with my taking up the game more seriously in my youth. Not only did it give me something I could do with my dad, just the two of us (my three siblings weren't needed), but it gave me something I could be good at. Since then I've played in tournaments, started chess clubs around the U.S., coached players, and most recently I'm teaching a chess class to homeschoolers.

So interviewing someone who is able to make a living at a life-long passion was special.

But I expected the interview to be special for another reason. Here was an entrepreneur, teacher, and coach who had to think tactically (short-term benefits and gains) and strategically (long-range planning) to be a strong player. And because Dennis has the Master title with both the National and International Chess Federations, he definitely qualifies as a very strong player. He was the 2009 Indiana State Co-Champion. He teaches chess, coaches in schools, has recorded videos for numerous organizations, and writes a chess column.

He didn't always make a living playing chess; he spent over a decade teaching philosophy at major universities before deciding to embark on a new career. And I can assure you, very few people can make a living at chess.

Here is what I learned from my interview with Dennis.

I asked Dennis how he'd measure success. I asked him because he was an adjunct professor at the University of Notre Dame, and he is now "making it" through a game (some argue it's a sport), chess only...teaching, writing, coaching, and so forth. I thought it took a brave spirit (he's not a Millennial, just starting out) to try to make a living doing something you love, something that doesn't normally pay enough unless you're one of the best in the world. And not in a small town (Midwest USA).

"I don't measure success by a career, I measure success based on if I'm making a difference in people's lives, in the bigger sense. I wasn't sure if making a living at chess was a legitimate career choice, but I like helping kids and much of teaching and coaching becomes mentoring.

"I also feel the aesthetic realm is important. Blogging, creating beauty [in chess games, problems, and so on], sharing beauty with the world are important. Of course, making a living is necessary, but the important thing is that I'm helping make lives better. There's also a religious slant, I'm able to share my faith with others through what I do."

His answer was on target, but I wasn't sure if "making a difference in people's lives" was equal to his purpose. Normally this type of answer is a high-level concept of a purpose, but not specific. It doesn't help the individual know what to do (or not to do). It's too vague, too broad an answer. To know your true purpose, your calling, you need more specificity. You may notice that Dennis chose to use chess as his vehicle for fulfilling his mission, but that choice in itself is not his calling.

So the question is, what type of a difference? Which people? What about their lives?

But overall I was happy to hear that Dennis did not account success as a product of his ability to make a living at his passion. Instead it was based on how well he helped others. It just needed to be more specific.

I thanked Dennis—and like any good teacher and coach, he decided to turn the tables on me. I, of course, didn't mind...but what I really liked was how he asked me about *my* measures of success. I had not mentioned my theories...

"How about you? What's your purpose in life?" he said.

I laughed.

I had never mentioned purpose or vision. I had only asked him how he measured success. He translated success as *living your purpose*. This was much more valuable to me than digging deeper into the specifics for what his purpose was.

He got it. All on his own.

It felt good to know I wasn't alone!

And as happens many times, once you find one kindred spirit, you find another. And another.

WOULD YOU CONSIDER THESE PEOPLE TO BE SUCCESSFUL?

Think of this as a mid-book quiz. See what you think. First consider the person listed—would you consider him or her successful? Then read the short biography. How about now? Successful or not?

Mohandas Gandhi

Gandhi fought for India's independence from Great Britain through nonviolent protests, from 1915 to 1947, when India finally won its independence. The next year, Gandhi was assassinated. He wasn't the first who fought for India's freedom—the movement he joined had been going on for 30 years before. And he not only shared the vision for a free India, he held an unpopular belief that freedom could be achieved through nonviolent means, although not trivial. Through civil disobedience, boycotts, and hunger strikes, his vision came true.

If that wasn't enough, his vision for how freedom should be achieved inspired others who followed, including Dr. Martin Luther King, Jr.

Mother Teresa

Born Agnese Gonxhe Bojaxhiu, she found her calling at 12, and at age 18 started her journey toward a vision. At only 40 years old, she founded the Missionaries of Charity, which ended up operating more than 600 missions in more than 100 countries at the time of her death. She won the Nobel Peace Prize, was given India's highest civilian honor, and was beatified by Pope John Paul II. She recently was acclaimed a Saint by the Roman Catholic Church.

Based on her calling, I'd easily argue she was very successful.

George Washington

General Washington could definitely be considered lucky, even by his own account. He survived very near misses, including having his horse shot out from under him twice. But was he successful? If his calling was to free our nation, you'd have to say as *the* general of the Continental forces that he was indeed successful. But perhaps it was his unwavering dedication to his principles and values that made him truly successful.

He led with nobility, courage, and humility. He refused to be the new "king" of the Americas and instead resigned his commission. He sought no rewards for his service to his country. No wonder his election as America's first president was unanimous.

And that brings up the topic of heroes (and heroines). Are our heroes by definition successful? Most historical heroes are given that honor because they accomplished great things, for good reasons. Hitler wasn't a hero to many, and probably none by the time he was finally defeated. Same for Charles Manson. To be a hero requires that you do good.

One of my heroes is Abraham Lincoln. If his calling was to free the slaves or to make our country truly great (we couldn't become the home of the free if we didn't move away from slavery), his handling of the Civil War would show him as successful. And like Gandhi's, Lincoln's success cost him his life because of the hatred of the enemies his vision spawned. But is being a hero enough?

Perhaps.

Especially if we define heroes as those who change the world for the better.

Heroes

Are heroes by definition successful?

Today there is a disturbing trend toward lifting up athletes, celebrities, and the famous as heroes. One of the biggest differences between the world in the near past and today is the dumbification of hero worship. In the past, heroes were identified by their deeds, values, mission, and vision. Today, many seem to be selected because of their fame or their ability to play a sport.

This is why I have been so happy to see people cheering for firefighters and our military. It gives me hope that we'll find heroes who are worthy. Don't get me wrong—I can think of more than one athlete (one of my favorites would be Ruth Riley) who I would say is worthy of hero status. But it's not because of their abilities, play on the court, championships, or trophies. It's because of what they do with their lives and, sometimes, how they use their fame.

Although being the best may make you famous (and rightly so), should it make you a hero? And does it make you successful?

While I'm listing heroes, Dr. Martin Luther King, Jr. would be at the top of that list. Not because of his nonviolent means of affecting change or his deep faith. I put him as one of my heroes because of his unwavering devotion to his vision for a better future. And what a vision!

Talent

Does being super-talented mean you are successful?

How about those athletes? How about geniuses? How about inventors and innovators? Leonardo Da Vinci, Albert Einstein (one of my heroes), Thomas Edison, or Nicola Tesla?

Louis Pasteur, Alexander Bell, Marie Curie, or Henry Ford? How about Paul Morphy, Jose Capablanca, or Bobby Fischer? Bach or Beethoven?

Does the gift of a world-class talent make you successful? Or is it the development of that talent that makes you a success? I'd say no to both. You are not a success simply because you were bequeathed a special talent or skill set. Being a "freak of nature" doesn't make you successful. Even taking your talents and developing them to their fullest doesn't do it. Nope.

It's all about why you were given those talents, and whether you fulfilled that calling. Hitler was granted a unique charisma and ability to galvanize a nation, but he didn't use those talents for the betterment of the world. Charles Manson also had undeniable talents—which he used for perversion.

How about those who reach the highest heights in spite of a lack of those talents, skills, or gifts? How about those who overcome adversity? In America we especially like to cherish the underdog who achieves great things (or even little things). The story of *Rudy* is founded on this. We like to lift up those who have had to fight to reach their place in the public eye.

But are they successful?

Again, not if the only thing we have to judge their success by is that they overcame adversity. Was there a reason for their determination and perseverance? Perhaps they made it as a pro athlete against many odds, but they ignored their talents in the arts. Did they deny us of a great artist to chase an athletic career for selfish reasons?

And simply using your talents isn't enough either.

We have to go back to your calling. Why do you exist and what is it that you want to achieve in life?

We're not discerning whether someone is a good person. We're not trying to determine whether they're likable or even a hero by today's standards. We're trying to determine whether, in the larger scheme of things, they are successful.

Summary

We all have a purpose in life, a calling. We all don't have a vision. It's not a requirement for our happiness or survival. But if we have one, it is one of the two ways we can know success. A calling can guide our life choices, and so can a vision.

A vision is a special gift. It is a world-changing, enormous, ground-shaking, audacious goal. With the responsibilities of having such a dream also come some definite benefits.

A vision will galvanize those who want to see it come to life. It's the ultimate common goal. A vision also focuses your work and efforts. It gives you the power to say no. With its laser-like focus, a vision also provides direction. A vision tells us what to do and what not to do.

A vision gives you hope. Many times we disparage. We worry. But a vision gives hope because there is the possibility of a better tomorrow. A tomorrow you've dreamt of. And along with the hope comes the passion of making a better tomorrow come true.

Since a vision isn't a requirement, it helps to know whether you have a vision or not. We all have dreams and goals, but do we have a real vision? The tests for it include the following: It incites passion in the sharing, it attracts naysayers and enemies, it scares people (any world changes create fear), it cannot be achieved alone, it is likely to outlive the visionary, and it will change the world for the better.

You don't have to have a vision, but if you have one…you need to find out. If you have a vision and ignore it, it will eat at you—just as ignoring your calling will. If you have a vision, it's part of who you are—part of you purpose in life.

What Not to Measure

Sometimes it's much easier to think of the negative in order to form a clear picture of the positive. There are only two things that you should measure to determine real success. But there are a lot of wrong ways individuals and organizations try to measure success.

Don't Measure Performance and Call It Success

So far we've discussed why you shouldn't start with performance (Efficiency) measures. I've also recommended against starting with the safer Effectiveness measures. The reason is because I don't want you to start at a lower level, a level that should be used as indicators of lower-level progress, not of success.

But besides the mistake of starting with these measures, you may find yourself tempted to use these measures *as your Measures of Success*.

That would be a worse mistake than starting in the wrong place.

If you measure performance or effectiveness and think that equals a Measure of Success, you'll end up measuring the wrong things, using the results to tell the wrong story, and having no clue whether you are moving in the right direction.

© Martin Klubeck 2017
M. Klubeck, *Success Metrics*, DOI 10.1007/978-1-4842-2586-8_8

It's like measuring milestones along the road to the wrong destination.

"Yes, we're lost, but we're making great time!"

How effective and efficient you are indicates just that—how well you do what you do. It doesn't tell you whether you're moving in the right direction, nor will it tell you if you are likely to reach your destination. It can't tell you if you're successful.

Don't Measure Things That Aren't Included in Your Purpose and Vision

As a process improvement consultant, I abhor compounds. When you say *and*, you water down the statement. If you ask a seemingly simple survey question like "What did you think of the class handouts and slides?" you are likely to get useless feedback. Whatever rating is used to answer the question, you have no idea if the response is about the class handouts or the slides. Or both.

I am always diligent to remove such compound words from my client's missions, goals, visions, and tasks. I am also careful to avoid using them in my own work.

When I say don't measure things that aren't included in your purpose *and* vision, I do so intentionally. If I were to use the word *or*, you should get the impression that your purpose and vision could be at odds, and you could measure them totally independently from one another.

This is illogical. Your vision will not be separate from your purpose. It will be an outgrowth of it. If you have a vision, we will have an easier time of finding your calling. If you have a clear purpose, possible visions will be clear. So you have a wide range of things that would fit into measuring these two things. Not all of them will be good Measures of Success. Some will be too low level. You may likely get confused over the goals, subgoals, tasks, and indicators. It's normal.

But what we can't do is measure things that don't fit at all into your mission or vision. At least we can't use them in any way as a Measure of Success. Here's a simple example: If your mission is to combat cancer, and your vision is to find a cure—anything you measure that does not align to one of these two is not a Measure of Success.

The amount of money your organization raises might seem like a good Measure of Success. I can even see your organization celebrating meeting its fundraising goals. I can see you bragging about how much you exceeded the fundraising expectations for the year.

But neither your mission nor your vision were about raising money. If you raise billions of dollars but you get no closer to curing cancer, you are a failure. If the monies you raise aren't used to effectively combat cancer, you are an abject failure.

Don't misunderstand—I realize you need money to pay for research, for medical trials, for treatments, equipment, and facilities. You'll want to pay administrators, doctors, scientists, and test subjects. Oh, you can definitely find a lot of ways to spend lots of money. But none of that really matters, does it?

Simon Sinek in his excellent 2009 Ted Talk about "Starting with Why" (he wrote a book on that later called *Start With Why*, published by Portfolio in 2011) shares the remarkable story of the Wright brothers. Samuel Langley had the government funding (lots of it), recognition, publicity, and the "best" aeronautical minds working with him. But two brothers working with passion and a dream won the race to solve the puzzle of heavier-than-air manned flight. The money didn't matter. I would consider Orville and Wilbur Wright successful. Langley wasn't.

The Wright brothers weren't "successes" because they *didn't* have a lot of money—they were successes because they achieved the vision. They fulfilled their purpose. I also believe the reason they were successful (and Langley was not) was because they saw it as their purpose in life. And they saw the fulfillment of man taking to the air as a vision they were destined to achieve. It was that passion and level of belief, of faith, which separated them from the others competing in the race to achieve heavier-than-air manned flight.

I've stressed that you should measure success based on your purpose and vision. But the logical subtraction is also true. You can't measure success by things that are not your purpose or vision.

There a tons of things that go into fulfilling your mission or achieving your vision.

And the problem is that most of these are easier to measure than the final destination. So, between being pushed to provide performance measures, you will also have to combat the request for measures of the steps you're taking along the path. It's not that you can't use these measures—but you can't let them replace or substitute for Measures of Success.

I was working with a very aggressive visionary and his team. The team included a PhD who had the responsibility of collecting, analyzing, and reporting metrics for the organization. When I explained how to measure success, she was distraught. She had already worked with the board of trustees, and she knew unequivocally that they were looking for measures that could show progress today. They didn't want to wait years for proof of how well the organization was doing.

When I explained how we had to measure against the mission and vision, she interpreted that to mean that we would have no indicators for years. I assured her, and I'm assuring you, that you *can and should* measure progress monthly, weekly, or daily if you want. The key is to align those measures with the mission and vision.

You will definitely measure programs, projects, objectives, goals, and even tasks! But you won't measure them in isolation. Nor will you use the accomplishment of any of these levels as a Measure of Success. It's not whether you complete the project or program. It's not about achieving the objective or goal. It's not a question of "whether you finished the task."

The question is whether and how well doing each of these things helped move the organization toward the vision and mission. Feel free to report on how efficient and effective you were at completing the efforts. But that completion is not equal to success. It can provide valuable insights into how you do what you do. You can use these insights to be more productive. I love productivity. I love finding ways to automate and simplify what we do. It's fun and very rewarding.

But these things don't equal success.

You can do a great job, but be mistaken in how much your efforts will help "move the needle" toward fulfilling your mission or vision. You *have* to measure at the top level (the mission and vision) to ascertain whether the things you're doing to get there are working. And how well they're working.

At the leadership level, we have to stay focused on the end. We have to keep our eyes on the biggest prize: our mission and vision.

So, while you're improving your processes, measure how well your efforts push you toward being successful. That will be much more valuable.

Here are some benefits:

1. *You'll determine whether the projects and programs you are undertaking are worthwhile*: If they help move you along the path to your mission and vision, then they are worthwhile. If they don't advance you toward success, they are not providing a return on the investment. And remember—you are definitely investing in these efforts. Even if you don't have to front any monies, your time is your most valuable commodity…don't waste it on things that don't bring you closer to success.

2. *Your goals and objectives are only guesses*: You can't *know* whether the goals and objectives you defined will actually lead to success. And that's okay. By measuring how well those efforts bring you toward success, you affirm your guesses. It's okay to have been totally wrong. If you thought hiring that live rock band would help toward your mission, but learned that it did not, that's okay. Learn from that failure. But rest assured: No matter how many people attended the concert, no matter what type of feedback you received, if it didn't move you along the path, it was a failure.

3. *By differentiating between performance and success, you can stay focused:* You can stop doing things that aren't working and try other things.

Unfortunately, we pick the wrong paths—a lot! Why would we measure things that don't give us insights into how well we're fulfilling our mission or moving toward our vision? Because...

- It's easier.
- You believe you have control over it.
- You had a great turnout.
- You had great reviews.
- You spent a lot of time and money on it.
- Everyone liked it.
- It raised a lot of money.

These aren't good enough reasons to keep doing similar things. They have to move us toward our ultimate and final destination. Otherwise, we have to stop doing them and try other things.

When we lose focus, we get lost. When we forget where we're headed, it's easy to get distracted and end up someplace else.

One of the most common mistakes we make is to allow the steps we're taking to be more important than why we're taking those steps.

We have to stay diligent and vigilant. We have to keep our focus at the right level—on the end, not on the means for getting there. And when we do measure the means, it has to be in relation to how well the means are moving us to that end.

The concept of celebrating small wins is an important one. I want you to celebrate. Celebrating provides recognition and rewards for those doing the work. This is critical to maintaining momentum and motivation. But we have to make sure these wins are defined by how far they've helped us along the journey. If we don't, we'll end up settling for doing good deeds instead of demanding true change—real success.

The completion of a task or even the achievement of a goal is not worthy of celebration; that effort has to move the needle!

Good truly can be the enemy of *great*. And when we measure good things we do and say they equal great accomplishments, we not only lie to ourselves, but we lie to our stakeholders who have been sharing, following, and supporting our vision.

What About the Normal Indicators of Success? Are They Invalid?

When I say *normal*, I mean *accepted* or *the norm*. I'm still waiting, but my good friend Don says he wants to write a book about the *new norms*. He means new ideas about how to do things. New ways to look at processes, process improvement, project management, and organizational development. But when he says *new norms*, it can (and will) also mean that what is normal today will become old or out of date, and the new ideas will become the norm.

Our norms for measuring success are poor choices. They are predicated on what marketing firms have been pitching for over a century. You should have what your neighbor has. If you don't, then you're not as good as he is. And of course, you want to have *more* than your neighbor—so it is obvious that you are successful (and he is not).

I can't blame this only on advertisers. It's been around since Cain and Abel. We seem to be jealous creatures full of envy. Rather than applaud another person's success, we display a jealous and envious nature. Not always. Not everyone. But it is a norm, especially when trying to define success. We look at how our neighbor is doing and feel less happy with our own lives in comparison.

And yes, I'm counting everyone and anyone as your neighbor.

When we drive around our own town, we ogle over the more opulent homes and mutter how we'll "be there some day!" We see someone driving a very expensive car and think, "I'll have one of those too." We look at movies and TV and wish we could have the lives of pro athletes, CEOs, and Fortune 500 business owners. So it is natural that we then measure personal success on personal wealth, fame, and fortune.

But these are all poor indicators of success. Of course, not everyone falls into this trap. Many people understand that true joy and happiness don't come from without—they come from within. They are happy with who they are. They don't need to be better than their neighbor to feel successful. They can truly be happy for someone else's success. And that doesn't mean these people are non-competitive. And it doesn't mean that they can't or don't amass wealth or fame or fortune. It's just not how they define themselves or how they define success.

Let's look at the current norm for measuring success and see what should change.

Wealth

This is the same for a business as it is for an individual. But it's easier to personalize the discussion.

Wealth is the accumulation of assets that have a monetary value. Of course, cash fits this criteria. As do stocks, bonds, property, jewelry, cars, and homes. Yachts, businesses, airplanes, and even small islands. *Wealthy* means rich. Some people can't get enough of the stuff. We have billionaires who can't get close to spending all the wealth they've accumulated.

Never mind the Christian parable about the farmer who amassed more than he could eat or sell and decided to build bigger storage and never work another day in his life. He died suddenly and all of his accumulated goods were useless to him. Even if he had lived for many more years, wealth would be a poor measure of success.

Having Wealth Does Not Mean Success

This should be easy to think about. If you are born with a silver spoon in your mouth, you weren't born successful. If at 30 you inherit uncountable wealth, you don't suddenly become a successful school dropout living in your mother's basement. If you win the lottery, you don't become transformed into a successful person. No, wealth in itself doesn't mean you are successful.

If you do nothing to "earn" your wealth, you were not successful just because you received it. We live in an age of entitlement. So many of our college-bound young people are accused of acting like spoiled brats—assuming a level of entitlement. Being wealthy definitely doesn't mean you are successful. If you are entitled, that doesn't warrant pride, much less being crowned successful.

So, being wealthy may provide status and fortune, but it doesn't mean you'll be a success—even in the public's eye.

Accumulating Wealth Does Not Mean Success

If you can take full credit for your riches, can you claim to be successful?

It should matter how you earned your wealth, right? If you did it through criminal avenues, were you successful? You might say yes! If you stole the wealth from other wealthy people…were you successful? How about if you stole it from the poor? Does the *how* matter? Or does only being wealthy matter? If you say, "Yes, you have to do it through legal means," how far does that go? How about if it were legal but immoral? Rather than steal all the life savings of 1,000 poor and elderly people…how about if you did it legally? Would that make you a success? Should success be predicated on other peoples' values?

And yet our society, our world today, doesn't seem to take into account how you accumulate your wealth. We are very lazy when it comes to measurements. We don't want to have to do research—we just want to look at some simple data and make a decision about the world. We just want to look at a person's balance sheet and determine whether they are wealthy enough to be successful.

Actually, we're even lazier than that. We just want to look at their home, car(s), or how they dress. We can notice if they throw around a lot of cash, give big tips, or donate a lot.

I remember my neighbors across the street when I was growing up. They had to have the latest status-symbol car. They had to have a Cadillac. I didn't know it until much later in life, but they in no way could afford that car. Yet that didn't matter. They wanted to feel good about themselves. They wanted to appear successful to the rest of us, so they went into debt to show that they had wealth.

Wealth, riches, and money are just a means to some end. When we give wealth more importance than it deserves, we end up measuring success incorrectly. We admire people whom, without the wealth, we would feel sorry for or abhor. We want to hang out with affluent people. We want to be like them. We want our children to be like them—all without knowing a thing about who they really are.

Wealth isn't evil. It's a very useful means. Businesses seek it so they can do more of what they do. Nonprofit organizations seek it—they have whole departments dedicated to fundraising.

Money, of course, does not make the world go round—that's a result of gravity, magnetic fields, and how the earth was originally formed. But money does make a lot of things easier. It's an enabler. It's a good tool. A means to an end.

The problem is that we forget that it's just an enabler. We equate it to the end. We give it more importance than it deserves. Wealth is not our calling. It is not a good vision. Wealth can possibly help us fulfill our mission or achieve our vision, but thinking it *is* our mission and vision is a large mistake. Many wealthy, unhappy, depressed, and suicidal people would attest to that.

Fame

Fame may be harder to resist than wealth. Fame plays on our need for recognition and our self-esteem. Fame makes us feel good about ourselves while wealth can make us feel guilty or dirty. When we see others who are poor or lack the basics, and we have an abundance, our conscience can weigh on us.

But fame is different. Fame is popularity. Fame means that other people think you're special.

The problem is, fame doesn't mean you're doing what you're supposed to be doing. You can gain fame even for doing the wrong things. Some of the most famous people in history were in jail or worse. Fame also requires a certain type of personality. Not everyone can deal with fame. Actually not everyone can deal with wealth either. That's why a lot of lottery winners end up losing it all. It's also why a lot of professional athletes, making millions of dollars a year, end up broke.

And success isn't based on personality. No one has to be famous—especially not to be successful in life.

Status

Status is pretty much in the same vein as fame. The difference is you can buy status. It's why my neighbors bought a Cadillac they couldn't afford. It's why we care so much about what other people think of us. It's why we get so upset when people disparage us. Our reputation is important to us—most times, too important. We worry over what people think and say about us. We go out of our way to gain a positive reputation.

We are categorized and grouped based on many factors: race, creed, color, height, weight, eye color, hair color, diction, and even our smiles. Most of these create biases. Of course, if you're already combatting prejudices, it won't make it any easier when you realize that most of these are used to help determine status—and bias based on perceived status is extremely devious. Status brings in more factors for bias; the style and age of your clothing, your haircut, your wallet, how much cash you carry, whether you have a gold (credit) card, and the car you drive.

Status is insipid. It will eat away at your self-esteem. If you try to obtain a preferable status, it will normally cost you money. So, those with wealth many times spend it to gain higher status…and also fame.

If you can buy it (fame or status), chances are it's not a valid measure of success. It could be an indicator of wealth, but not of success.

Power

Power is different than fame, wealth, or status, although having those may help you gain more power. Many wealthy people think they can "buy" power. They believe if they have enough money, they can boss people around, telling them what to do. They believe that money equals power, but of course it doesn't. You can use wealth to buy the semblance of power, but if the money runs out, the façade ends. Even if you don't run out of money, if the people you are exercising power over decide that *they* have enough of your money, the façade ends. If others just decide that the exchange of money for their subservience is no longer worth it, the façade ends. The point is, it's a façade.

There are two basic types of power: *positional* power and *personal* power. Both types are based on influence.

Positional Power

Some people with fame try to leverage that for power. They want to control others and be in charge. They use their fame to wield a false power. As long as those who they want to have power over remain in awe of them, they can maintain the semblance of power. But unlike using wealth, power based on fame is strictly a result of how others see you. Status, like fame, can provide a temporary feeling of power. If others give you power over them because of your status—then you can enjoy power for a while.

Status is a form of positional power. Because you hold the position of CEO, you enjoy a level of power based on your job title. Positional power only goes so far, though. In the military, every officer has a level of positional power over any enlisted. As you climb the ranks, you have more positional power over those with lesser rank. But there are many (true) stories about how positional power is not true power. If you only have positional power, you might be fine as long as you're not in a life-and-death situation. If you are in battle, and all you have is positional power, you may find that no one follows you when you try to take that hill. Then again, if you don't have personal power, you probably wouldn't lead the charge. Chances are you'd try to be in the back of the pack, trying to lead from the rear.

I actually know a consultant whose new idea for leading was to "lead from the rear." She coached leaders on not being in the front. To sit in the background and encourage their team and not lead the effort. Her concept was that by "leading from the rear" the rest of the team would feel more engaged and own the process (and the results).

You may have guessed that she was trying this in academia, not in the military. This concept is so rife with problems that it's hard for me to pick where to start. Sticking to the question of positional power, though—this is a great example of giving up your positional power. The consultant thought this was a good way to use humility to draw out the team and gain buy-in. Leading from the rear may work if you have a lot of personal power—but if your source of influence is your position, it's a recipe for disaster. It equates to abdicating not only your power but your responsibility. And if you give up your share of the responsibility for success, you will lose whatever possibility you had at personal power.

She thought that by sharing or spreading your power among the team, they would all be better off. I actually think she disliked the concept of leadership. She believed every decision was better made through consensus—and I can assure you (from experience) that that is not true.

Sometimes you need someone to make a decision. Sometimes someone has to make the tough call.

On the flip side, if you have personal power, you *should* be careful when to use it and when to let others take the lead. But chances are you already know that.

Personal Power

True power is based on your leadership abilities, charisma, and ability to inspire others. It's called personal power. Your power is a result of your ability to lead others and their willingness to follow you.

But does personal power equal success?

No—success won't be based on the level of personal power you have, but it can be a measure of how you use the power.

"With great power comes great responsibility."

And the thing is, people with personal power (and who are responsible— there are many evil people with a ton of personal power over those lost souls who choose to give it to them) understand that that power in and of itself is not success. If you misuse it, abuse it, or waste it, you are pretty far from successful.

Personal power, or non-positional influence is the key trait of a good leader. There are, of course, others: decisiveness, compassion, empathy, and courage to name a few.

The ability to lead is a trait, like athleticism or height. You're born with it. Sure, you can get better at it, just like you can improve your athleticism. But as with height, there's only so much you can do. If you're not born with any, chances are you won't develop it to a larger degree by trying harder.

Health

I'm not up to arguing against health being an important factor in everyone's lives. I know too many people who are ill or fighting serious illness (cancer, for example). Being less than "healthy" sucks. Sorry, that's the truth.

But is our health a way to measure success? I think about my friend Ed. He's turning 89 this year. He's been fighting cancer for over 50 years. More than one type. I can't even imagine that he would be considered unsuccessful because of his periodic poor health. And there are many more like Ed. Sickness and injury are things to overcome. They aren't harbingers or determiners of success or failure.

Sometimes we deem people successes (or success stories) if they overcome adversity. And poor health—especially disease or injury—is a very common and powerful adversity. We have all been sick at some time, to some degree. We all know someone who died early in life due to injury or sickness. We honor those who overcome infirmity. We cherish those who beat the odds and survive "terminal" illnesses.

And I stand right there with you, applauding those who have overcome adversity. Poverty, addictions, illness, or injury. We love such people. And rightfully so. And Americans may love them even more. We love the underdog. We love seeing people achieve the unexpected.

But this is not success. Sometimes it's simply survival. Sometimes it's hard work and perseverance. You can call it luck or a miracle. But it's not overall success.

How about the other half of the universal wish all parents have for their children?

Happiness

Health and happiness. What a nice wish to bestow on others. Is happiness the right way to measure success? We've covered this a little already, so I won't belabor it. Happiness can be a good indicator that you are on the right path—because fulfilling your purpose should afford you the greatest level of contentment and therefore happiness. True happiness.

So, how happy you are, and how often you are happy, may be indicators that you're doing the right things, the right ways, and for the right reasons. But it is not equal to success. However, out of all the ways we normally judge success, this is the closest. It's the only one that is a good indicator that you are on the right path. Of course, if you're working diligently toward your purpose, you may also achieve wealth, fame, and status.

I was asked to speak to a group of professional women during a 7-for-7 evening event. There would be seven speakers giving seven-minute presentations on various topics important to professional women and women business owners. I was given the topic "Happy on Purpose." It was a quick and easy decision for me on what I'd cover during my seven minutes.

"To be happy on purpose," I told the women, "you have to fulfill your purpose."

I thoroughly enjoyed the event. It was a late afternoon event in a ballroom. The seven speakers sat up on a dais. We were provided a podium, a stationary mic, and a quick introduction by one of the organizers. I was honored to lead off the event. Going first, I passed on the podium and mic and walked out in front, floor level to address the women.

I had two goals: to energize the room for the rest of the speakers to come and to introduce the women to the idea that the only way to true happiness was to be found in being about the calling they'd been given. Of course, that meant they had to find it first. But once they knew what it was, they had to spend their time fulfilling it. It's when we're lost and off the path that we suffer from anxiety, depression, and fear. Being lost is never fun. It won't make you happy. It will make you miserable.

To be happy on purpose, fulfill your purpose.

It's amazing what fulfilling your purpose and achieving your passions do for the rest of your life. They can attract many positive things to you.

Contentment

Dave Ramsey says contentment isn't an emotional state, it's a spiritual state. I think happiness is also a spiritual state rather than an emotional one.

Contentment may be the same as happiness or it may be a fuller realization of what makes us happy. I think contentment is harder to attain than happiness because we can have fleeting joy and believe we have happiness. But contentment requires that we have a long-term feeling of satisfaction. Many people try different techniques to obtain peace of mind because this gives us a level of contentment. Or perhaps achieving contentment allows us to have peace of mind. Whichever comes first, they are highly sought-after states of being.

Meditation, yoga, and deep contemplation are all techniques we try. Week-long (expensive) retreats, introspective sessions with psychologists, and even hypnosis are ways we try to reach contentment and peace of mind.

But it may be a lot easier and less expensive to reach this state. To be content, to be truly happy, only requires that we fulfill our purpose. By doing what we are meant to do we can truly relax and enjoy life and ourselves. When we are fulfilling our missions, we attain a high level of contentment, and our minds can be at peace.

It sounds really simple, because it is.

All you have to do is figure out what your purpose is and then succeed at fulfilling it. If you have a vision, you have to work diligently to achieve it.

I said achieving happiness and contentment was *easier* than we make it out to be, not *easy*.

So are contentment and peace of mind measures of success? Again, like happiness, these are good indicators that you are on the right path. Barring anything else, if you satisfactorily measured your level of happiness, contentment, and peace of mind, you could say that you were successful. But by now you realize that it's not a complete (or highly accurate) measure of success. Just think of all of those people who believe they have reached peace of mind because they have left all of the stress and worry of life behind by becoming a hermit. Or the person who meditates for hours daily and has attained a quiet contentment.

And I'm not sure any CEO would choose these three indicators as measures of success for their *organization*.

How about if we put all of them together? What if we made a balanced scorecard using wealth, fame, status, power, health, happiness, contentment, and peace of mind?

You guessed it. The answer is still no.

These are plausible *indicators of success*, but they don't work as measures because they don't tell the whole story. They only tell us how we feel, not whether we're successful. A big part of the problem is that we apply our own lenses to them and try to apply our lenses to others. Our lenses are formed in part by our experience, upbringing, values, and beliefs.

The number one goal is to fulfill our mission. The number two goal in our lives is to achieve a vision. Everything else is comparably unimportant.

If these are "indicators" and possible measures of success—what's missing? Why don't we just measure each of these?

Because as indicators they do not add up to success. They can help us know whether we're on the right path, but that's the trick. We *have* to be on the right path to truly be successful. And of course, being on the right path doesn't mean that you will arrive at the desired destination. So, your measures of success have to do more than tell you whether you're headed on the right path.

These are extremely helpful, but they're not your Measures of Success.

Your Measures of Success have to do more than let you know you're on the right path—they must tell you whether you will reach your destination and when. So don't ignore these indicators—but remember there's more to do.

JEFF AND SARAH, OWNERS OF A PIZZA PARLOR

This may have been the hardest interview I had. Not the interview itself, just getting time on Jeff and Sarah's schedule. You may have thought getting time with a CEO, CIO, COO, or a professional sports general manager would be the hardest to get, but you'd be wrong. Between running their own business and working it—theirs is truly a family-owned and family-operated business—their dedication to their faith, and their devotion to their children, Jeff and Sarah were the toughest to catch.

How do you measure success?

Sarah

The business? Based off of where we started from—sold everything we could to buy the business, to the point of near bankruptcy. I was working at the post office part time, due to morning sickness with our oldest child, so the business was our only means for income.

And knowing that was a catalyst to making it work.

We're not very material people. Our gauge of success is knowing that your family, your children, and your husband are there with you, and happy. Don't know how I can ask for much more than that.

We have been blessed. We have food. We realized the ability to keep the shop, and while doing so, teach our children a good work ethic. This and dragging the kids to church every week pays dividends later. The work ethic and drive is important. To strive and not become complacent; willing to put in the effort. If we teach our children those things, that would be successful.

Watching our children adopt our values: our belief in God, our work ethic, and not being envious of their neighbors. These things make us successful.

When we started, we couldn't find trustworthy help. We couldn't find employees we trusted—Jeff had to be there every day all day, six days a week. I was going to college full time, but I worked as much as I could.

While we were making a living, we weren't living our lives. Jeff decided to cut our hours, eliminating our lunch offerings, a big part of our business. He did it so he could be a bigger part of his family. The kids would have to spend their whole summer break at work…that would be our lifestyle if we put money and material things first. We decided to try the less hours so we could spend more time as a family.

I shared my theories on success and how to measure it.

I completely agree with that.

This didn't surprise me. Everyone seems to get it immediately. When I ask how they measure success, most people don't know how to articulate it in a simple way. But they all have the underlying truth in common: they all measure success by how well they fulfill their purpose. Each time I share the truth of it, the reaction I hear the most is gratitude. Thanks that they now know the name of what was always at the core of their success. Their purpose, their calling, their mission.

We have to keep striving to be what we're meant to be, that's why God gives us a new day every day. I have to figure out what I can do better tomorrow, and I then try to do that. We have to continuously reassess. Sometimes in the mess, we find beauty. You have to pick yourself up and dust yourself off.

Why am I here? A calling to spread God's word. It's what we're most passionate about. Jeff is the youth pastor at our church. I've been teaching Sunday School since

I graduated from high school. I love sharing how stories and concepts from the Bible can still relate to our lives today. The Bible can make a difference to kids, today.

Having the kids learn the basics of the Bible. It's not outdated. It shouldn't collect dust on a shelf…there's a personal message there for each of us. Having teachable moments for others…seeing others appreciate the love of Christ, and then appreciate it themselves, is very powerful.

Seeing kids get it, that's why I'm here.

Jeff

My success would be measured by the path I have made for my children: a safe environ, healthy, ethical, good morals, hard workers, and honest. If this comes to be, the entirety of my life will have been a success.

I shared my definition for Success Metrics.

I would agree with that. Once I became married and had children, my calling in life became clear. I have an obligation to take care of my wife, keep my family financially secure and protected. And to do these things to the best of my abilities.

My calling in life is to be a good father. To raise my children in a way that would be acceptable to God first of all and to man as well.

I cut back on our hours, not only to spend more time with our children, but to also do what we're supposed to do, per our faith. Biblically speaking. We need to do both— we need to have a work/life balance where we can spend time with our family. So, my children work with us and we teach our children the value of hard, honest work. There's a point, though, where you realize which one is the most important. I missed the first three children's lives…I missed all of their school functions and their activities.

We have to balance accumulating wealth and spending time with our family. There has to be a time when we say, enough is actually enough. Having more wouldn't be better since we wouldn't appreciate or enjoy it.

It's very important to be able to spend time with our children.

Although I cut back our hours, and closing down our lunch market, I'm doing better. We changed our hours, cutting back six hours a day. The result? I'm less stressed, I now have a home life with my family—my wife and my children. I feel healthier (and younger) than I've ever felt. There is definitely such a thing as working too hard and too long. Funny thing is, when I focused on my calling, I didn't only do better with my personal mental, physical, and spiritual health. We also didn't lose any of our overall income, which was a happy surprise.

I'm a bit of a workaholic, which I come by honestly from my dad. But I'm learning to focus on my family, and that makes sense since it's my purpose, my calling.

In Jeff and Sarah's case, their business is simply a means to an end—the end being their calling in life. And that's totally fine. They are not concerned about making the business a franchise. They're not concerned with wealth. They are concerned about their faith and their family—their calling.

Summary

Why is it easier to describe something by what it's not than by what it is?

Regardless whether it's easier or not, there are good reasons to look into what not to measure—mostly because you will be tempted to do it wrong. You'll want to simplify your life by using measures you already have. You'll want to ignore my advice because you think the ways you've always done it are good enough.

Actually, I have faith that you don't believe that. Otherwise, you wouldn't be reading this book, and you definitely wouldn't be still reading at this point. But you'll have to sell others, and that won't be easy. So, it will help if you know why the measures they want to use aren't good enough.

You can't use performance measures. Don't measure things that aren't included in your purpose and vision. The normal ones that people use fall short, even: wealth, fame, status, power, health, happiness, and contentment. There are a lot of things you shouldn't use.

Perhaps we should look at what happens when we get it right?

Success Stories

I worked with our district library to develop a strategic plan looking out at least ten years. As a board member, I offered my services pro bono, but that didn't keep me from pushing them as hard as I do any of my clients.

When it came time to measure success for the executive director, the board of trustees, and the library as a whole, we had to stay focused on the mission and vision. It wasn't an easy road, and we risked slipping off at any one of the numerous curves along the way.

As the new president of the board, I pushed us to look at the mission and vision at every board meeting. And at those meetings, I wanted to have periodic updates on the organization's progress toward becoming successful. Achieving the vision and fulfilling our mission.

From the library's website: "The mission of the Niles District Library is to provide our community with access and guidance to resources that inform, entertain, and enrich. Our vision provides us with clear direction and motivation, because we see our library as building a community of life-long learners who will make Niles their life-long home."

I'll confess up front that this is not what I would advise as the true mission and vision. It's a good public rendition, though. When I teach my clients to share their mission and vision, I stress the avoidance of wordsmithing the perfect mission or vision statement. Here's why.

© Martin Klubeck 2017
M. Klubeck, *Success Metrics*, DOI 10.1007/978-1-4842-2586-8_9

Why We Should Not Have a Formal Statement

Your mission describes why your organization exists. It's your purpose.

Your vision is a very scary, large, hairy, audacious goal with all the trappings we've covered. It's the world-changing, selfless goal you want to achieve.

In each of these cases there is a strong constant: passion. Your purpose, the reason your organization exists, should create passion in those who share it. And perhaps more importantly, in those who hear it. When you share your mission, your audience should get excited about the possibilities. They should want to join your team, wishing they could be part of your organization. When people hear about Google, Apple, or IBM, this happens. There are other awesome organizations, nonprofit as well as Fortune 500 companies, that attract the best (and the rest) because their purpose is inspiring.

Your organization's vision should do the same, but at an exponentially higher level. The vision should be shared with even more passion and be received with equally greater levels of passion. Why? Because although the mission highlights why you do all the great things you do on a daily basis, (the *why* behind the *what* of your organization's existence), the vision is much more. The vision impassions those who want to make the world a better place— those who still believe in the power of humans to right the wrongs of their ancestors.

I've never seen a well-crafted, wordsmithed statement that could elicit anything near the level of passion that either a mission or vision should. How about you? Does your organization have a mission statement? Is it on its website? On your business cards? Were you asked to memorize it? Read it. Share it with someone you knew. Let me know (feel free to email me) if it elicits any passion at all. Does it create passion in you? Do you have passion when you share it? When you hear it?

I'm betting not.

I'm always looking for a good mission. So if you have one, please send it my way.

Officially sanctioned statements make it almost impossible to have passion. Too many words are used. Too many large, polysyllabic words. We try to fit too much meaning into the statement. We want it to tell a large story, the story of our existence and of our future. So we try to shove everything into it. The statement becomes a ridiculously long run-on sentence, with little to no meaning. It does nothing that we want it to except fill a check in the box.

Instead of only telling the why, we try to squeeze in what we do, how we do it, and when, and even who does it.

Your mission and vision have to be shared with passion and heard with passion.

You can't do that with a wordsmithed, single sentence.

You can't do that in a paragraph.

There are some extremely talented writers (Stephen King would be my choice) who might be able to write your mission or vision in a page or two. They could take your story and make it a short story that does the job. But even they would need more than two or three paragraphs.

Your mission and vision have to be shared verbally. It has to be shared by you and your peers. It has to be shared by the organization's leadership. And the passion will not come through in what you say. It comes through in how you say it.

The words are just words. They don't have passion imbued within them. Even putting them together in a string, a sentence, a paragraph, or a page won't do it.

Passion comes from the person sharing those words.

Passion is found in your eyes, in the quiver of your lips and the increase of your heart rate. Passion is found in the goose bumps on your arms, the way the hairs stand up a little, how your body temperature rises.

Passion is elicited through how you tell your story. Imagine any story from your youth or past that created strong emotions in you. Imagine if the person who shared it with you didn't care. If the person didn't believe in the vision they were sharing. If the person didn't care about your mission. How much passion would the story create for you if the person sharing it lacked passion?

Your mission and vision have to be shared by your leadership, employees, and shareholders. They all have to know it and they all have to believe in it. It should be the main criteria for hiring and firing personnel. It's how a board should select their executive director. It's how every key position should be filled—from CEO to the front-line manager—they all should believe in your purpose and your vision. They don't have to agree on the *how*. You actually don't want them to agree on the *how*. You want them to challenge each other and the status quo. You want innovation and creativity. Not just "out of the box" thinking—you want them to feel free to throw the box away totally.

But the biggest *whats*—they have to agree on.

The underlying *why*—they have to believe in.

None of this will happen without passion.

That's why I don't care about the formal statement. It's why I didn't fight for the library to write something "better." The simple answer is, I don't really care.

What I do care about is how they tell the story, how they share it. And like those who wish to rig an election, you should share the mission and vision "early and often."

Measuring Success

Let me tell you a story.

At one of our board meetings, our executive director was excited to tell us about a program her team had implemented. She even led off by telling us it was a large success!

"I wanted to let you all know that we had one of our biggest successes this past week. We had a young college student playing Michelangelo, of Ninja Turtle fame. He was awesome. We had over 400 families sign up *in advance* via Facebook. As you might guess, we had more than that the day of!"

I smiled. Not because she was sharing program updates. I was happy that she was. I wanted to hear more about the programming, activities, and work the staff was doing than about how much money they spent or how they spent it. But I smiled because I knew this was going to be a teaching moment.

She misread my smile.

"Oh, and our board president helped out too! We knew the large turnout would mean long lines so we enlisted Marty to dress up as Ironman (costume purchased from a local store), and he did a great job."

I did. Really. I loved it. I did the "robot" (all those years of dancing when I was a teen finally had a use) and posed for a ton of pictures with little kids. I never spoke a word since I don't sound anything like Robert Downey, Jr.

What a blast!

This time she read my smile correctly—I was remembering the fun.

She turned to me and said, "I know you like statistics."

I had to correct her. "Actually I don't like statistics at all—I like metrics. But I have to ask you, why do you say it was a success?"

She looked at me puzzled. I could see her rewinding her presentation and checking—yup, she had already shared with us how many families attended.

"We had one of our biggest turnouts...actually it was our largest turnout ever for a kid's event."

"And..." I prodded.

"Doesn't that make it a success?" she asked, no longer sure of herself.

"Perhaps. Why did you hold the event? Was the purpose of the event to have the largest turnout ever?"

"No..."

"Well, we shouldn't consider it a success unless it did what we wanted it to. Unless it fulfilled its purpose, we can't say it was a success."

So the question has to be asked: why do we measure things like number of attendees? Or customer feedback ratings? Or number of hits on our website?

In a recent workshop on vision setting, I was working with a young entrepreneur. She is a salon owner. And when we found out what her mission was I was impressed. Her calling is to help women develop self-esteem. She says by making them look good, they can feel good about themselves. But when I asked her how she measured success, her first attempts were off target. She thought to measure success by the number of customers she had, number of repeat customers, and whether she was getting referrals. I had only one question: Did any of these measures tell her how well she was fulfilling her calling? Did they tell her whether her customers felt better about themselves? And how much did her efforts account for those feelings of self-esteem?

So, why do we use only these measures to try and define success? It would be okay to use these measures to answer specific questions—but those questions aren't "were we successful?"

The answer can be a little depressing. The reason organizations use measures that don't really define success is because they're easy to collect and analyze. And the converse is also true. The measures that *should* be used to define success are hard to collect and use. Easy vs. hard. Wrong vs. right.

Does that seem pessimistic? I think it's a realistic assessment after years of working with organizations on metrics. Too often I've been asked to develop metrics around data solely because it's readily available.

"Can you make a set of metrics from this data?"

"Why? What question are we answering?"

"Oh, no specific question. We just have a lot of data and we should be able to use it to better the organization."

This is why, at my keynote presentation to a room full of institutional researchers, I opened by explaining that I "hate business intelligence and institutional researchers." I was (unsuccessfully) coached not to use the word *hate*. I was told it was too strong. But I made sure I smiled when I said it. And I mostly meant it.

I told the room of researchers that I hated them because they (and business intelligence teams) kept encouraging leaders to look for their answers in the reams of data they have available. Instead of helping leaders find what their questions were, they provide ready access to Big Data and hope that they'll find answers. But if you don't know the question, the answer won't help.

Or: if you don't know where you're going, any map will do.

This may seem obvious…but I assure you, it is not.

It's one of the biggest battles I fight when consulting on metrics. Getting leaders to stop using measures that don't answer their questions—and to take the time to figure out what those questions are.

Back to Ninja Turtles, Iron Man, and how the library should measure the success of the event.

"So, why did we hold the event? Why did we pay the young man to dress up as a mutant turtle?" I asked.

Our executive director had to think a bit.

I decided to help her.

"What part of the vision or mission were you trying to help achieve with this event? Or with any of the similar programs your team has been implementing?"

This she knew easily.

"We're trying to introduce more people to the library and our services."

"Why?"

"Because we want to be the hub for our community, so we can create life-long learners who want to make Niles their home."

"Why do you want to create life-long learners?"

"If we create a community of life-long learners, we will create a healthy community. A great place to live."

"So, why do you hold events like this?"

She had now recovered her focus and confidence.

"Two reasons. One is our mission. Events like these help us to inform, entertain, and enrich. Granted, this may have been mostly on the entertain side of things. But it also provided an opportunity to introduce people to the library and the resources we offer. It builds on creating that life-long learner community."

I whole heartedly agreed.

"So we should be able to measure the success of that event by how well it helped to inform, entertain, or enrich our community's lives and how well it worked to introduce people to the library."

"Yes."

But that wasn't what we measured. The number of attendees did nothing to answer the question about whether the event was informative (doubtful—there wasn't any informative component), enriching (it could definitely have been enriching for the children and their families) or entertaining (another high possibility). We needed to measure these outcomes instead of attendance.

Of course, we had a better chance of success if we had higher attendance, but the attendance was not the measure of success. It was only a means to hopefully be successful.

And we also had to collect demographics. Of the 400 families, we had no idea how many of them were from our community.

Looking at the vision and the goal of introducing more people to the library's services and resources, we would need to measure how many new members we acquired as a result of the event. We could measure how many new library cards were issued. We could also count how many questions were asked and answered, whether we saw an increase in loans or service use during the event, and a slew of other related measures.

It's nice to bring people in for an entertaining event. Our library has been really proactive in this area. We have magic shows, princesses reading books to children, local authors and artists doing talks. We have yoga, drawing, chess, and teen-focused movie events. Our programming is frequent and well attended. But if we forget the purpose, all we end up doing is providing events without a reason. And if we don't measure against the mission and vision, we won't know whether the events were successful.

So, for the library we have to measure whether the events are helping us fulfill our mission. Are we doing better at informing our community because of the event? Are we doing better at entertaining? Are we doing better at enriching? And to be really accurate, our mission doesn't say that we will inform, entertain, or enrich—it says that we will provide access and guidance to resources that inform, entertain, and enrich. By holding the events, we are providing access to an entertaining resource. But that's only one-sixth of the mission.

And worse, if we look closer we'd remember that "entertain, inform, and enrich" are actually the *hows* for the library. We'd be falling short of measuring if we were satisfying the *why*. If we correct that and look at the hoped-for result of creating a community of life-long learners, perhaps. But we need to measure that also. How well did it help us toward our vision? These are the basics to building the correct story.

One of my peers, Stacey Barr, is a metrics consultant out of Australia. I love the way Stacey thinks. We are as in sync as I think possible for two people from different backgrounds, different experiences, and different countries. We both came to many of the same conclusions about the right way (and wrong ways) of doing metrics.

Her second book is due out early 2017 and keeping in line with the coincidences around our journeys, I found that her book, *Prove It*, is about proving "how our organizations are performing." And Stacey offers that the way to do this is to do what few people do—"measure your mission."

Stacey gives specific ways of measuring your mission, and the good news is that it's based on avoiding what she calls *weasel words*. Yup, you've guessed it. Weasel words are those unclear words I told you to avoid.

Here's an example she shared of a good mission measured:

> *The National Alliance to End Homelessness (NAEH) in the US also has a very clear mission:*
>
> *The Alliance works toward ending homelessness by improving homelessness policy, building on-the-ground capacity, and educating opinion leaders.*
>
> *And to prove how well they are fulfilling this mission, they used measures like these:*
>
> *Average Length of Time Persons Remain Homeless*
>
> *Median Length of Time Persons Remain Homeless*
>
> *Percent of Persons Who Return to Homelessness*
>
> *Number of Homeless Persons*
>
> *Percentage of Homeless Persons Who Gain or Increase Income*
>
> *Number of Persons Who Become Homeless for the First Time*
>
> *Using measures like these, it's much easier to prove the impact that change programs have. To contribute to ending homelessness, one change program raised average incomes of people from $910 per month to more than $2,000 per month within 18 months. And another change program for assisting people to remain in permanent housing exceeded their target of 75 percent and achieved 77 percent.*

This *is* a good example. The Alliance could go off the tracks very easily because their mission shares the *hows* as well as the *what*. The mission is to end homelessness. That's it. Nothing more. If the Alliance had stopped there, with the what, measuring would be very easy, and you wouldn't need either of our books. How can you measure whether you are successfully ending homelessness? You have to measure the current level of homelessness and how that level changes. You should also measure anything that shows a reduction in homelessness. But if you add in the *hows* as the National Alliance to End Homelessness did, you risk becoming distracted, confused, or just off track.

For example, the *how* was "by improving homelessness policy, building on-the-ground capacity, and educating opinion leaders." I can easily imagine the Alliance measuring the quality of the policies, measuring "on-the-ground capacity" and the level of leadership's education. But we wouldn't know if any of these worked if we were measuring them instead of simply measuring homelessness.

Think that's too easy? Even Stacey, my "metric-soul-mate" says, "Using measures like these, it's much easier to prove the impact that change programs have. To contribute to ending homelessness, one change program raised average incomes of people from $910 per month to more than $2,000 per month within 18 months. And another change program for assisting people to remain in permanent housing exceeded their target of 75 percent and achieved 77 percent."

Because I have so much faith in Stacey, I'm going to bet that these measures not only showed increases in average income and percentages of those remaining in permanent housing—they also showed a decrease in overall homelessness. The problem is we have to assume that if the percentage of people moving into permanent housing stayed at that rate, they would be subtracted from the numbers of homeless.

And granted, these are *so* much better than the possible misstep of measuring the *how*. These are logical in that they should lead to less homelessness. If you're measuring how many homeless are now remaining in permanent housing…you have to believe that should give us an indicator of progress. But it's still not the answer. It will tell us how well the program for providing permanent housing is working…but we have to still bounce that against the total numbers. The goal wasn't to *maintain* but to *end* homelessness.

This holds true for the other positive numbers she applauded. Even if average incomes have risen by more than 100 percent, are these increases in pay translating into fewer homeless?

Although I am hesitant about the conclusions, I love the measures Stacey pointed out:

1. Average Length of Time Persons Remain Homeless

2. Median Length of Time Persons Remain Homeless

3. Percent of Persons Who Return to Homelessness

4. Number of Homeless Persons

5. Percentage of Homeless Persons Who Gain or Increase Income

6. Number of Persons Who Become Homeless for the First Time

So we see that one of the examples given was directly related to measure 5. The problem with this is that this is an indicator of a specific *how*.

The problem with both of the examples is that she tried to take them and show how effective the programs were…when really you didn't need to come up with anything complicated. These measures should tell you directly whether you're proving successful. I believe the reason she slipped a little is that our customers always want proof that *their specific programs and efforts* are resulting in success. They want to know that what they are doing is responsible for the change. But if our goal is to end homelessness—if homelessness is eradicated—we've won! Of course, if we had nothing to do with it, if we did nothing positive and the change still happened, we couldn't claim success, could we? No, we couldn't.

But anything we do toward our mission and vision has to be tied first back to the actual results. That's why I believe Stacey is actually on the right track and I look forward to reading her book.

Look back at those six measures again.

Are any obviously good measures of success?

If number 4, "Number of Homeless Persons" were zero, and stayed zero, I think we could claim success. If our mission is truly ending homelessness— that's our one key measure.

Look at number 3, Percent of Persons Who Return to Homelessness. It's interesting that we're looking at a percentage. We'd hope for 0 percent, of course. If any return to homelessness, then whatever we did to help them not to be homeless was only temporary. I'd much rather measure homelessness over time to show that we didn't *chase the data* (do whatever was necessary to have a moment in time when there were no homeless). Return to homelessness speaks to the known problems with ending homelessness altogether. Much like the problems with ending indebtedness.

Dave Ramsey, *the* Dave Ramsey who does his best to help people get out of (and stay out of) debt, is a-w-e-s-o-m-e. Why? Because his mission and vision is straightforward and clear. *No debt.* Change the world from one in which people dig really deep holes and then ask for a new shovel. Instead his motto could be, "If you find yourself in a hole, stop digging."

I love listening to his radio show. I really love his advice to people who end up enabling their loved ones. They give money to someone who has problems with debt. He also admonishes people to not try and force loved ones to get out of debt. If they're not ready to actually change, helping them (or forcing them) out of debt today will likely end up putting them in more debt later. They haven't changed their ways, and therefore they will slip back into the behaviors that put them in debt to begin with.

It requires a change in behavior. A change of life.

Homelessness for some requires the same. There are some who have fallen on hard times, and if they are given a residence that they can afford or a job that pays enough for an abode, they are unlikely to return to homelessness.

But there are others who suffer from addictions or mental illness. There are those who, even when given a home, will return to homelessness.

That's the secret to mission-based efforts. You can stay focused on what really matters: the fulfillment of your purpose. It isn't enough to have some effective programs if you don't do what you said you would.

Giving money to your indebted friends or family who have a problem with spending doesn't actually solve the long-term problem. Short-term measures may look good, but our mission is not to look good, it's to change the world.

So, we have to actually show progress toward ending homelessness.

We have to show progress toward ending indebtedness.

We have to show progress toward our mission and vision.

How to Get 'Er Done

The good news is that there are specific steps to take to measuring success. Anyone can do it.

Identify Your Purpose

A short review because we've covered this already: As we've discussed, this isn't as simple as we would like. We have to get to the *why* behind the *what*. We don't need wordsmithed perfect statements engraved in marble. What we need is a clear understanding of our purpose. We have to understand the reason why we (our organizations or ourselves) exist.

We have to ask *why* as many times as it takes to get to the root cause, the root need, the underlying purpose for our existence. Each person and organization should take the time to find the answer to this fundamental question.

Start with why your organization was founded. Has your mission changed? If it has, how has it changed?

Find the purpose. You should be able to finish the statement, "Our organization exists because…"

Once you know what your purpose is, we can measure how well you are fulfilling that purpose.

Determine How to Measure Whether You're Fulfilling That Purpose

Pick a true calling. It should then be easy to determine the right measures. Remember that we are answering the *why* question. Why do we exist? Why does our organization exist? See if you can put *because* in front of any of these very successful companies' mission statements.

Google

> *To organize the world's information and make it universally accessible and useful.*

I love Google. It's gone from a noun (the name of a search engine) to a verb! "Wait a sec while I Google that." But what about the mission statement? It sounds like a cool thing to do, but is it the purpose? Is the reason Google exists to organize the world's information? Is it to make it universally accessible? Is it to make the world's information useful (by organizing it)? What is the purpose?

Organizing the world's information sounds like a big *what,* or *how.* So that's not the *why.*

Making the world's information universally accessible could be the *why,* but it could be a *how* also. Notice that I'm taking the existing mission statement and trying to make sense of it. I'm trying to find the *why* behind the *what.* And as in most cases, that *why* is at the end of the statement instead of the lead. Even in such a short statement, it's pushed to the back.

Making the world's information useful (to all). That could be a *why.* That could be the purpose. But I'll dare say that there is probably a *why* behind that. Why is Google making the world's information universally useful? The *how* is nicely stated—to organize the information and make it universally accessible. What a great mandate!

But why? Is it simply to make it useful? Or is making the world's information universally accessible and useful a giant *what* for achieving a truly world-changing *why?* Can we help mankind rise to its greatest heights possible by making the world's information available to all?

Is it a fulfillment of Andrew Carnegie's dream of making all information available to everyone? He funded the first public libraries because he believed in the power of knowledge and that knowledge should be accessible to everyone. It shouldn't be only for those who could afford it.

Google seems to be on the same path, with the same destination.

What easier way to find Google's mission statement than to Google it?

Google's mission is to organize the world's information and make it universally accessible and useful. Our company has packed a lot into a relatively young life. Since **Google** was founded in 1998, we've grown to serve millions of people around the world.

Company – Google
https://www.**google**.com/about/company/   Google ▾

Andrew Carnegie wanted knowledge to be free and available to all because he believed everyone had enormous potential for creating a great world. And knowledge was the key.

Of course, I'm not in charge of Google. I can't tell you what its purpose is. But I can tell you that the mission statement listed feels a little shy of fully defining the purpose of the organization.

The funny thing is that these mission statements were supposed to be examples of motivational, inspirational ones of great companies. But wouldn't Google's mission be even more inspiring if we knew the *why* behind the *what?*

Which is more inspiring?

> *Google exists to make the world's information accessible and useful for everyone.*

or

> *Google's purpose is to give everyone the power to make the world a better place.*

Feel free to add the *how*, but please put it at the end!

Google's purpose is to give everyone the power to make the world a better place. How? By organizing the world's information, making it accessible and useful to everyone.

If I'm right, their mission was there for all to see, but it wasn't described correctly. The *why* behind the *what* was hidden. And that's a shame.

When we know the *why* to our existence, it becomes much easier to find our compatriots. Instead of focusing on your competitors, knowing your *why* allows you to focus on your contemporaries. It helps you find collaborators of your purpose. Other organizations (or people) with the same (or compatible) mission as you should become key nodes in your network.

Whom should Google be teaming with?

I already mentioned that the mission of our public libraries may be fully aligned with Google. Who else?

I immediately thought about Wikipedia and then the Wikimedia Foundation. Just as I searched Google for Google's mission statement, I thought I might find Wikipedia's mission statement on the entry for "Wikipedia" on Wikipedia.

I actually found it in more than one place.

And like many organizations, it was hard to tell the vision from the mission (and that's just fine):

> *Tom Morris, Wikipedia administrator*
>
> *The Wikimedia Foundation's vision is...Imagine a world in which every single human being can freely share in the sum of all knowledge. That's our commitment.*
>
> *The mission of the Wikimedia Foundation is to empower and engage people around the world to collect and develop educational content under a free license or in the public domain, and to disseminate it effectively and globally.*

You're probably getting pretty good at this by now and realize that what is listed as a mission has a lot of *hows* in it. But I'm okay with that. What I'm looking for now are collaborators—others with missions and visions that align with yours.

In this case, it seems (to me, an admitted outsider) that Wikimedia and Google have common goals and an aligned purpose. If I were collecting names, I'd start with: public libraries, Google, and the Wikimedia Foundation. I'm sure there are others. There are many computer programmers that believe everyone should have free access to the power of the computer. They believe in open source software.

There are for-profit companies that are based on providing knowledge and making learning available to all.

When you know your mission and vision, you can align your efforts with others. It helps you to achieve your vision—remember, you can't do it alone! Google can't achieve its vision without help from others. Wikimedia has at its foundation the concept of crowd-solving—it relies on all of us to participate to make information and knowledge available to all. Our public libraries need financial support from the community as well as active participation. And all of these should be working with each other to make it easier to achieve success.

But does this work with less altruistic endeavors? How about organizations that have as their primary goods and services making money? How about Amazon?

Amazon

To be Earth's most customer-centric company where people can find and discover anything they want to buy online.

I love Amazon. I love Amazon online. I love that I can buy something and it arrives at my door step in two days. And if there's something wrong, I can return it. I love their customer service. I happily pay a fee to have Amazon Prime. Sorry if this sounds like a commercial—but I wanted to establish my bias up front.

I hate their mission statement.

How can their purpose, their reason for existence, be to "be Earth's most customer centric company?" That's not a purpose…it's not a mission.

How about the second part of the statement? "…where people can find and discover anything they want to buy online."

That's a really nice business model, but it's not a valid *why*.

It also sounds like a really cool thing for me. I'd love for them to be the most customer-centric company in the world *and* also be the place where I can find, discover, and buy anything I want online! Woo hoo!

But, that's still not a *why*. It's a *what* and a *how*. It gives an in-depth view of what the company plans to offer and how it plans on offering it. The problem, though, is these aren't the underlying *whys*.

There are so many possible good reasons for Amazon to exist, I'm hoping there is a mission somewhere in there that isn't being promoted. Digging a little I found this:

Learn how Amazon is making books available around the world through digital reading.

I thought about Amazon's Web Services (massive storage that scales to your needs), the Kindle, and the programs that get books into readers' hands. I thought about the Echo, the voice-activated companion stationed in my living room.

If Amazon existed to simply be the place where I can find, discover, and buy anything I want online, what's up with all these other serious ventures? These don't match up logically.

I'm leaving out altruistic or charity efforts Amazon is involved in, such as its Joining Forces Pledge, which included the pledge "to hire 25,000 veterans and military spouses over the next five years, and to train 10,000 active-duty service members, veterans, and military spouses (not employed at Amazon) in cloud computing through AWS Educate memberships and offering a path to AWS certifications."

There is also Amazonsmile—another altruistic endeavor by Amazon in which you can have Amazon donate to a charity of your choice. Even small local ones. By using a different link to get to Amazon (www.amazonsmile.com), Amazon will give a small percentage of what you spend to that charity. No added costs or fees to you. Not taken from the supplier of the goods. Just Amazon giving per your wishes.

I leave these out because most super companies spend good amounts of money and resources on charitable ventures. And although I love that they do so, none of them seems to consider this to be their purpose. This isn't why they believe they exist, although they do believe it's a responsibility they have to society.

But Amazon sells books. More books than any other bookseller in the world. But that's not part of Amazon's mission? Amazon is even in the business of publishing (printing) on-demand books! So what's up with that?

No. I believe there's definitely more involved with the mission of Amazon than to be a ubiquitous online seller. I do agree that this is their specialty. Online sales is their market niche (and that niche is a vast valley of possibilities). It's how Amazon makes their mark, although they are branching out (online servers, Kindles, book publishing, and the Echo are examples).

And you might justifiably ask: Is it important for Amazon to know their purpose? They're one of the biggest players in the industry. They're growing steadily. With their focus on customer service and providing what people want/need—will they really benefit from knowing their mission?

Yes.

Yes, they will.

Knowing their purpose will actually improve their standing with their loyal customers. It will enable them to increase that customer base and grow champions to their cause.

What would you offer as a possible mission for Amazon?

Is it to make goods and services available to everyone—eliminating the inability of some to get what they need or want because of geography, knowledge, or transportation?

I like that a lot better, but it still doesn't speak to the other areas Amazon is branching out to—or does it?

Perhaps those focus areas have more to do with Amazon's vision for the future than they do with Amazon's reason for existence?

Seems I'm not the only one who wants to analyze Amazon's mission and vision. Lawrence Gregory of the Panmore Institute did as well (http://panmore.com/ amazon-com-inc-vision-statement-mission-statement-analysis):

> *Amazon.com Inc.'s vision and mission statements have pushed the company to become the largest online retailer in the world. This success is attributed to stringent measures to ensure that the mission and vision statements are fulfilled.*

In this article, Gregory actually lists "To be Earth's most customer-centric company where people can find and discover anything they want to buy online" as Amazon's *vision* statement.

He lists Amazon's mission statement as follows: "We strive to offer our customers the lowest possible prices, the best available selection, and the utmost convenience."

In either case, the problems are the same. Although the analysis in the article says that the vision and mission are "good," the author doesn't judge it the same way I do. He doesn't consider "purpose" at all for the mission.

And from a further inspection of Amazon.com (go to the bottom of the home page. Under Get to Know Us, click the About Amazon link), we find out more deeply what Amazon is really about. Still no useful mission and vision statement, but it gives us a much better understanding of why Amazon believes it exists.

I keep getting the vibes of Amazon being a provider or products and services to all. Full accessibility (as long as you can get on the Internet).

Chipotle

Chipotle is another company (that's supposedly in the business of making money) that I like. Why? Because they have really good food! And the employees seem to genuinely enjoy working there. So I was happy to see that their mission statement fit my expectations of what they were all about.

> *Using higher-quality ingredients and cooking techniques to make great food accessible to all people at reasonable prices, to provide Food With Integrity.*

Providing *food with integrity* is a pretty cool catch phrase—a nice tagline. Let's break down the rest of the statement.

"Using higher-quality and ingredients and cooking techniques" is an obvious *how*. Not the *what*, and definitely not the *why*.

"to make great food"—now there's a clear *what*. Making great food. Nothing wrong with that!

"accessible to all people"—this part is very interesting. Wonder if this is accurate. Does Chipotle really believe that their purpose is making great food accessible to all people? I'm guessing that means globally.

"at reasonable prices" sounds like a *how*.

How to make it accessible? One way is to make it affordable.

When you put it together, it sounds like a great purpose. *To make great food accessible to everyone at reasonable prices.* Usually *reasonable prices* means mediocre food. Or unhealthy food. And if you're a small mom-and-pop restaurant, believing in providing good (healthy) food at reasonable prices, you wouldn't expect to provide that to all people. This is starting to sound like a mission aligned with Whole Foods's mission.

And then we have the really nice tagline of "provide food with integrity," which translates to healthy foods. No skimping on safety and health considerations. High-quality ingredients, processes, and delivery. All affordably provided so everyone can benefit from it.

Why?

Because people deserve high-quality foods at affordable prices? Or because everyone deserves high-quality foods, period. And being a fast food (and delicious) choice means we can have healthier eating and therefore healthier people.

Why?

Because the current choices for affordable food are either not healthy, not of high quality, or just not very tasty.

Okay, so let's say the mission is to provide food with integrity. How do we measure success? If it's based on how well we fulfill our mission, then our measures would grow out of that purpose.

Chipotle's measures of success won't be centered on stock prices, profit margins, or sales. No, the measures should answer the question: Are we providing food with integrity? Or: How well are we providing high quality food at affordable prices?

The recent (early 2016) claims of E. coli outbreak and battles with the CDC would be critical to their measures of success. Mistakes happen. So it's not a question of whether tainted food (still not seeing actual evidence of it) was used—but how Chipotle dealt with the possibility.

Trader Joe's

The mission of Trader Joe's is to give our customers the best food and beverage values that they can find anywhere and to provide them with the information required to make informed buying decisions.

Does this sound familiar? We've looked at more than one food provider (Whole Foods and Chipotle), and their missions seem very similar. "Best food" and values, or at "affordable prices." Trader Joe's has a twist, though—although when you review it, it isn't really a twist at all. If your true mission is providing quality and healthy foods at affordable prices for everyone, it makes total sense to help the public (the customer), discern whether you are succeeding.

So is Trader Joe's giving its customers the "best food and beverage values that they can find anywhere?" Is that the *why*?

As you should know by now, that's the *what*. The *why* is hidden behind the *what*. We get a glimpse of it when we realize that the second part of the mission is really a critical how.

"…and to provide them with the information required to make informed buying decisions" is not the *why*. It could be a *what* but it looks more like a *how*. If the customers know what healthy is, customers have the ability to make good choices. It allows the customer to not only pick your products and services if they want to be healthy, but to determine whether you are fulfilling your mission.

Of course, providing information to their customers is a big *how* for fulfilling their mission…but it's a great *how*. Unless the mission is actually to educate the public so they can make informed buying decisions.

So why is Trader Joe's giving their customers the best consumables values anywhere? You could say to have good profits. To corner the market. To compete with Whole Foods. That would be a better *why* than the statement. Better in the sense that it's more of a *why* than the first clause. Not better in finding out the underlying *why*.

We've spent a decent amount of time explaining that making money is a necessity. It's a big *what*, a serious *how*, to staying in business. If you want to spread your message and expand your *why* to a larger audience, you have to be profitable. You have to not only keep the doors open, you have to do financially well.

But that's not Trader Joe's underlying *why*. How do I know? The second clause gives us a good clue.

Why, if the purpose is to make money, do we care about informing our customers so they're better educated and can make better buying choices? If all we wanted was our customers' money, we wouldn't care about educating them.

Making the best buying decisions doesn't necessarily mean that we are the best choice every time.

No, there's a hidden mission here. And that hidden mission first has to be uncovered so we can actually measure success.

BALLOTOPEDIA

I have to start this interview with a confession. I love this company.

Last year, one of the leaders contacted me and asked if I'd be willing to work with them to create metrics for their organization. We met via web conference multiple times, and each time I was encouraged by their forward-thinking and their altruistic mission.

According to their website, "Ballotpedia, the Encyclopedia of American Politics, contains over one quarter of a million encyclopedic articles on local, state, and federal politics and public policy. Our nonpartisan, nonprofit organization has compiled this information over the last 10 years." And: "Ballotpedia is the online encyclopedia of American politics and elections. Our goal is to inform people about politics by providing accurate and objective information about politics at all levels of government. We are firmly committed to neutrality."

I asked Colin, the COO, if he'd be willing to be interviewed. His agreement came without hesitation.

So I asked the question, as I had many times before.

"How would you measure 20 years from today that Ballotpedia was a success?"

"That question was what actually led me to your book [Metrics: How to Improve Key Business Results]! And I believe after working with you, speaking with you, that I now have a better handle on that.

"We [the leadership of Ballotpedia] talk about it a lot—are citizens being better informed about the political process and is that a good enough reason for us to exist? Even if there are no changes in policies or how politics is conducted, or what politicians do…are we a better society if people are just better informed?

"Or should our success be based on changes or improvements? Should we measure success by civic participation, voter turnout, reducing incumbent entrenchment— eliminating unchallenged elected offices?

"Incumbents can make a career out of the office for as long as they want because there is no healthy challenge to their position.

"Should we measure success by the level of civic engagement in the process? We continue to discuss this as a leadership team—we wonder if we need a new mission statement. Currently, Ballotpedia is simply 'the Encyclopedia of American Politics.' That implies that real-world changes like increased voter turnout is beyond our mission. Is it enough that people know more stuff? Is how they use that knowledge beyond us?

"I, personally, don't think it is beyond us. I think we may be moving toward the direction of deliberately encouraging more participation in the political process. Ballotpedia is absolutely committed to neutrality when it comes to electoral outcomes and policy

changes, but not when it comes to civic participation. We definitely encourage people to read our pages and then go use that information to change the world.

"Success has to be based on our mission. If we're measuring success by something other than our mission, then we are either measuring the wrong things, or we have the wrong mission."

I smiled pretty wide at this time. I was glad that we weren't doing a web conference—I was sure I looked like a kid on Christmas morning. I was very, very happy.

"We're making deliberate efforts to make things we want to see happen, happen. We want to see fewer uncontested local elections. With our larger number of email subscribers after the 2016 election, we will be emailing them about filing deadlines for local offices to encourage people to run for office. There are city council elections, school board elections, and other local positions that are up for election somewhere in the country in every single month of the four-year cycle. We're also going to email people on election dates to remind them to vote. Many people don't even know these elections are happening until after the fact. I myself forgot to vote in Wisconsin's school board primary last February. We're telling people about these elections to encourage participation in the political process."

Awesome. Really.

Although Colin definitely "got it," I wasn't sure if he had defined his mission correctly. "Colin, you said Ballotpedia is the encyclopedia of American politics, but is that your mission or is that how you fulfill your mission?"

"This is exactly what we've been discussing as a leadership team. Is being the online encyclopedia of American politics our mission or how we fulfill our mission? Is building the encyclopedia the how or the why? We don't know yet. We're still discussing it.

We're deciding if, philosophically, we believe it's enough to provide information or if it's the means to an end. It will always be part of our mission, even if we decide that the end goal is to improve civic participation. We believe the way to do this is through being the encyclopedic, comprehensive, and non-biased provider of information. This includes things like providing a Ballotpedia.org profile of every elected official in the country. There are over 18,000 school districts, 19,000 municipalities, 5,000 counties, and an unknown number of special districts with elected officials, and we want to write about them. It comes out to about 525,000 incumbents—and all of their primary and general election challengers—that we want to profile."

"So, like Mohandas Gandhi, your *how* is essential to your *why*. His mission was to free India from British rule, but there was only one way he'd do it. His *how* was critical to his success. Gandhi believed in nonviolent civil disobedience. This was his means for bringing about his mission/vision. Like Gandhi, Ballotpedia has at its core a *how*: to educate the public with a comprehensive non-biased sharing of information and knowledge."

"We don't have a vision around an engaged public, yet."

"Perhaps your mission is to inform and educate the public. And providing the encyclopedia is your *how*."

"*That's possible.*"

"And your vision is to have a public fully engaged in the political process."

"*That could be. We discuss how would we know if 'our job was done.' What would the world look like on the day when Ballotpedia's job is done and we can close up shop? We don't know the answer. Another way to look at it is, if a competitor came along and we could look at them and realize that there was no longer a need for us. If they've done everything we thought we should—what would that look like? What would they be doing?*

"*So the question becomes, are we done if we have a fully informed public, or do we still have more to do? Are we done only when that information bears fruit and we have a fully engaged public?*"

Colin and I spoke for a while longer. One of the reasons I asked Colin for the interview was that I knew his leadership team was doing a great job of working on their mission and vision. I have total faith that they'll find their way. They have a mission—they just have to finish clarifying it, for themselves and others. I made some educated guesses to help, but I can't define their mission. Only they can.

The thing about Ballotpedia, and other young companies, is that they have a great opportunity. Their mission many times is to achieve a vision. Why do they exist? To achieve a world-changing vision.

When an organization has a purpose of changing the world (for the better), it has the potential to achieve great things. I fully believe Ballotpedia is destined to achieve great things. But achieving great things isn't success. Success will only be theirs if they fulfill their mission. If fulfilling that mission means achieving a world-changing vision—even better!

If we're measuring success by something other than our mission, then we are either measuring the wrong things, or we have the wrong mission.

Summary

I tried to share with you some examples of good mission statements. The reason for this was to give you a basis for measuring success. By far, most of the mission statements I've encountered over the last 25 and more years are woefully lacking in clarity and inspiration. They don't provide direction or purpose. They lack focus.

That doesn't mean they *can't* provide direction or focus, just that most don't.

The reason for these failings is simple. The mission statements these organizations create are more an exercise in literary exposition than a tool for providing guidance. Too often, the statements are long drawn-out affairs without clarity. They try to be all things to all people. They try to provide an explanation of what the organization does and how they do it. If lucky, the mission statement will include the *why* somewhere in it.

But it doesn't have to be this way. There are good mission statements (hopefully I've shared enough to convince you of that). And you can make a good mission statement.

Actually, I suggest you don't call it a *statement*. I have fought against the embossed, engraved, chiseled statement. I have recommended that you do not hang statements over the entryway. Don't put it on your business cards. Instead, make it simple, clear, and short. Make it easy to understand. Don't make it a "statement" that you have to wordsmith. Make it something each and every member of your organization does not memorize, but instead can interpret and express with earnest passion for its fulfillment.

Each employee—from the CEO to the cleaning staff—should be able to express the mission of the organization in their own words. This is crucial. An organization, from top to bottom, should not only know the mission but believe in it. That's why it's not good enough to have everyone memorize a "statement." Instead, everyone needs to be able to share the mission in their own way, in their own words. They have to own the mission.

The best documented missions you'll find clearly express the organization's purpose. The passion should be evident. Passion is the key to success.

Why Should You Share Your Success Metrics?

At work my boss has a saying: *We have to drink our own champagne.* I'm used to it being *We have to eat our own cooking.* The concept is simple—we have to go against the parental adage of *Do as I say, not as I do.* If I want others to follow my advice, I have to follow it myself.

And that makes total sense to me.

So I'm starting with the *why* rather than the *what* or the *how*.

Why should you share your Success Metrics? I can tell you that you will run into a lot of resistance—internally and externally—to sharing your Measures of Success. So let's start with why you should.

Yup, you have to go against all those who will want you to hide and horde your metrics (including that inner voice in your head).

© Martin Klubeck 2017
M. Klubeck, *Success Metrics*, DOI 10.1007/978-1-4842-2586-8_10

Before you share the results, you should take into account why you're sharing them. There are three basic reasons why we share metrics:

- To gain support

- To improve something

- To get feedback on our progress

In the case of gaining support, we have to consider what we need support for. A simplistic answer is that we want support for achieving our vision or fulfilling our mission. But it goes farther down the chain of actions.

We need collaborators, supporters, and doers. Almost all missions and visions need resources, and those resources are normally purchased, so we end up focusing on fundraising. Even for-profit organizations focus on making more money so they can do the things they want. But the money is a *how*. We need to raise money to obtain the resources we need. The resources are another level of *how*. We need the resources to allow us to get certain things done.

And those things we want to get done are also *hows*. So, fundraising is way down the chain of things we need to do. Even so, we end up focusing on these things instead of the *why*.

That said, we still need them, and we need help in obtaining them.

A good way to obtain support is to share your Measures of Success, because they provide insights to your efforts. By compiling the data into measures, and measures into information, and finally information into a metric, you can tell a complete story.

The best way to obtain support is to share a complete story of how you're progressing toward your *why*. The bigger the support, the bigger the story. And in the case of obtaining the near impossible (your vision), you'll need the largest levels of support necessary.

Think of it this way. You start out by sharing what it is you're trying to achieve…and not just the biggest *what*, but you'll focus on (and lead with) the *why* behind it. The passion you use when you share your mission and vision is contagious. It builds excitement in those who hear it. They want to become involved, to help you. They want to support you.

But that's just the desire. In most change models, we work along a contin-uum—from an awareness of the need for change to the reinforcement for that change. And be assured, for you to fulfill your mission and achieve your vision will require a massive change.

When you share your *why*—you create a passionate awareness of the reason for your efforts. This awareness is a great start—it enables you to create a team of collaborators. But it's not enough. You need to create a desire for the change. You need to inspire this desire in those you need to participate. After you create a desire for the change, you need to create momentum and motion. This step is a little farther along the continuum of change.

You not only want your audience to desire the change, you want them to desire it so much that they are willing to work toward it. They have to want to participate. They have to want to give of themselves, of their resources and time. They not only have to believe in your *why* and your *what*, but they have to believe that it can happen if all of the stars align properly.

And the way you help people believe—the way you give them faith in your dream—are your Measures of Success.

This is one of the reasons we don't share the lowest level measures, the ones we sometimes confuse with success. Imagine if all we shared was how much monies we raised? If our vision is to cure cancer once and for all—how do we pull the world together to achieve this dream? There are more fundraising events going on around the world than you can count. We encourage people to give by telling them stories about those who have fallen to cancer and those who have conquered it. We give them passion and hope. But we haven't achieved the vision yet. Money does not cure cancer.

Think about inventions that have solved the biggest problems. They didn't require immense amounts of money. Remember the Wright brothers? How about Marie Curie? Or Jonas Salk? Mother Theresa, Nelson Mandela, Martin Luther King, Jr., and Mahatma Gandhi all were successful visionaries who were *not* famous for fundraising. Their visions were not predicated on a large amount of money.

Even so, if you want to raise funds—significant funds to help make your vision a reality or to fulfill your purpose—the best way to do that is to share your Measures of Success with potential supporters.

To get more volunteers and to make those volunteers more engaged, share your Measures of Success.

Your mission and vision are your best tools for making your dreams come true. Sharing your Measures of Success is the best way to seal the deal. Close out the sale with your metrics.

Another excellent use of your Measures of Success is to keep all of your stakeholders aware of your progress. Your supporters will want to participate through volunteering or giving funds because they believe in your cause.

But even your fringe supporters will want to chip in if you show them your progress. Everyone likes to back a winner—and by showing your progress, your stakeholders can see that you're continuously moving forward.

Yes, that means not sharing with them the amount of money you've raised. At least not as your main presentation. No, you'll want to share the progress toward the mission and vision. And after that, progress toward your long-range goals (the biggest rocks). Then you can share the subgoals and objectives. Only after that would you share how well you're doing at the task level.

It allows all of your stakeholders to stay in the loop and to gain a level of confidence that the impossible is becoming more and more possible.

Besides motion, we want to maintain momentum over a long period of time. Remember, a vision is a very long-term goal. So we need a way of maintaining engagement for more than one generation of believers.

OUT OF THE LOOP

Each year at a university the employees ran a massive fundraising campaign for cancer research. Year after year they increased their goals (how much they tried to raise), and year after year they exceeded them.

But that's all they heard about. It helped…but it was way too low a level. Telling them that they raised more than they did the year before wasn't a good enough motivator. The amount of effort eventually was more than the university could afford.

Oh, stories of survivors were shared at the big closing event, bringing appropriate amounts of tears and cheers to the event. And at the end they all celebrated the amounts they raised for such a good cause.

But they didn't tie it back to the goals above the fundraising—at least not enough. And the Measures of Success for those parent goals were never shared. They didn't focus on the parent goals. They didn't highlight them. And they didn't share the metrics that would tell them about the true levels of success.

To this day they don't know if their efforts positively affected the actual goals—the things the money was being raised for. They don't know if the monies they raised moved the needle toward success at all.

And I fully believe that was a grievous mistake.

Not sharing the Measures of Success with the stakeholders is a missed opportunity.

Who should you share your measures of success with? Everyone.

It will sway some enemies to your camp. At worst it will annoy the rest.

It will motivate new stakeholders to join your cause.

It will encourage more supporters to join in.

It will give confidence and resolve to your leaders.

It will make your workers and volunteers proud.

Strategic Planning: Alignment and Comprehensiveness

Strategic planning has gotten a bad rap lately. And I understand why. Too often an organization's strategic plan becomes dust-covered shelfware. They aren't actually strategic in nature, or they aren't really a plan. No wonder people have so little faith in strategic planning.

Most people's experience with strategic plans is that they are a waste of time, effort, and money—especially since they normally hire a high-priced consultant to help them create their plan.

This is in large part due to poor plans and incompetent consultants.

A strategic plan should be made up of long-range (ten or more years out) goals in support of a larger, overarching vision. And those long-range goals should be supported by mid-to-short-range goals. I'm okay with a plan stopping there. You can take the very short-range objectives and tasks and put them in a tactical or operational plan.

Strategic Plans Have to Include Long-Range Goals

By far, most plans don't include a vision or long-range goals! Most are at best a collection of short-range goals—usually no farther out than 18 months. There has been a lot of material written on the concept of SMART goals. This is supposed to combat the lack of "well-written goals." But even when you write the goals well, if they're short range, they're not *strategic*.

So, the first error is that the strategic plan is not actually strategic. The goals are usually not long range.

Strategic Plans Have to Have Aligned Goals

The second common error is that the goals are not aligned to the vision. The goals are a smorgasbord of things people want to get done. Rather than worry about alignment to the vision, the writers of the plan try to make sure that everyone is happy. Every department leader, every participant, gets to stick one or more goals into the plan.

This is a ridiculous and poor attempt at gaining buy-in for the plan by letting everyone put a goal or two into it. There is no regard for the logic of the goals—no alignment from one to another.

A good strategic plan (actually, any plan that is truly strategic) is made up of aligned tasks, objectives, short-range, mid-range, and long-range goals, and finally the vision. One builds to another. Your tasks should be aligned clearly to objectives. Objectives should be aligned to short-range goals. Every short-range goal should be aligned to a mid- or long-range goal. And the mid- and long-range goals have to align to the vision.

This assures that you're not accomplishing goals that don't help move the organization toward the vision.

Yes, you can do things—tasks and objectives that don't support the vision. Usually these are necessary to fulfill your mission or to "keep the lights on and the doors open." But these are *not* included in your strategic plan!

A Strategic Plan Is Comprehensive

The third mistake I see frequently is a lack of comprehensiveness. Even if the goals are all clearly aligned, you have to ask yourself whether they are comprehensive. This means that when you look at all the tasks, objectives, and goals together, you should have a high level of confidence that you'll actually achieve the vision.

I'm looking for at least a **95** percent confidence level that you will achieve the vision if you succeed at achieving all the goals below the vision.

You can check comprehensiveness at every stage. Take a look at your task list (possibly in your tactical plan). If you complete every task as well as you want, as fast as you want, will you achieve the objective they lead to?

Here's an easy example: You have a high school band that wants to participate in a regional contest. This is a short-range goal (the contest is in six months). If one of your objectives is to raise $1,000 in the next four months to pay travel fees, we may have tasks like the following:

1. Have a fundraising car wash.

2. Solicit donations from local businesses.

3. Ask the school district to give matching funds for whatever you raise.

To be comprehensive, you will need to have a high level of confidence that if you do each of the tasks, you will succeed at the objective. So, if you have the car wash, solicit funds, and get matching funds—do you believe you will raise the $1,000 by your deadline? If you're not confident, you'll need to add some tasks (and you can remove tasks if you think they won't be as productive). You may also try to accomplish these even faster (in two months?) so that if you fail to raise the target amount, you can try other things.

Comprehensiveness is not a guarantee. It's a guess. That's why you want to have at least a 95 percent confidence that you will succeed.

Bi-Directional Strategic Planning

When you're filling out the plan, you will need to identify gaps in your plan and then fill them. If you have goals that aren't clearly aligned to the vision, you will need to identify the missing goals. If the goals you have identified aren't comprehensive, you will need to identify what is missing. The plan should lead you, with a high level of confidence, from where you are today to where you want to be in the future.

From your current state to the vision.

When you are trying to fill in the missing puzzle pieces, you can work from the bottom up and from the top down.

Bottom Up

In our scenario of the band fundraising for a competition, we can start at the bottom—raising $1,000 for travel expenses. We would see if raising that money aligns to a goal above it.

- Mid-range goal: Participate in at least four competitions per year.

- Short-range goal: Participate in the upcoming regional band competition.

- Objective: Raise $1,000 to cover travel expenses.

Does the objective support something above it? Yes, it does.

Notice that each "parent" goal should answer the question *why?* Why were we raising $1,000? To pay for travel expenses, so we could attend the regional competition. Why were we participating in the regional competition? Because we want to participate in at least four competitions a year.

If you don't have a parent goal for the mid-range goal, you'll have to ask the magic one-word question: *why?*

Why do we want to participate in four competitions each year?

If it's not already documented, we will be identifying a missing goal. Let's say the reason is to qualify for national competition. Great! Yup, you guessed it... we'll have to ask "why" again.

We want to qualify for nationals because eventually we want to win nationals.

Do you think that's a valid vision? Nope. It might be a good long-range goal, though. The *why* for winning nationals may be that we want to be one of the best band programs in the U.S. And that should even have a *why* behind it.

But let's stop there for the moment and take a look at what we have for goals and subgoals (Table 10-1).

Table 10-1. Goals and Subgoals

Long-range goal	Be one of the best band programs in the U.S.
Long-range subgoal	Win the national "best band" competition
Mid-range goal	Qualify for nationals
Mid-range subgoal	Participate in four competitions each year
Short-range goal	Participate in the upcoming regional band competition
Objective	Raise funds to cover travel expenses ($1,000)
Tasks	Hold a car wash, solicit businesses, to provide sponsorship, get the school district to provide matching funds

In Table 10-1, all of these are aligned. Alignment is easy when you work from one to another. They are obviously not comprehensive, though. Even if you have a high level of confidence that the three tasks you identified will lead to raising the needed funds to cover your travel expenses, there must be other things you'll need to do to participate in the upcoming regional competition. So, even from the objective to short-range goal your plan is not comprehensive.

You are missing things like getting permission slips, gaining support from the school board, arranging for travel (bus and driver), and ensuring you have all the equipment and band members you need.

The short-range goal of participating in the regional competition doesn't accomplish the mid-range subgoal of competing four times a year. You'll need to plan to participate in at least three more competitions.

We've not covered anything about making your band one of the best in the nation—yet. When we look at the mid-range goal of qualifying for nationals, we should notice that we're missing a lot of goals under it that will make us good enough to qualify! So, now that we worked from the bottom up, we can change directions and work from the top down.

Top Down

Of course, you can work from the very top (vision) down, but you can also work downward from any level, just as you can work upward from any point (not just the task level). If we look at "Qualify for nationals" and work down, we need to identify the *whats* and high-level *hows* for accomplishing the goal. We'll come up with things like these: practice N times a week, buy new uniforms, add subject matter experts to our coaching staff, and study the best programs. We would lay these out in our plan and see if we think those would be enough.

You can, of course, work your way farther down. How will we "study the best programs"?

1. Identify the best programs.
2. Reach out to the best programs.
3. Arrange visits to the best programs.
4. Attend clinics and camps put on by these programs.

And if we're a high school band, we might add objectives and goals around learning from the best college bands. And we will hopefully also add some creative and innovative ideas for improving.

We don't stop fleshing out the plan until we have a fully aligned and fully comprehensive plan. Remember, you don't have to go down to the objective or task levels. You can leave these *hows* up to your subordinates. And these can be in a tactical or operational plan.

You may be wondering how having a good strategic plan helps with measuring success.

Shame on you—I thought you were paying attention.

Measures of Success in Your Strategic Plan

So now we have a valid mission, vision, and even a good strategic plan.

What we're trying to figure out is how to measure success. As I've said throughout the book, the only way to measure true, overall success is by measuring how well you are fulfilling your mission and achieving your vision.

A good strategic plan is built from your vision. So, if you measure how well you are achieving your vision, you will be measuring success, and you'll also be measuring how well you are carrying out your strategic plan.

At each level of goal within your strategic plan, you can measure progress to the overall vision. If you wrote measurable goals, you will easily measure attainment of those goals. So, that part's actually very easy. The difficulty occurs when we stop short. Let's continue with our band example.

Let's say we measure our completion of our tasks (lowest level).

1. We held our carwash! And we actually had a great turn-out of volunteers and donors who brought us their dirty cars to wash.

2. We solicited more than 100 businesses and succeeded at getting 63 of them to sponsor our band.

3. We were not as successful in getting matching funds from the school district. They didn't have the funds to do this. Instead they offered to buy us new uniforms and provide the bus for our trip.

The bottom line turned out to be: We raised $879.56. So, we didn't achieve the $1,000. If we stopped there with that measure, we would determine that we were unsuccessful. But if we climbed the next rung on the ladder and remembered why we were raising the funds, instead of simply measuring the funds, we'd be measuring the parent goal also. And we'd realize that the parent goal's attainment was more important because the *only* reason we were raising the money was to attain the parent goal.

So, when we look at the parent goal of covering the travel expenses, we find the following:

- Because the school district will donate the bus, we only need $400 for the bus driver and $200 for gas. So, we actually have over $250 in surplus we can put toward the next competition.

- We also got new uniforms, which had nothing to do with getting to this particular goal but does help us with a different higher-level goal.

We can't measure any of these goals (objectives or tasks) in isolation. That would be extremely misleading. Even if we had raised more than the $1,000, if it turned out that gas prices went up, the bus needed repair, and we forgot to estimate lodging costs—we could fail at attending the competition. Although we succeeded at the objective, we would have failed at the goal.

And the *goals* are what we're striving for…but only because they hopefully will lead to their parent goals, which will lead to the vision.

So don't get bogged down in the lower-level tasks or the measures at these levels. Stay above the noise and work with the long-range goals. Build your Measures of Success at the top level and work down. Evaluate every effort against the parent goal.

Don't celebrate raising $1,000, and don't lament falling short of a target. Instead, check the results against the parent goal: Can we attend the competition? If yes, celebrate. But don't celebrate too much because that wasn't the underlying *why*. Celebrating small wins is great—if you don't forget that they're only small milestones on the journey to your vision.

Summary

Why?

Why in the world do you have to share your measures with others? It's your data. It can make you look bad. It can let others see how badly you're progressing to plan, how you're failing to fulfill your mission, and how poorly you're doing at achieving your vision.

Yup. That's true. But it won't be that way. I have total confidence that it will instead show how well you're progressing to plan, how you're doing a great job of fulfilling your mission, and how you're making great strides to achieving your vision.

Why am I so positive that your glass will be half full vs. half empty?

Because you are embarking on this journey. You have read through this book to this point and believe in your mission and vision. You understand that you can't do it alone. You understand that there's something bigger than your resume at stake here. You are aware.

And that awareness leads to desire. A desire to succeed.

And that desire will lead to passion. And that passion will lead to success.

So, I'm not worried that your Measures of Success will show that you have a lot of room for improvement. If they do, it just means you're like everyone else. But I know your measures will show that you are moving toward success. They will show that you are on the right path—that you know your destination.

Just think of your favorite sports team. If they hide their record, does it help? If they share their record and remind you that they too want to succeed and achieve great things, you won't mind that they have a long trip ahead of them. We all do.

And that's not just the first step in the battle—it's the most important step.

Who to Share Your Success Metrics with (and How)

There are three reasons we share metrics: to gain support, gather insights for improvement, or provide feedback on our progress. In each case, you may want to find a way to share your measures (and your success) with others. Organizations especially benefit from sharing their success.

Success begets more success, especially for organizations. By sharing an organization's success with its stakeholders, the organization tends to attract more supporters, shareholders, and employees. Apple, Google, and Whole Foods are great examples.

Their success makes people want to be involved with them. When they hire, they get the "best" in their respective fields because the best want to work with and for them.

© Martin Klubeck 2017
M. Klubeck, *Success Metrics*, DOI 10.1007/978-1-4842-2586-8_11

When an organization shares its success, it needs to take into account who exactly it's sharing it with. Although the measures are the same (how well the organization fulfills its purpose and how well it is moving to achieving the vision), there are options around how to share those measures.

Shareholders

Shareholders are an interesting group. You would think that shareholders wouldn't care about how well the organization is fulfilling their mission (or working toward achieving their vision). Shareholders only care about their stock value, right? Shareholders have invested their money in the company with an expected return. The more the better, right? Why would a shareholder care about the organization's mission and vision? All they care about is the bottom line, right?

RON, THE FORMER CEO

I recently had a conversation with a former CEO of a global financial business solution company, a member of the financial industry, about how he defined success for his organization. This is a company with shareholders, but they also have a customer base that relies on them to help their investments grow. This company's focus, processes, and business model are centered squarely on making money.

So I was not surprised that Ron (yup, another Ron) had profitability as one of his Measures of Success. What *was* a surprise was that he didn't see this as the key measure, or the most important measure. He listed it at an equal level with his other four measures: client satisfaction, employee engagement, industry influence, and community acceptance. So, if they are all equal, only 25 percent of the input toward measuring success had to do with how much money the organization made. I enjoyed Ron's determination—he had a hard time finding his way past the importance of profit. He reminded me more than once that if the company failed to make a profit, it would literally close its doors. And when he spoke about the employee engagement and client satisfaction, he couldn't help but point out that these factors would logically help improve the company's financial position. Engaged workers would lead to more profit. Satisfied clients would lead to more clients and more profit.

Ron also connected *community acceptance* and *being a strong, positive example for the financial industry* back to profitability by stating that both helped employee engagement and therefore profitability. I thought that this, though logical, was less directly correlated. Community acceptance and being a strong, positive example for the financial industry seemed to me to be more altruistic and less bottom-line driven.

After the interview I told Ron my theory behind measuring success—that it was based on how well you fulfill your mission or achieve your vision. His demeanor changed. He became more engaged. He offered a more succinct and complete mission: *To improve our customers' lives through investing.*

If his company was highly profitable, was widely accepted by the community, had high client satisfaction, contributed to the industry, and had impressive employee engagement—but failed to improve the lives of their customers—they wouldn't be successful. So, although the measures Ron had used were good ones, they weren't what the organization really needed.

By the end, Ron admitted that the things they measured were the things that were easy to measure. Even the five good measures he used were easier to measure than determining whether their customers' lives had improved—especially based on what his company had done for them.

Back to sharing with shareholders.

The point is, it's not enough to show how much money the shareholder made the last year. And shareholders should want to know more than the return on the investment. They should want to have a high level of confidence that the organization will continue to provide a return on their investments. Otherwise, the shareholders may just move their stock investments to another organization. So how do you show the likelihood of continued or even increased returns?

Past performance is not an indicator of future results.

What can you use to show that the organization will do as well or better next year? And the year after that?

Measures of Success will do this for you.

If Ron's organization fulfills its mission, it's highly likely that the other measures Ron was using will reflect that success. If you fulfill your mission, your workforce will be engaged and have a high level of self-worth. If you fulfill your mission, your clients will have higher levels of satisfaction, and you will have better relationships with the surrounding communities. If you fulfill your mission, you will have a positive influence within the industry. All of this will logically lead to higher profits.

And the organization will attract more shareholders—not just because the profits will be good, but because people will want to be a part of the organization. People will want to join your staff. More people will want to be your clients. And people will actually want to move into your neighborhood!

I'm not telling you to leave out the data on the returns the shareholders have received over the last year or two. I *am* telling you that you should definitely share how well the organization is doing with meeting its mission and vision.

It will pay dividends!

Note   All puns used in this work are intentional.

Board of Trustees

This one always shocks me. If anyone involved in an organization should want to see how well the organization is fulfilling its mission and achieving its vision, the board of trustees should be that group.

As a board member and later the president of a board, I was fascinated by the lack of engagement for most of the board! I couldn't figure out why people volunteered (or accepted invitations) to be on a board if they didn't passionately believe in the organization's mission and vision.

And if they were passionate apostles of the organization's mission and vision, they couldn't help but be engaged.

So, the only thing I could surmise was that they must not have believed in the purpose of the organization. But I was only partially correct. It wasn't just that they didn't believe—they were blissfully unaware of the organization's mission and vision.

And I guess this shouldn't be surprising, because most of the staff and even the executive director are often unaware of what the underlying reasons for the organization are.

As the top leadership (it hires and fires the CEO, president, or executive director, after all), the board has to be more than aware of the mission and vision. The board has to *own* the cause. The board has to be the "keeper of the faith." The only way the organization can succeed in its quest is to leverage the connections and contacts of the board.

How should you share your Measures of Success with the board? Frequently! These are the measures the board should be reviewing each meeting. They should be the first thing they look at and should be central to their agenda. This should be the criteria used to hire and fire. Raises and bonuses should be based on how well the organization is progressing toward success.

You don't wait for the annual report to share these measures with the board.

And the board should in turn use these measures to promote the organization's cause to others. This is the best tool for creating new collaborators and partners. It's how you get funding. It's how you market the organization to the customer base.

The Measures of Success should be provided in a dashboard—preferably online, so all stakeholders can see them. But they *have* to be reviewed on a regular basis by the top leadership. These measures are how they know how well the organization is doing, how well the director is doing, and how well the board itself is functioning. Why? Because the Measures of Success we have been discussing are the only evidence that the organization is truly successful.

If you are not fulfilling your mission, you are not succeeding.

Did that come across as optional? It shouldn't have. Sharing your measures of success with your leadership is mandatory. Every board meeting should start with a review of how well your organization is fulfilling its mission. There's nothing more important for the board to examine.

Oh, there may be regulatory things (laws, policies, and procedures) that require the board to look at financial records, fiduciary conduct, and inclusive and discriminatory issues. The board may be directed to carry out many oversight functions. And that's all well and good. I'd love for every board to meet, and better yet exceed, those expectations.

But if that's all the board does, it's a poor excuse for a leadership function.

Leadership has to make fulfilling the mission job one! Job two for the board should be to ensure that the mission is being fulfilled while adhering to the values of the organization. What good is it to achieve greatness while losing your family, friends, or self-respect? Winning is definitely not everything (nor is it the only thing). And the third most important thing for the board to do should be to ensure that the organization is working effectively and efficiently toward achieving its vision for a better tomorrow.

That's it. The rest is housekeeping—oversight and overhead.

Fulfill the mission and achieve the vision while living by the values of the organization.

Employees

By the way, sharing your Measures of Success with those who report to you is equally important. And yes, that's mandatory too.

First came shock that the top leadership can function without regularly receiving updates on their mission and vision. Then came bewilderment over the lack of communication with employees. It's as if leadership wants to keep the employees in the dark about…everything. Most leaders who actually have measures fail to share those measures with the staff.

It's as if the leadership believes the measures are privileged information—only for those with a big enough business card. I've heard a ton of excuses, but the most honest one is the argument that the data "makes us look bad." It's why leadership doesn't want to share the measures with anyone!

Keeping the results of the Measures of Success from employees is ridiculous.

The employees are in the best position to validate or invalidate your Measures of Success. They have unique relationships with vendors, suppliers, and customers. They are involved where the "rubber meets the road" and have great insights to how well the organization is fulfilling the mission or achieving the vision.

Though leadership has a lot of power to effect the organization's progress, the staff are the ones who implement the things leadership sponsors.

Employees know more than they are given credit for. They have more insight into how well the organization is doing than leadership realizes.

The number one lament of leaders is that they want an engaged workforce— but they don't give that workforce any power to make decisions or change the organization. They don't share the Measures of Success with those workers. It's hard to be engaged in an activity that you are not included in. If you want an engaged workforce, you have to allow them to be engaged. You have to share the information they need to fully participate.

This is why the Measures of Success are so valuable to the organization. And their value is only realized if shared with everyone. These measures are not an indicator of any individual's performance. They are measures of the correctness of the path the organization has chosen. These are indicators of how well the organization is doing today and how well it will do tomorrow.

The employees need to have this information in front of them. This is the best reminder of the *why* behind the *what*. It gives meaning to the work they do, day in and day out. Without it, the work becomes drudgery. Without clarity around the *why* behind the work—it becomes a chore. It becomes something to avoid.

Understanding the *why* is paramount to success and to engaging your workforce. If you truly want an engaged, loyal, dedicated workforce, you have to share more, not less. And the first thing you have to share is how well the organization is doing what it was created to do.

If you want to disengage your workforce—turn them into zombies or disgruntled organizational anarchists—then keep them uninformed. Don't share the purpose behind the work. Don't explain why. When asked, just tell them, "Because I told you to." And if those nosy employees figure out the mission or vision, make sure they don't have a clue about whether you are actually making any progress toward it. Instead, use misdirection to distract them from your Measures of Success. Make them collect data on other things—like how long it takes them to do a task, response time, time to resolve, and the results of customer satisfaction surveys. Focus on these things that only tell them how well they're performing tasks—usually mundane tasks that could be contracted out.

To *really* disengage your workforce, hold them accountable for Measures of Efficiency. Review each month how much time they waste on breaks, how many times they come in late, how often they have to leave for family or health reasons. Show them, by what you measure and share, that what you care about are the things that have nothing to do with the actual success of the organization.

No wonder workers hate metrics programs.

No wonder organizational metrics programs fail to reap any of the promised benefits.

Focus on what's truly important and share the feedback on how well you are doing freely. Be truly transparent. Transparency is a great start—but it's not the end. You have to be sharing the right information. You have to be collecting the right data and building the right Measures of Success.

Customers

Another great thing about using real Measures of Success is that you can share them with everyone. Especially your customers! You don't have loyal customers if you don't share your mission and vision. You may have customers that like your bargains and coupons. Some may promote you to others because of your awesome customer service. But the way you earn truly loyal customers is through belief in your mission and vision.

Whole Foods found this out early in their existence. When they only had one store, it was devastated by a flood. In 1981 Austin, Texas, saw a massive flood that should have ruined Whole Foods in its infancy. They didn't have flood insurance. They had no stock (it was all destroyed or ruined). They had to clean up the water and fix the damage. They had no money to do this, and no money to restock the store. Actually they had $400,000 in losses.

Then the unthinkable happened. The staff came in to help clean up the wreckage. There was no assurance that the store would reopen (with no money, it was more likely that it wouldn't). There was no assurance that the staff would have a job afterwards.

That was impressive, but then *customers* showed up with brooms, mops and shovels. Customers. They volunteered their time and energy. Why in the world would customers take time out of their lives to help a store recover from a flood?

Because they believed in the mission and vision of Whole Foods.

Suppliers restocked the organization on credit. Why? Because they believed in the future of Whole Foods.

And the mission and vision of Whole Foods is not to make money.

General Public

Very few companies, for-profit or nonprofit, share their measures with the public. But there isn't any reason not to. Especially if your measures are Measures of Success. Just the fact that you're trying to achieve something important will be good publicity for you. And if your mission is a good one (hopefully it is!), then all the better to share it with the general public. Most businesses want more customers—either as consumers or shareholders.

Sharing your purpose and vision will only help you attract more of both. And sharing how well you're doing with fulfilling that mission and moving toward that vision will also earn you many brownie points with the public. People like to know the *why* behind the *what*. And sharing your measures of success is a great way to communicate those *whys*.

Imagine if the American Cancer Society shared their true Measures of Success. What if you could go find the information on how well they're doing with eradicating (curing) cancer? Isn't that what their mission is? Isn't their vision to remove cancer from our lives?

Does anything else matter? Does anything else matter as much as this true success? Number of screenings provided? Amount of money raised? Number of specialists, clinics, or hospitals?

The number of survivors gets close—because we can say those are "success stories" in our journey to saving everyone—but to be truly successful, we want no casualties. So having saved some people is a step in the right direction. But we can't claim success at that point, lest we become complacent.

Are we getting closer to a cure? Are we getting closer to eradicating the threat? And shouldn't we as a public be highly vested in the ACS's progress?

How about police departments? Lately they've been maligned for the actions of some who abuse their power and authority. But perhaps that happens because they lose sight of their calling. I have to believe no police officer could commit these wrongful acts if they kept their mission in the front of their eyes. And how could the public attack the police, figuratively and literally, if they remembered the mission of the police force? The mission is well known, in a short catchy phrase: *To protect and serve.*

Let's dig deeper into what that means.

To Protect

To *protect* the people of the town, city, municipality, or state. Protect them from harm—as in the military (based on our constitution)—from enemies, foreign and domestic. And our police forces also protect us from harm brought about by natural disasters. Like firemen, they run toward danger rather than away from it.

To Serve

What does it mean to serve? In the military, we have the core value of *service before self.* Which means we serve *others*—those we have sworn to protect—before we think of ourselves. If this is also true for police, then they have to be great examples of server-soldiers.

Perhaps you don't buy this? Perhaps you're saying that the police you know don't live up to this mission statement. They may protect some, but mistreat others. They may serve a few, but most citizens are not afforded this treatment. I'm not going to argue for or against either position—because I have no idea about your particular situation, police force, or experiences. All I can tell you is what I believe the police mission, their purpose for existence, dictates.

So, with the problems we currently have and the civil unrest around incongruences between actions and mission—wouldn't it be highly beneficial for these public servants to share their Measures of Success? Wouldn't it help if the public could view the evidence about how well the police were protecting and serving the people of their communities?

It would do even more than provide a basis for better communications. It would clearly define to the community and to the police force what was important. Not number of arrests, tickets, or amount of funds raised through penal fines. By providing Measures of Success and focusing on these, everyone involved would know exactly what the mission of the police force is and how well the current employees were doing at fulfilling that mission.

Other Stakeholders

It should be very clear by now that you should share your Measures of Success with everyone who may have even the smallest interest in your mission or vision. That includes any and all stakeholders.

We usually focus on customers (because they buy our products or services), leaders (they pay our salaries and keep us employed), board of trustees, and sometimes other employees. But we forget to include other stakeholders.

There are many others who are effected by our success or failure. We have vendors, suppliers, peers, competition, a surrounding community, and the rest of our industry. These may not be as directly involved in your organization, but they are stakeholders. They have a vested interest in your success.

Your success will affect them—hopefully in a positive way.

If you share your Measures of Success with everyone, than these stakeholders will be included.

But most organizations don't share metrics at all. Sharing entails allowing others to see and access them—even though they didn't ask for them. We reluctantly provide metrics when requested, so it's a truly rare instance when we make our metrics available to others. And not just externally (stakeholders and customers). We rarely share our metrics even internally.

One simple rule I encouraged in my book *Metrics: How to Improve Key Business Results* was that *those who provide the data own the data*. And as the owners of the data, they had to receive the metrics that were derived from their data. You have to close the loop and ensure that those who provide the information get to see the metrics created from them.

An example of inequity would be leadership reviewing metrics on different functions, departments, or topics and not sharing those with their workforce—especially workers who were providing the information.

I know I'm asking most of you to do something that is totally out of the norm.

I'm asking you to share your Measures of Success with, well, everyone.

If you're a wildly successful organization, you might consider it.

But what if your measures of success show that you aren't as successful as you might like?

One of the most common excuses I hear for not sharing metrics is that they don't make the organization look good. The metrics may even make the organization look *bad*.

Even if this is true, you should still do it. Hiding the evidence doesn't mean the crime wasn't committed. If the metrics tell a negative story, they represent an opportunity for growth and improvement. But more importantly, they represent the state of the organization at the moment. We shouldn't hide these metrics from others or from ourselves.

I've seen organizations (at various levels) decide to hide their metrics from even themselves as if by ignoring the indicators things would magically improve.

The idea isn't to collect data, analyze it, compile it to develop indicators—and then only share (or show) them if things look good. If you don't know where you are, it's impossible to plan your journey to where you want to go.

We all should want to reach the place where we are fulfilling our purpose. This is our first destination.

The first trip to fulfilling our purpose is normally not a long trip. Many times we're well on our way—even though we may not have known where we were going. Usually instinct gets us on the right path, going in the right direction.

Sometimes we get sidetracked or end up detouring, but eventually we get back on the path.

Of course, if we know where we're going to start with, we have a much better chance of reaching that destination!

Once we are comfortably on our way or have reached the destination, we can start planning for our next trip. This one is a much farther distance from where we are today. This journey has a destination: our vision. It's a long journey, and it's very likely that we may not reach it. But that shouldn't stop us from trying. We should embark on the journey without reservation.

Such a long and arduous journey is scary. It's not easy to go on the road when we know it will take us such a long time to get to where we want to be.

These two trips define our success. How well we do at reaching these destinations measures our success. How well we plan the journey, how well we travel, and whether we make it to our destination are part of the story.

Abby (Abigail Jillian) Sunderland's failed 2010 attempt to become the youngest person to sail solo around the world provides a level of insight. Some thought her plan was ill conceived, that the timing was poor. That her equipment could have been better.

But was she a success or a failure? If her only goal was fame and fortune—the fortune part can be said to be a failure, although she definitely achieved a level of fame (including a book-signing tour). If the only goal was to be the *youngest* to circumnavigate the world in a sailboat, again she failed. But if her purpose or vision dealt with the adventure—with trying—we may have to judge her level of success differently.

Another adventurous spirit who failed to succeed at a goal was one of my heroes, Amelia Earhart. I love using her quotes in my visionary newsletter:

> *Never interrupt someone doing what you said couldn't be done.*

And:

> *The most effective way to do it, is to do it.*

Amelia Mary Earhart was an American aviation pioneer, author, and symbol of American fortitude. She was the first female pilot to fly solo across the Atlantic Ocean, earning her the U.S. Distinguished Flying Cross. She was a symbol for women in America and abroad. She was a hero in part for her achievements, but mostly because she dared to try.

From the Amelia Earhart official website (www.ameliaearhart.com):

...the world will always remember Amelia Earhart for her courage, vision, and groundbreaking achievements, both in aviation and for women. In a letter to her husband, written in case a dangerous flight proved to be her last, her brave spirit was clear. "Please know I am quite aware of the hazards," she said. "I want to do it because I want to do it. Women must try to do things as men have tried. When they fail, their failure must be but a challenge to others.

She set records and broke others:

- First woman to fly across the Atlantic then did it solo

- Broke women's altitude record

- Wrote two books

- Set two women's speed records and another speed record

- Awarded *National Geographic*'s gold medal

- Awarded the Distinguished Flying Cross

- First woman to fly solo nonstop from coast to coast across the U.S., setting a speed record while doing so

- Broke her own transcontinental speed record

- First person to fly solo from Honolulu to California

- First person to fly solo from Los Angeles to Mexico City

- First person to fly solo nonstop from Mexico City to Newark, New Jersey

- First person to fly from the Red Sea to India

But we can't judge her success on these achievements alone. We have to view them in the context of her calling and her vision. She was called to fly. She was called to be a symbol for woman's rights. She lifted the American spirit—for men and women.

She dreamed big. Very big. Her dreams were big, audacious, hairy, and scary. They definitely brought her enemies. But they changed the world and continue to do so.

Was she a success?

She did not complete her last goal. She died trying.

Was she successful?

Summary

All measures provide benefits. They provide insight to processes, identify potential areas of improvement, and can provide important feedback. All of these benefits require one simple step—the measures have to be shared.

But sharing is one of the hardest things to get leaders to do.

Leaders are reluctant to share their measures—any measures—with anyone. They don't want to share with their competitors, their stakeholders, or their shareholders. I've seen leaders who don't even share their measures with their own employees.

And those are "everyday" measures. There is a reluctance to share performance measures, operational measures, or customer satisfaction measures.

How likely is it that leaders will willingly share their Success Metrics? Yet that's exactly what I'm pushing you to do. Of all your metrics, these require sharing the most. Your Measures of Success will be wasted if you don't share them, far and wide.

Success Metrics only reach their potential—power, benefits, or influence—if you share them.

Don't wait until the twilight of your career or your organization's life.

Sharing your metrics will help you to be accountable for your success. Most people fail to find their purpose in life, and if they do, they rarely measure their fulfillment of it. Sharing your purpose, your vision, and your Measures of Success makes it easier for you to be accountable to yourself.

Share early and often.

Using Success Metrics to Improve

One of the most important uses of metrics is to help your organization improve. To improve, you need to understand how to use your measures. The first, second, and third steps you take after collecting and analyzing your measures are: investigate, investigate, and investigate.

The first step—and the only proper response to metrics (good or bad)—is to investigate. Success Metrics are no different. We don't pull out our metrics and declare success, nor failure. We use them to provide insight into our progress. We use them to see which of our processes and procedures might benefit from a tweak or two. We use them to find our way. They are signs along our path: warning, danger, detour, right way, wrong way, yield, stop, and suggested speeds. None of these normal road signs dictates action—you can still do whatever you want. They do suggest caution (most of them do) or possible tweaks. They provide awareness of a need for different behaviors than what you were doing before you reached them.

Metrics provide an awareness that you may need to change your behaviors before you encounter a problem.

© Martin Klubeck 2017
M. Klubeck, *Success Metrics*, DOI 10.1007/978-1-4842-2586-8_12

What Do You Do with the Results?

The preceding two chapters cover why you should share your results and with whom (*everyone*, in case you're skimming). Now we'll talk about how to use the measures. It may seem too obvious to warrant being written, but I find that, especially when it comes to metrics, you can't take the obvious for granted. People and organizations just don't seem to do the logical, common-sense things that seem so obvious.

We want to measure success for a few reasons:

- To give clear insight to the likelihood of reaching our destination.

- To know whether we need to make course corrections. If we fall off of the path and are heading in the wrong direction, we need to know.

- To know whether and when we have arrived. We want to celebrate when we're successful and to know whether we should try again if we're not.

Are We Likely to Reach Our Destination?

Measures of Success need to provide insight into our progress and clarify whether we're on the right path. We need to have a high level of confidence that the path we're on will help us reach our destination. Some of us also want the path we travel to be the most direct one possible. We want to avoid the two-lane roads, stop signs, and construction zones. We want to travel on the four-lane highways where we can hit the fastest speeds allowed.

Measures of Success should tell us which type of road we're on. They should tell us how fast we're traveling and whether we're on a smooth, open road.

Are you likely to fulfill your mission? Are you likely to achieve your vision?

The good news is this is actually very easy to determine if you've fleshed out your mission and vision. If you've identified the goals necessary to fulfill your mission, your progress measures will be easy:

1. Are you achieving the goals you've identified?

2. Are those goals providing the expected progress to the mission or vision?

And this works throughout the full plan for your journey. If you've planned out each milestone on the journey, you can measure attainment of each. You may reach some of them early—ahead of schedule. Others you may be late for, or decide to forego altogether. This is especially true if you determine that the planned milestone isn't going to actually help you reach your destination.

Here's an example.

Let's say our vision is to provide a shelter for abandoned pets. That's not really a big enough or scary enough vision. It's definitely a lower-level *what* to some larger *why*. So, we'd dig deeper and find the *why*—pets are abandoned at an alarming rate, and these abandoned pets deserve better. The solution to this problem may be to assure that all abandoned pets are rescued within five days of abandonment. This time frame was determined because most abandoned pets have a life expectancy of seven days. By rescuing them within five days, it is projected that we'd save over 90 percent of them (and possibly all of them). What long-range goals do we need to achieve to be successful?

1. Develop a mechanism for identifying abandoned pets within three days of abandonment.

2. Create a process for attaining the pets.

3. Have a temporary refuge for recovered pets.

4. Have a system for finding new homes for the pets.

Changing the world is like trying to change the course of a river. You can use rocks to make this happen. Big rocks are like your long range goals, medium-size rocks are like mid-range goals, and small rocks are your short range goals.

It doesn't matter whether any of these rocks are already in the works or actually accomplished. We're not planning out every step—yet and this is only an example, so don't be surprised if you have ideas for other goals.

We should now be able to take each of these big rocks and break them down. We'll do it for one of them:

1. Have a temporary refuge for recovered pets.

    a. Determine size of needed facility.

    b. Raise monies for facility.

    c. Purchase or rent a facility.

    d. Find volunteers to work the refuge.

    e. Identify veterinarians for on-call duty for the facility.

And of course each of these can be broken down further. When doing the breakdown, we find that we may be missing some of the items we need. We also may find that some of the subgoals actually belong to a different goal (identified or not):

1. Have a temporary refuge for recovered pets.

    a. Determine size of facility.

        i. Research estimated number of pets abandoned daily.

        ii. Research estimated size and type of pets abandoned.

        iii. Identify all types of possible pets.

    b. Raise monies for facility.

        i. Hire a fundraiser.

        ii. Create a fundraising campaign.

        iii. Identify possible funding sources.

        iv. Implement fundraising campaign.

    c. Purchase or rent a facility.

        i. Determine whether an existing facility will satisfy the need.

            1. If yes, find out how much it will cost to rent or buy.

            2. Determine the best direction to go.

        ii. If not, plan how to have a facility built.

            1. Find an architect.

            2. Estimate costs.

    d. Find volunteers to work the refuge.

    e. Identify veterinarians for on-call duty for the facility.

And lo and behold, we're missing some items: determining the location for the facility, equipment and materials needed to house the pets, food and water for the pets, and finally shots and medical care. These all need to fit under a big rock. If there isn't one that they logically fit under, we're missing a bigger goal.

And the beat goes on. This can take a while, and the results should be thoroughly vetted. When you look at the details, the breakdown, you'll find that you have a very effective plan of attack, remembering that you will have to make adjustments along the way. It's rare that you won't need to make changes or modifications to the goals and steps.

But let's get back to measuring and determining whether we're on the right path.

Most times we end up measuring the lower-level goals, objectives, or tasks. In this scenario, we may measure the amount of funds we've raised. Or perhaps the effectiveness of our fundraising campaign. This isn't a problem in and of itself. It becomes an issue when it's the *only* thing we measure because we forget the larger goals. We forget the *why* behind the *what*. We forget why we were doing the lower-level tasks.

Let's say we diligently measure how many funds we raise each month and each year. Let's say we even use one of those neat-looking thermometer displays where we keep moving the marking up higher and higher until we reach the top—our monetary goal.

Then what? We celebrate, right?

But are we there yet? Of course not. Because its part of our plan, we expect that we're moving in the right direction. Let's check and see how much farther we have to go.

Are we likely to reach our destination? We know we needed funding to get from here to there...but we also needed to achieve many other steps along the way. If we squander the funds we raised on vaccinations, paying staff, or creating an awareness campaign (all good things), but fail to actually put the temporary refuge in place, chances are we won't succeed.

How about being sharp enough to actually measure the attainment of the facility? We can still measure the funds—so we know when we've raised enough—but we need to map that to the achievement of the facility. Even then, there's more to do. Even if we measure our progress toward the facility—is that enough?

Unfortunately, we don't measure against the vision. We stop short.

Okay, so we have the facility! Time to celebrate, right? *Yes!* Definitely.

But we're not done.

How many abandoned pets are we rescuing? How many are left behind? Were our estimates correct? Do we have a big enough facility? Is it in the right place? Do we have the equipment and materials we need? Are we moving the big needle?

All measures have to point to the mission and vision. They must measure our progress toward the top goal, the biggest rock, the vision.

Do We Need to Make Course Corrections?

Are we on the right road? Besides the detours life throws our way, we have opportunities to try different paths. Is the path we're currently on the best one for our journey? Should the path be changed?

One example for the nonprofit sector would be looking at our funding stream. Is the current source of our funding the right one for us? Should we be looking for a different source? Are we primarily funded by grants? Should we look at a capital campaign? Should we try to raise enough to create an endowment?

A for-profit organization may look at their product line or service offerings. Are they the right ones? Do they make sense in light of our mission and vision? These are the type of questions any company should ask when presented with new technologies or innovations.

Computer-based technology has been running wild for the last couple of decades. Because of this, things change frequently and quickly. If we're focused on tasks and short-range goals, we won't notice when we need to make a course correction. But if we keep our focus on the destination, the longest-range goal, the vision—we'll have good indicators when things are running off the rails. Because we're measuring where we're headed vs. where we are, we can identify those rough spots on the road.

Are We There Yet?

I don't know why this incessant question, asked by my daughter when she was five, bothered me. I should have gotten used to it. Of course, if I had provided her with a GPS that told her exactly how close we were to our destination and estimated what time we'd arrive, she may not have asked as often.

The same goes for customers of our metrics—but only if they know to ask it. If we're measuring our journey and if we're getting closer to our destination, we should expect to hear this question all the time.

Why don't our leaders ask this question?

My five-year-old asked it because she was impatient, but she was also excited about reaching our destination. Shouldn't our leaders (and the entire organization) be excited about reaching the destination? Granted, it's a longer journey than most five-year-olds are subjected to, but I would still hope that leaders would be impatient to succeed and excited at the prospect of reaching the destination.

So, our metrics should do the same—and if they don't, our stakeholders should be asking over and over again, "Are we there yet?"

Honestly, I'd be overjoyed to have customers emulate my five-year-old! What a great problem to have. Then, when it became annoying, we could provide the GPS equivalent so we don't have to deal with repetitive questions about when we'll finally get to where we're going. I love my GPS. I even use it when I know where I'm going and don't need it to tell me where and when to turn. I like it because it visually provides an estimated time of arrival. My daughter likes to tell me to turn it off. "Don't you know the way home from here?" she'll prod. But I leave it on because I can see clearly how many miles and time is left to the journey.

Your Measures of Success should do the same.

Using measures of performance, like miles per gallon or average speed, do nothing to tell whether you're closer to achieving your goals. The right answer is to use your Measures of Success to check your progress.

Are we there yet?

How to Leverage Your Sharing of Results to Make a Change

One way to allow and encourage others to assist in your journey is to share your Measures of Success. This includes sharing with your workforce, your leadership, suppliers, vendors, and stakeholders.

By sharing your Measures of Success, you inform everyone of the *why* behind the *what*. It lets everyone know where you're going and how well you're doing at getting there. If your vision is a good one, then others will want to help you achieve it.

There are many renditions of the adage *You improve what you measure*. There's *What you measure you get* and *What you measure you can manage*. And I'm sure there are more of the same. But I can assure you that they have the same underlying principle. If you make the effort to collect the data, analyze the measures, and formulate metrics that you share readily—it will get attention.

And that attention is a good thing. Even if your measures show that you're floundering, they will still encourage others to get involved. Like the adage *Any publicity is good publicity*.

What's the best way to leverage your results? Share them.

Yup. It's that simple.

And because your Measures of Success will tell the story of your mission and vision, it will also help others understand what you're all about and what you're trying to accomplish. Of course, they will also show that you are serious about it all.

Measuring the Effects of Your Changes

We love to make tweaks and adjustments. Everyone likes to get their two cents worth. But are the changes we make effective? Are they doing us any good? Are they moving us closer to our destination, or are they just a distraction?

Part of the problem with the way most organizations (and individuals) measure success is that it doesn't really help us have any idea of how well we're doing or how well the changes are working. And because we don't know, we end up making changes for the sake of changing.

These changes become resume builders and opportunities to bolster our annual review. We can test out our pet ideas for improvement without actually knowing whether they provide anything useful.

Measuring a level of efficiency doesn't actually mean the same thing as moving toward success. We overly focus on making mini-improvements—trying to be more efficient and effective. This over-focus allows us to believe our efforts and adjustments are more important than the actual goal we're seeking to achieve.

Think about it. Normally we have goals, subgoals, objectives, and tasks. If we're really lucky (or if we actually plan out our strategy), those efforts will be aligned. If they are aligned, each should build to the other. In this scenario (a good one), we still get distracted by our small wins. We perform a task accurately and think we're done. We can move on to a different area instead of working up toward the next item in the same alignment. We may complete an objective, celebrate, and shut down that path. We fail to stay on track to the top-level goal. We don't end up working toward the vision.

We become too satisfied with the short-range successes, missing the big picture.

If this happens at this level, how much easier is it to go astray if we're implementing little changes to our process and procedures? These efforts aren't directly aligned to our set of goals or our vision. These tweaks and modifications are sidebars to the real story. They're nice anecdotes—not the actual story.

Yet we treat these changes as if they're more important than the goals. No wonder strategic plans languish on shelves gathering dust.

How can you combat this complacency?

It's actually easy: Measure all your changes and all your efforts against your mission and vision.

Efficiencies are nice, but their worth has to be measured against your destination. Are they helping you get to the end of the trip faster? More effectively?

With better, faster, smarter, larger results? Or are they just pretty cool things that don't move the needle?

If they don't move you closer to your desired destination...they aren't so great.

A VISION FOR A TEN-YEAR-OLD

Let's do an analogy. What if the vision for my (now) ten-year-old daughter is to be an Olympian volleyball player in eight years? What steps should we take? How would we measure success? It becomes quickly apparent that the vision should be tweaked—it's too dependent on variables that shouldn't matter. Better would be to have a vision to be an *Olympic-quality* player. And whether she makes the Olympic team becomes an indicator of success rather than the goal.

Please note, this is not the best analogy since the vision I'm using wouldn't pass the tests for a world changing vision. It's really just a long-range goal.

So what steps do we have to take to get her there?

Lots of training and practice. Coaches. Joining teams that get the greatest exposure and competition to push her to be the best she can be.

There are lots of tasks we can do along this journey.

And we have a model—at least a current one (it could change in eight years) for what it takes to be an Olympic volleyball player.

Height helps, but although we can't do much about that, there is room for shorter players with special skill sets. So, to optimize our chances (in case she doesn't reach six feet or taller), we would train her on all the skills involved.

We would also work on her physical abilities, taking into account what's safe at each age. Weight training, jump training, agility drills, and speed conditioning. We'd work on her hand-eye coordination. We could build a serious training program to give her the best chance at realizing her dream.

And along the way we could measure progress.

How have the changes we've implemented affected her chances?

Is she jumping higher? Moving quicker? Does she have more explosive movements?

Does she have better skills? Is her passing efficiency higher?

All of these will be compared to what she has to be able to do to make the Olympic team in the future. We won't celebrate an added inch to her vertical leap without relating that to her overall vertical leap and then comparing that to the requirement for an Olympic player.

You've heard the adage: *Shoot for the stars.* Even if you don't make it, you'll probably make it to the moon, and wouldn't that be a great achievement?

In other words, shoot for *starter on the Olympic volleyball team* and if you don't make it, you'll still be a much better volleyball player for trying. Wouldn't that be a great achievement?

Would it?

Will Smith (of acting fame) says there's no need for a plan B, it only detracts from accomplishing plan A.

In the case of a vision, he is dead on.

Although not reaching your vision isn't failure, it sure isn't success either.

So don't get distracted by small wins and incremental improvements. Measure success against the mission and vision. Build confidence that you are moving the needle.

Repurposing Leadership's Role

What is the job of leadership? *Too lead* is way too simplistic. What does that mean? Traditionally, we find leaders trying to figure out their role, and many times they settle a little shy of where they should be.

Business and organizational leaders try to keep their organizations healthy and make improvements before the end of their tenure. CEOs may be one of the shortest-tenured positions in many companies.

There are exceptions, cases in which the boss, the leader, stays with the same organization for a very long time. And in these cases they get a lot done. But even these leaders find themselves normally focusing on areas they feel are critical to keeping the organization doing well and making incremental (small) improvements.

I especially enjoy working with nonprofits because they are naturals for having a higher purpose and a world-changing vision. But I also find them extremely hard to help sometimes because they aren't led by an individual—they have a board of trustees. This board means that the organization's long-range vision is run by committee.

After 20 years in the military, I have collected a large number of idioms. One of these is *If there is more than one person in charge, no one is in charge.* But this is our government at work. All nonprofits have to have a board of trustees (or board of directors) who are ultimately in charge. The board hires and fires the executive director. The executive director is in charge of the daily operations and has the responsibility of making things happen—making things work.

I have been on our district library's board of directors for over five years now. For the first four years, I was a member, doing what the board president dictated. And what he dictated was to continue running the organization and the board the way they had for the last 20 years and more. The board, like all boards, was required to ensure that the organization was being fiscally responsible—that the monies were being spent in the right ways. We also reviewed and helped define policies as needed. Procedures weren't our concern, as that was the purview of the executive director. Other than those two areas, we only got "involved" if there was a problem—usually a big problem that the executive director needed our input or participation to solve. For example, asking for a new bond or tax levy, or approving how our savings would be used.

During each monthly board meeting we spent the majority of our time reviewing every line of the budget—expenditures and income—even though we had an annual audit, even though our board treasurer reviewed all the books every month.

We then spent what time was left on policy. Occasionally we stayed late to work on any problems or issues.

So how does the role of leadership change when we measure success?

Boards of trustees are a great example. The whole purpose for a board of trustees changes from primarily one of fiduciary accountability to being a fully engaged team of visionaries. Catalysts, connectors, collaborators. Spokespeople. Leaders!

This should be extremely logical and in some ways obvious. If the top leadership of the organization aren't the visionaries for the organization, who will be? The farther down you go in the chain, the more the focus becomes on the day-to-day. It's the same in the military. The soldiers on the front lines aren't thinking about how to end the war, they're focused on taking that hill and keeping their teammates alive.

The four-star generals at the Pentagon plan how to win the war. And those generals aren't telling the guy in the foxhole how to do his job.

The same is true for all organizations. But the smaller the organization, the more likely that the top leaders will confuse their role with the foot soldier's.

In most businesses, the founder had a vision. But as the business grew and became a large corporation with a board of trustees and a CEO, the leaders forgot the vision. They forgot the role of the founder—to provide the direction of the organization.

It's time to repurpose leadership. It's time for leadership to get out of the weeds and do what only they are positioned to do—lead!

It's actually not hard to lead. The hard part is focus and persistence.

You Have to Focus

This can be difficult because leaders think they are responsible for every facet of the organization's functions. In a conceptual sense, they are—but in a practical sense, the people responsible for the front-line work are the front-line workers. The people responsible for leading the front-line workers are their supervisors. And so on and so on. But the clear responsibility of the leadership of an organization is to provide the organization's focus.

Yet to provide this focus, leadership has to know what the mission and vision of the organization are. Leaders have to know why the organization exists.

This is an easy thing for the founder of the organization—who usually knows why they started the organization. But years later, when the leadership is hired in to lead the organization, do these leadership experts learn the *why* behind the *what* before they attempt to put their own stamp on the organization?

This is one of the benefits of growing your leadership from inside the organization. You hope that when you develop from within that the people that end up on top have experienced the real work that makes the organization function, that these internal promotions understand why the organization exists. They are fully versed in the organizational values and principles and are believers in them.

If you hire from outside to lead your organization, many times you get an experienced leader who doesn't know why your organization exists. This same leader may believe that her personal success is defined by how much of a personal stamp she can leave on the organization.

Really?

Do you want the top leader of your organization to be focused on making her mark on your organization? Shouldn't her focus be on the mission and vision of the organization? Should she be helping the organization, your suppliers, your customers, and stakeholders all stay focused on the organization's purpose?

Leadership has to stay focused on the mission and vision.

It's easy to get distracted by the crises of the day or week or month. And guaranteed—there *will* be crises. It's the nature of our world that we are given challenges in our lives. And yes, leadership has to show strength in these times to help the organization through the crisis.

But rather than putting the mission and vision aside at these moments, these are great opportunities to refocus the organization on what's really important. The organizational values and principles will help guide us in the *hows* that we choose—but we have to keep our purpose and dreams in the forefront when we're trying to deal with threats to our existence.

Even the front-line soldier does her job better if she understands the *why* behind the *what*. It's the vision for the future that helps a totally volunteer military do its job.

This is how those who do evil in the world get people to do their bidding. They share a purpose and vision that is compelling. The reason they are evil is that they lie. They use propaganda to distort truths and create a false cause to follow. They manipulate and use people to their own ends.

Of course, there are those who fully believe in their own distortions. And they may be the most dangerous.

Enough gloom and doom.

The point is, everyone in the organization needs to know why they do what they do. Not how their actions help the next person in line or how it helps develop a solid product or service. Everyone needs to understand the bigger *why*—the reason the organization exists.

Everyone needs to understand the organization's vision for the future. They all need to understand the greater cause and the ultimate destination.

And both of these have to be provided by leadership. Leaders have to not only stay focused themselves, they need to ensure the organization as a whole remains focused.

You Have to Stay the Course

Perseverance. Determination. Discipline.

Wow, those are tough for anyone!

Do you exercise regularly? Do you eat healthy? Do you read? Are you a life-long learner?

Do you have bad habits? Are you trying to stop? Are you trying to change?

These things are not easy.

I have a simple goal: inbox zero. And I want to keep it that way. I want every day to reach inbox zero at least once. (Right now, I'd settle for once a week.)

Change at an individual level is hard enough. When we stretch that across an entire organization, it becomes nearly insurmountable.

But the only way to achieve greatness—to be successful—is to persevere. There are numerous quotes by the great achievers throughout history that admonish all of us to persevere.

> *Success is no accident. It is hard work, perseverance, learning, studying, sacrifice, and most of all, love of what you are doing or learning to do.—Pele, soccer great*

Never stop fighting until you arrive at your destined place—that is, the unique you. Have an aim in life, continuously acquire knowledge, work hard, and have perseverance to realize the great life.— A. P. J. Abdul Kalam, former President of India

We must have perseverance and above all confidence in ourselves. We must believe that we are gifted for something and that this thing must be attained.—Marie Curie, pioneering scientist

Great works are performed not by strength but by perseverance.— Samuel Johnson, author

I do not think that there is any other quality so essential to success of any kind as the quality of perseverance. It overcomes almost everything, even nature.—John D. Rockefeller, American oil magnate and philanthropist

A noble purpose inspires sacrifice, stimulates innovation, and encourages perseverance—Gary Hamel, American management expert

The point is that it's a long journey. To successfully reach our destination, we need to stay the course.

Celebrating milestones along the way helps. Measuring progress to the final destination helps even more.

Summary

Now that we know where we're going, we can ensure that our journey is well planned, efficient, and effective. Using Success Metrics we can feel confident that we're on the right path. We can determine whether we are likely to reach our destination. We can also determine with a comfortable level of confidence when we might reach that destination.

Course corrections become possible when we pay attention to the journey. When we forget our destination and ignore the path we're traveling, we can easily become distracted and lose our way. We can spend inordinate amounts of time on the wrong path. If you're adventurous, this may seem like fun—but if you're trying to be successful, it can be detrimental.

Because we're now sharing our Measures of Success, we can leverage that activity to help us make necessary changes. Because we share our progress, any stakeholders can understand why we make changes. And these changes can be measured against our progress to determine whether the hoped-for outcome was realized. It's great to have an open mind and to try new things. Innovation is simply awesome! But change for the sake of change is rarely a good thing. We need a way to tell whether the changes we're making are reaping rewards or not. A great use of Success Metrics is to determine the effects of the changes you make.

When we measure well, we grow. When we grow, we change.

Leadership has some of the greatest potential for change. Leadership's role can be totally repurposed if we focus on our mission and vision. It doesn't have to change—but most times I've found that leadership is fulfilling the role of management. An organization's top leaders should spend the majority of their time leading, not managing. Not solving problems. Not signing checks.

An organization's top leadership should be spending the majority of their time helping the organization become successful. Many of the required steps to achieve true success can't be done by anyone else in the organization. The leaders have to embrace their role and fill it. It's not easy because most of the things they do aren't short term. Like a good grade school teacher, a leader's positive impact on the organization and its stakeholders will likely take decades to show. Unfortunately, most leaders today don't want to wait that long to show they are doing good works. They want results now. And to compound this problem, many times the organization's shareholders and board of trustees expect to see evidence immediately also.

The closest you'll come to showing short-term success is by showing progress to the long-term mission and vision.

Index

© Martin Klubeck 2017
M. Klubeck, *Success Metrics*, DOI 10.1007/978-1-4842-2586-8

Get the eBook for only $4.99!

Why limit yourself?

Now you can take the weightless companion with you wherever you go and access your content on your PC, phone, tablet, or reader.

Since you've purchased this print book, we are happy to offer you the eBook for just $4.99.

Convenient and fully searchable, the PDF version enables you to easily find and copy code—or perform examples by quickly toggling between instructions and applications.

To learn more, go to http://www.apress.com/us/shop/companion or contact support@apress.com.

Made in the USA
Las Vegas, NV
02 September 2021

29495706R00138